Development and Cultural Change:

Cross-Cultural Perspectives

An ICUS Book

Science and Values series

Humankind has pursued truth about the extended, material world in recent centuries through scientific methods. Using the knowledge gained through these methods, man has achieved a remarkable degree of mastery over the world around him. Yet all this material progress holds limited promise for solving the deep and widespread societal problems which trouble humanity today. To ease this malaise, there is a need for a clear, universal value-system to guide mankind in personal life, in sociopolitical relations, economic relations and in the application of the power made available through science in the service of mankind.

Books in the Science and Values series seek to create an academic environment in which value considerations can be brought into scientific discourse and application. In particular, books in this series offer different perspectives regarding the dilemma of a "value-free" scientific approach while the world faces global-level environmental and societal crises. It is hoped that this series will help bring the value perspective into the application of man's knowledge.

Books within this series represent an attempt to direct scholarly discourse toward the essential interface of Science and Values precisely because this interface is so important yet so difficult to clarify. Each book differs in its relation to the overarching theme and none is expected to be able to consider all of the aspects elaborated in this statement. Nonetheless, in their cumulative impact the Science and Values books should make significant contributions toward harmonizing these two disparate domains.

Development and Cultural Change:

Cross-Cultural Perspectives

Ilpyong J. Kim

Ilpyong J. Kim

An ICUS Book

Paragon House Publishers

New York

Second Printing

Published in the United States by
PARAGON HOUSE PUBLISHERS
90 Fifth Avenue
New York, New York 10011

An International Conference on the Unity of the
Sciences Book.

Library of Congress Cataloging-in-Publication Data

Development and Cultural Change.

   "AN ICUS book."
   Bibliography:
   Includes index.
   1. Economic development. 2. Economic development —
Social aspects.   I. Kim, Ilpyong J., 1931-
HD78.D48   1986   330.9   86-4986
ISBN   0-89226-030-0
       0-89226-041-6(pbk)

Contents

Introduction

Ilpyong J. Kim

It was during the Eleventh International Conference on the Unity of Sciences (ICUS XI) in November 1982 in Philadelphia that Morton A. Kaplan of the University of Chicago and chairman of ICUS XII asked if I would put together a panel on development in Asia. I subsequently discussed the request with several colleagues at the University of Connecticut and with Arnold Harberger, a member of the Department of Economics at the University of Chicago. What emerged from the conversations was the possibility of organizing the panel "Developmental Experience in East Asia and Latin America," which later functioned as Committee IV of ICUS XII in Chicago in November 1983.

In selecting a number of case studies of East Asia and Latin America, we initially thought to address the question of why certain countries are successful in development and others are not. The original idea of assessing socioeconomic development in terms of success and failure was subsequently abandoned and we came up with a new theme. The paper writers would address the issues of government's role in economic development, the interplay of politics, economics, legitimacy, and policy process in the course of political and economic development, with special emphasis on cultural changes.

The objective of organizing the committee was not to provide a systematic comparison of developmental processes in East Asia and Latin America nor to generate a grand theory of development. Rather, it was a modest effort to conduct a case study of development in each country, with attention to unique characteristics of culture, geographical environment and the historical background, that might lead to a better understanding of recent development. It was my expectation that the case method adopted would make some significant contributions to the thinking on the nature of socioeconomic development, the causal effect of cultural change, and the role of government. In other words, what causes development, and how the process in turn brings about other changes in a society.

The concept of development encompasses all aspects of societal transformation, including socioeconomic, political, and cultural transformation as well as the introduction of science and technology. We use the term *development* here interchangeably with the term *modernization*, although some scholars use it in a more comprehensive sense. *Development* is usually defined somewhat like *modernization*: the process of structural change in a society whereby inanimate sources of energy supersede animate sources. Thus, the meaning of *development* includes such notions as industrialization, commercialization, urbanization, acculturation, and rationalization by the increase of skills and knowledge to control nature and the environment. A society might be characterized as traditional, transitional, or modernized (or underdeveloped, developing, and developed) in terms of its political, economic, sociocultural, scientific, and technological status.

The study of development in the 1950s, unlike today, was much more narrowly focused on economic development and was measured by the indices of the gross national product (GNP). W. W. Rostow's *Stages of Economic Growth* (1960) might be characterized as representative of the theoretical concerns of economists and social scientists then. In the 1960s, even as development came to mean a reduction of poverty, an increase in equality, and a solution to unemployment, the focus of the study of development was still on linear economic growth in terms of GNP, as evidenced by the concern of the First United Nations Development Decade. During the Second United Nations Development Decade, the 1970s, the study of development "caught up" and shifted to a basic-need approach, emphasizing quality of life and ecological balance.

In the 1980s we are increasingly concerned with the problems of development, and recognize the importance of a multidisciplinary perspective. Theorists stress that it is about time to change the focus of our thinking (about the Third World) from simple economic development to human development. Some radical theorists believe that *development* should be redefined, according to the Third World view, as a process of liberation of individuals, classes, and societies from poverty, deprivation, dependence, and exploitation. The study of development in the 1980s, as Frederick Turner asserts in his paper, should be more concerned with improving the quality of human life around the world. Some of the old issues of development like economic growth and political participation remain central, but other issues, like the roles of science and technology, as Alexander King stresses, should be considered equally important.

In the 1970s a new approach to development attempted to explain the causes and effects of underdevelopment in the Third World, especially in the Latin American countries. This world-systems analysis or world-economy approach looks at underdevelopment in the Third World in terms of the exploitive relations between the core nations of the industrialized North and the peripheral nations in the underdeveloped South. The approach traces the history of conquest and occupation, and capitalist expansion of the colonial period, thus establishing the root cause of underdevelopment. Foreign investment, technical assistance, trade, and aid are considered as modern forms of colonialism. World systems partisans advocate better terms of agreement between the North and South on the issues of investment, technical assistance, trade, and aid within the framework of the New International Economic Order (NIEO).

The conventional approach to development, on the other hand, takes such internal problems as population growth, excessive military expenditures, luxury consumption, corruption, and management inefficiencies and deficiencies as the causes of underdevelopment, and external factors like aid, trade, and investment as possible remedies. Thus, the conventional approach is still concerned with low-level productivity and high-level social waste inefficiency within a given cultural context as the cause of underdevelopment.

One of the most interesting cases of development in the twentieth century is that of Japan, and many explanations have been presented to show why Japan was able to modernize and other nations were not. The Japanese experience is unique because of Japan's culture, tradition, and national character, according to most observers, and they stress that Japan therefore cannot serve as a model for the developing countries. One of the characteristics of the Japanese modernization is cultural values and institutions that were the indigenous sources of development as well as the contributing factors in societal transformation. The traditions and institutions fostered adaptive capabilities as well as imitative and assimilative capabilities. The Japanese were capable of accommodating to changing external circumstances and of borrowing foreign values and institutions and modifying them to suit their own needs.

The Japanese were open to the cultural influence of China when Confucianism, Buddhism, and Taoism were introduced to them during the early stages of their cultural development. That experience eased the way for the incorporation in the late nineteenth century of the values and institutions, including science and technology, of the West so as to transform a traditional to a modern society. How a people acquires and increases transformational capacities is beyond the scope of this introduction, yet it is a subject to keep in mind when considering the developmental experience of contemporary societies in different cultural contexts.

Edward C. Stewart's paper, "Japanese Culture and Modernization," which was presented at the panel "Resurgence of East Asia: Problems and Pitfalls of Modernization" of ICUS X in Seoul, Korea, in 1981, addresses how cultural values influence the modernization process in Japan. Stewart details the relationship between the country's deep culture and its development process, characterizing deep culture as the main thrust in cultural values and patterns of thinking, which in turn influence modes of production, styles of management, and systems of marketing—all of which have bearing on the causes and effects of modernization process. Stewart writes about the psychocultural aspect of development, rather than the socioeconomic aspect, which contrasts the other papers in this volume.

Paul Kuznet's paper, "Economic Development in South Korea," discusses every facet of that country's development and the economic success that has been achieved as the result of flexibility of development policy and favorable external conditions. Had it not been for policy changes as well as the previous acceleration of productive potential for economic growth, the economic success of Korea would not have been achieved in the late 1960s and early 1970s. However, the most important factor, among others, was the Confucian tradition and its influence on government that played an active role in economic matters that must be taken into account in an analysis of development in East Asia. Because the government's activism has cultural and political as well as economic causes, the Korean model of development may not be applicable to other developing countries (DCs). The other important factor in Korean development was the government's heavy emphasis on expansion of exports, according to Kuznets, and this aspect of the Korean model is more likely to be applicable to other countries.

John Fei's paper, "Economic Development of Taiwan, 1950-1980," is an assessment of a transition process from pre-World War II agrarian colonialism to the epoch of modern economic growth based on science and technology. Taiwan's economic development is divided into three phases: import substitution (1953-63); external orientation (1963-80); and technology-sensitive external orientation (1980-present). Certain economic, geographic, and political characteristics seem to have been determinants of economic growth during each phase. The development of Taiwan, like that of Korea, fortunately had advantageous human resources, a highly educated labor force and market-oriented enterpreneurs, that contributed to accelerated economic growth, but government economic planning and policy formulation seems to have been more instrumental in achieving the so-called miracle economy in Taiwan as well as in Korea. It was government intervention that brought about the shift from the import-substitution phase to the external-orientation phase, thereby achieving rapid expansion of exports, which resolved unemployment problems and sustained economic growth in the 1970s.

Sidney Klein, in "Economic Development in Hong Kong and Singapore," characterizes the two islands as "economic microchips" because they are extremely small in size and population but increasingly more powerful and impressive in performance. Much of Hong Kong's economic progress since 1945 has been attributed not only to the skills and capital brought in by its refugee newcomers but to the human capital created by the government itself by the provision of social services. The latter factor has been the main source of development in Hong Kong, but the government maintains a very low profile. A source of the rapid economic growth in Singapore, as in Hong Kong, has been the high-quality, hard-working labor force, but the Singapore government plays a greater role in economic affairs than does its Hong Kong counterpart.

At a certain stage of development during the 1960s and 1970s it was essential for the government to take a greater part in economic affairs to stimulate growth, as demonstrated in the cases of Korea, Taiwan and Singapore. In the 1980s it may be necessary for the government to adopt a liberalization policy, as in Korea and Taiwan. More important, the cultural values will continue to persist in the countries of East Asia, and the role of culture in the process of development must be considered in the analysis of East Asian development.

The East Asian region, including China, Japan, Korea, Taiwan, Hong Kong, and Singapore, is influenced by Confucian values—discipline, hard work, achievement-oriented education, dedication to duty, and responsibility—all of which made significant contributions to the modernization process of East Asia. However, there are in Confucian culture elements that impede progress and development. Such elements include greater emphasis on the hierarchical ordering of social relations than equality; on the inculcation of a conservative ideology rather than openness to innovation; and on a humanistic educational system rather than pragmatic money making or manual labor. Sociocultural factors can contribute to or hamper progress toward development of the societies in East Asia, but East Asians have selected the positive aspects of Confucian culture to help them to adapt to alien science and technology, thereby acquiring the capacity to meet the requirements of development and modernization.

The second part of this volume addresses the question of why some countries are not successful in development. The case studies of the Philippines in Southeast Asia and of Chile in Latin America can be contrasted, for these two countries have many common features that explain the problems they are encountering. They share a Latin culture. Paul Sigmund's paper, "Development Strategies in Chile, 1964-1983," discusses the administrations of Frei, Allende, and Pinochet. The comparison of their approaches to development informs us of the issues and problems, and helps us to understand Chile's development strategies of the past two decades. Sigmund illuminates the active role of the government in the formulation and implementation of developmental policies. The interventionist policy was unsuccessful and, as a result, the Pinochet administration abolished subsidies, protective tariffs, and wage controls, and returned the nationalized firms to the private sector. Liberalization, that is, less government intervention, did not produce the expected results either.

Charles Lindsey's paper, "Economic Crisis in the Philippines," was not presented at ICUS XII but was solicited at the suggestion of the reviewer of the book manuscript. Alexander King also asked for the inclusion of a case study on the Philippines because the recent history of that country has many features that allow for comparisons with Chile. The declaration of martial law by Philippine President Ferdinand E. Marcos in September 1972 put an end to democratic processes and brought about the ensuing economic crisis. The assassination of former Senator Benigno S. Aquino, Jr., on 21 August 1983, triggered the severest political and economic crisis in the republic's history. Lindsey traces the origins of the economic crisis, examines the impact of the assassination, and analyzes the response by the government, domestic capitalists, the International Monetary Fund (IMF) and World Bank, transnational banks, and foreign governments, particularly that of the United States, all of which are important issues in the economic development of the Philippines. Chile and the Philippines provide excellent case studies of the interplay between politics and economics.

Alexander King served as honorary chairman of Committee IV of ICUS XII and chaired alternately with me the discussion sessions. In "The Values and Shortcomings of National Development Comparisons" King points to a number of contemporary issues in development against the background of our committee sessions. He also makes invaluable suggestions for the further study of development with cross-cultural and multidisciplinary approaches. His primary concern, however, is to address the issues of technological development and the population explosion in the process of development in the developing world. There will be increased disparities between the industrialized North and the underdeveloped South in technological development, King concludes, unless the Third World countries solve these problems.

Looking to the future of development studies, Frederick Turner proposes that fourteen issues be taken into account. According to Turner the future of development studies remains critically important because the issues involved are so vital to improving quality of life. He states: "The conclusions of developmental studies are and will long remain short-range or middle-range at best, yet here they can bring far more balanced insights to researchers and policy choices to public officials."

For a better understanding and analysis of development in the Third World it is necessary to come to grips with the experience and processes of development of a country and/or region in the context of its culture, history, and government by means of cross-cultural and cross-disciplinary perspectives. The discussions of Committee IV of ICUS XII clearly demonstrate that there is great diversity in the approaches to development. What we learned from the presentations and discussion sessions, among other things, was that the process of Third World development is not a unilinear extension of what Europe and North America experienced but something more complex. It must be dealt with in different ways. Scholars must bring to the study of Third World development a broad and long-range perspective to analyze and shed light on the problems and prospects.

Acknowledgments

In chairing Committee IV of the International Conference on the Unity of Sciences (ICUS) and editing the conference papers, I became indebted to many scholars, colleagues, and friends. Morton A. Kaplan of the University of Chicago, the chairman of the conference, suggested the panel "Development in Asia" and persistently encouraged me in reaching the goals of a successful panel and an edited volume. Frederick C. Turner of the University of Connecticut arranged for the participation of the specialist in Latin America and helped in organizing the Latin American papers.

David RePass, head of the Department of Political Science at the University of Connecticut, was very supportive of my effort when he assigned me to teach the graduate seminar in comparative political development during the fall semester of 1983. I learned a great deal about development from the graduate students, the current literature, and discussions with departmental colleagues, some of whom have read the contributed papers and made helpful suggestions. Florence Selleck has been always cooperative in dealing with necessary paperwork and correspondence. Betty Seaver of Storrs, Connecticut made a major contribution to this volume when she agreed to serve as a copy editor. Alexander King, chairman of the International Federation of Institutes for Advanced Study in Stockholm, was kind enough to serve as honorary chairman of committee and also contributed a paper, "The Values and Shortcomings of National Development Comparisons," that is a summary of his thinking in regard to the panel discussions. Richard R. Wojcik, ICUS executive director, has been consistent in his aid and unfailing sense of humor. Bert F. Hoselitz, of the University of Chicago and editor of the international journal *Development and Cultural Change*, reviewed the collected papers and gave wise counsel toward improvement of this volume, for which I am most grateful.

Last, my family, Hyunyong, Irene, and Katherene, have been very supportive of me throughout this entire enterprise, and I cherish their understanding. I am responsible for any shortcomings or omissions.

1.

The Japanese Model of Modernization: Present and Future

Edward C. Stewart

Introduction

Since 1945 the United States has been the dominant technological power in the world. With the major industries of many other countries left in ruins by World War II, U.S. industrial capacity provided the major means and resources for their reconstruction. But by the 1970s, the U.S. industrial plant was considerably older than those of West Germany and Japan, and lost part of its competitive edge as performance declined. The Japanese industrial plant underwent far more drastic structural changes than that of the United States or those of European countries. In industry after industry the Japanese expanded capacity and improved productivity, and then used their economic capability to penetrate and saturate markets. The strategy prevented their capital equipment from aging to the same degree as the Americans', but by the late 1970s, many industries were compelled to contract sharply as the rapid expansion of particular industries ended. The strategy has resulted in the elimination of capacity in some industries, has been costly to the Japanese economy, and will require a restructuring of Japanese institutions to accommodate the shrinkage in agricultural employment, to meet the needs of disadvantaged groups such as women, and to adapt to the changing values of the successor postwar generation as it gains access to power in government and the private sector. The future of the Japanese economy seems to rely more on social and cultural than economic factors, in the same way that the success of the eco-

1

nomic performance of the last thirty years has originated in the culture and society and not in its technology, which is imported from the West although perfected in Japan.

The Japanese people, living on crowded islands, lead a precarious life despite external signs of economic vigor. Japan must rely on imports for much of its foodstuffs and, in 1978, was dependent on foreign sources for 86.3 percent of its energy requirements. The country's economic success cannot be attributed to abundance of resources, as has been said about the U.S. success, nor to geography. Japan has no tradition of intolling merchants or business that might have been expected to produce the current state of modernization. An inquiry into Japanese success must probe the cultural and social factors that, in the face of great odds, have produced the contemporary economic situation. Numerous studies exist on Japanese industry and modernization, but the scholarship leaves a gap between the industry and economy on one hand, and the culture and social systems on the other. In this paper, the cultural base of the industry and its modernization are explored.

Deep Culture and Japanese Modernization

The modernization of Japan provides a case study of intrinsic value for theories of development, and as a source of ideas, concepts, practices, precedents, and methods that can be transported to other economies to improve their performances. The objective of using the Japanese case for applications abroad must skirt several difficulties. The first is that the Japanese economy can be considered to have occupied a niche in the economies of the world that it will lose in the course of events, coming to occupy a different position vis-à-vis other economies. Thus, the dimensions of its success are rigorously associated with contemporary contextual conditions that are unlikely to recur. Any lessons derived from the Japanese case must carefully consider the economy's occupancy of a special niche. The second difficulty consists of the cultural base of the Japanese case, which may make the model nonexportable to other countries, the United States for instance. The appropriate discovery and avoidance of this difficulty require an objective description of Japanese modernization—and avoidance of a narrow or biased perspective, which is the third difficulty found in some studies, among them Vogel's *Japan as Number One* (1979). This book was apparently written to alarm or educate Americans and to upgrade the Japanese, and its narrow perspective misleads. Especially troublesome in regard to such a perspective is the almost flippant use often made of concepts from Western social science such as *competition* and *achievement* without making them suitable for Japanese culture and society. Thus, the analyses are seriously flawed until the cultural equivalence of concepts is established.

For the purpose of this study, the important aspect of culture is the distinction between surface and deep culture. When the results of cultural patterns are observable, we speak of *surface culture*. How people dress, facial expressions, and hand gestures are examples. Much of culture lies below the surface, however, and cannot be seen but can be inferred from careful observation of behavior and/or surface culture. The inferences drawn represent *deep culture*, comprising both values and patterns of thinking. The individualism attributed to Americans, or the sense of reciprocity of the Japanese, will be treated as values serving as criteria for guiding action.

The Center of Gravity of Japanese Deep Culture

An old distinction between East and West can be put to good use in searching for the center of gravity of Japanese culture. In the West the center of identity tends to be organized on a materialistic basis, and displays a sharp distinction between self and nonself. In the East, and particularly in Japan, the sense of self is diffuse, existing in reciprocal relations between self and others, resembling a center of gravity or a polarized field of forces, and dissimilar to the thing-like qualities of the Western self. Boundaries between the Japanese self and nonself exist, but they are permeable to the influences of situations and groups and hence seem to shift. Social involvement provides one anchor to identity, but in a polarity to it, within the form of a social moratorium, Japanese selfhood finds itself in the state of isolation through introspection, meditation, and self-reflection. The pursuit of these solitary inquiries, when carried to extremes, produces an awareness of one's immediate feelings and emotions unperturbed by social norms. The deepening awareness of the world of emotional subjectivism, and the enjoyment of emotional anarchism reveals the truth.

> For the Japanese, truth is associated with what might be called mental exorcism, whereby one is supposed to eradicate all the inner pollutions that are clouding the true self. . . . The self that emerges in introspection and exorcism is thought to be the source of great potency. (Lebra 1976, 161, 163)

Many Japanese find satisfaction in work deriving from energy expenditure, and attach value and moral significance to a steady flow of physical or mental energy, to perseverance and to endurance reaching the point of masochism. The commitment bordering on excess relies on an optimistic belief that by virtue of single-minded effort and concentrated discipline one can achieve anything one undertakes.

> Familiar proverbs say that "A shaft can pierce a rock if pushed by a concentrated mind," and "Single-minded faith can reach heaven." (Lebra 1976, 163)

These observations on Japanese selfhood, particularly the process of mental exorcism, may by traced to the beliefs and rituals of Shinto, which center on ideas of defilement and purification, both physical and spiritual (Lebra 1976, 163). The center of Japanese identity has been proposed to be based on the concept *kami*, a word of uncertain derivation (Keane 1980). The celebrated scholar of the eighteenth century, Motoori Norinaga, defined *kami* as spirits that abide in shrines and are there worshipped. Human beings, birds, trees, plants, mountains, oceans—all may be *kami*. Norinaga observed that ancient usage called *kami* whatever seemed strikingly impressive, possessed excellence, or inspired a feeling of awe (Keane 1980, 4). This view of *kami* is amplified by the Shinto scholar Jean Herbert, for whom *kami* represents a sacred entity:

> [*Kami* is] the deification of life-force which pervades all beings, animate and inanimate. Kami is the invisible power which unites spirit and matter into a dynamic whole while it gives birth to all things without exception. (Herbert 1967, 25)

In his study of the *kami* concept, Keane concludes that the basic meaning of *kami* is the "core" or the "substructure" of Japanese culture. Although *kami*-faith cannot be clearly expressed, it has been retained without change, transmitted from generation to generation without support of dogma, reason, or logic. Intuitively and emotionally grasped, *kami* remains the elusive spiritual center of Japanese identity, removed from the reach of behaviorism and materialism, which compose the Western basis of the self.

In the practical context of groups and organizations, the Japanese identity possesses a psychological or attitudinal center in contrast to the American identity's centering on performances and skills. In addition, Americans place stress on technology as instruments for the worker and manager; Japanese managers tend to place a strong emphasis on loyalty, attitude, sincerity, and other similarly vague and unobservable qualities of the individual that suggest attitudes to Americans, who are likely to pass over them lightly and concentrate on behavior and events. Thus, American managers will speak of social and technical skills and competencies, often in the context of hardware technology, and consider how these contribute to performance. In instances where Japanese managers make selections on the basis of attitudes, American managers make selections influenced by observable skills and performances. The influence of the spiritual center in Japanese industry is illustrated by recent research conducted by the writer.

A plant located southwest of Tokyo was studied to determine how its personnel were implementing the safety system that had been adopted from a U.S. corporation. The safety system, designed and developed by Americans in the United States, had been transferred by American technicians to the entirely Japanese plant, and it was working well because the safety record of the plant personnel was very good. The purpose of the study was to gain greater understanding of the interaction between an American system and the values and operational procedures of the Japanese personnel. It did not aspire to solve problems. Given the conditions under which the study was carried out, it is believed that the managers and workers who participated reported accurate information and conveyed true attitudes.

The results of the study showed that the personnel of the plant identified three features of the safety program. First, technical devices that made the machinery safer. Second, the skills taught to and required of the operators of the machinery to make their operations safer. Third, the organization of work space and the analysis of conditions contributing to accidents. The workers fully accepted the system and admired it, particularly the third feature. They also appreciated the concern of management, which had taken the initiative in implementing and maintaining the system. But several of the workers, when asked for suggestions and proposals, offered ideas contrary to the conceptualization undergirding the safety system, which relied on technology, skills, and analysis of production operations in time and space. Workers mentioned the need for mental discipline and training, and understood the causes of accidents to be the failure, for reasons of fatigue or preoccupation of some kind, of concentration discipline, a translation of *kokoro gake*. The study reveals the two centers in American culture, behavioristic and technological, and in the Japanese culture, an appreciation of the same features but still an inclination to preserve the spiritual center of the individual as the significant factor.

Distinctive Influences of Japanese Deep Culture: The Human Being and Nature

The value orientation that describes the relationship between the human being and the world has important implications for many activities in the arts and crafts as well as in technology and the sciences. For the Japanese, when the world is interpreted as nature, the values are clear. The Japanese people have displayed a deep love for nature since very early in their history. Japanese culture provides a special status to forms and experiences that are natural and recall the asymmetry and even the imperfections of natural beauty, as if the human being can remove the imperfections by integrating in complete harmony with nature, not only in spirit but in acts that refine the natural appearance of natural manifestations.

Refined appreciation is significant for understanding the Japanese love of nature revealed in miniature gardens (*hakoniwa*), miniature trees (*bonsai*), flower arrangement (*ikebana*), the tea ceremony (*chanoyu*), short poems called *haiku*, and even in the art of cookery (Watanabe 1974, 279). These objects and activities, although naturalistic, reveal careful control and precise articulation to accommodate Japanese perception and values of the human being rather than any naturalistic qualities of heaven and earth, the three forming the three principles of *ikebana*, representing Japanese cosmology. But in the Japanese traditional view, there was no absolute division of heaven and earth, nor an absolute "onceness" of time. There existed varieties of beings and seasons, and everything came and went in cycles (Watanabe 1974, 280-81). Despite the violence of nature and the pessimistic teachings of Buddhism, the Japanese found respite and refuge in nature from the toils of life and suffocations of the group.

Nature for the Japanese was an object of appreciation and even a best companion, not an object for mastery (Watanabe 1974, 280). Even today, nature occupies a privileged position in Japanese thinking, appearing to function as a metaphor for the social nexus that comprises Japanese identity. The boundary between the human being and nature loses clarity for the Japanese because the human being is perceived as an integral part of the world and continuous with it. "The Japanese regard this world, with its diverse phenomena, as in itself absolute, and tend to reject viewpoints that seek the absolute in some realm beyond phenomena" (Nakamura 1977, 61).

The absoluteness of the phenomenal world originated with the indigenous Shinto religion. The ancient Japanese, believing that all things were invested with spirit, personified even nonhuman spirits and deities, *kami*, but considered human *kami* the primary entity. When Buddhism came to Japan, the original Shinto commitment to the phenomenal world prevailed over the Buddhist concept that there exists a realm of ultimate enlightenment transcending the phenomenal world. The Japanese interpreted the lofty concept of *hongoku* to mean "innate Buddha-nature" or "origin of Buddhahood," retaining it within the scope of the phenomenal world, for nothing was intrinsically hidden from the human being. (Nakamura 1977, 61). Watanabe writes about the same idea with a discussion of flower arrangement, *ikebana*, which represents the unity of nature. The human being lives in it as part of the unity (1974, 280).

The phenomenal integration of the human being and the world prevented the Japanese from developing an objective and detached view of the natural world, and as a result they did not initiate studies of nature. The world was not an object of study even though life on the Japanese islands was often threatened by natural disasters. Despite being often visited by earthquakes, the Japanese did not initiate the scientific study of earthquakes. Seismology began only after Japan was opened to the West, and Western visitors were exposed to earthquakes (Watanabe 1974, 281). The Chinese, who experienced a similar value of the human being's coexisting with nature, studied earthquakes at a very early date, and seem to have invented a machine to do so (Bloom 1974, 850).

Thus, coexistence of the human being and the world does not seem sufficient to explain the different developments of science and technology in China and Japan. The critical factor seems to be phenomenalism of the Japanese, which the Chinese did not share to the same degree. Chinese intellectual history provides examples of absolute concepts, of good and evil for instance (Lebra 1974), that are strange to the Japanese sense of phenomenal relativity. The Japanese sense of continuity with nature found expression in techniques of perfecting trees and gardens, and in the crafts such as swords and pottery, but did not launch the study of the world. A second fact helps explain the difference. Chinese culture ascribes a special status to the human being by developing qualities particular to deities, recognizing historical figures, and producing writings, but the Japanese indigenous faith of Shinto has no absolute being in its pantheon of deities, no founders, and no sacred scriptures (Maruyama 1977, 75). Thus, the Japanese people did not develop a philosophical or intellectual tradition but remained constantly open to foreign ideas.

The Chinese approached the Western position more closely but did not attain the concept of the human being's special station and of the objectivity of the world, and its separation from the human being, which appears to subsume the development of science.

> In the Western idea, man was not an ordinary part of nature. He was a specially privileged creature, and nature was subordinate to him and even to his sin. He was the master of the natural world, which was at his disposal to analyze, examine, and make use of (Watanabe 1974, 280).

Protestantism accepted the study of nature for the improvement of humankind, giving religious sanction to the human being's objective inquiry of the world. The separation between the human being and the world occurred early in Western history. In the fifth century B.C., Pythagoras, writing in the vein of a long tradition, separated the internal world of the subjective and mystic mind from the external objective world that could be treated with mathematics. This view, persisting until now, permits the human being to imagine the detached and objective realm of scientific principles and laws that can be applied to independent technology derived from research. Lacking these values in a significant way to develop, science and independent technology evolved slowly, developed from consistent opportunities mixed with some need, stimulated by the symbiotic relationship between man and his physical and social environment, and guided by the Japanese talent for craftsmanship and design. In addition, and particularly in modern times, the Japanese have relied on transfer of science and technology, which provides models that are imitated and improved in the direction of adapting them to the Japanese context.

During the postwar period, Japanese scientific and technological development have made giant strides. In science, and including nuclear physics, the Japanese have substituted brainpower and craftsmanship for lavish use of capital and natural resources (Campbell 1964, 776). In 1975 Japan had 399,842 scientists and engineers, and a research and development budget of U.S $10,022 million. Assuming that all the scientists and engineers are engaged in research, the difference between the two countries diminishes somewhat when additional factors are considered. Americans concentrate more on the basic research end of the spectrum; Japanese stress the development end, where engineers are more important. Further, a large proportion of American research and development is for defense, of which the Japanese have almost none. Finally, the United States conducts much high-energy physics research, which is capital intensive by necessity; Japan avoids it. Thus, the two research and development enterprises are not strictly comparable, but there are qualitative differences.

Social Relativism

The elaboration of the center of gravity of Japanese deep culture creates a misleading picture of the Japanese sense of identity until corrected with the present discussion of *social relativism*. In searching for a "thematic distinctiveness" of Japanese culture, Lebra used the concept of *ethos* (1976, 1). The concept was perhaps first systematically used by Bateson in 1935, in the sense of the characteristic spirit, prevalent tone, or sentiment of a people or community (Bateson 1958, 2). Later Bateson identifies ethos as the emotional emphases of the culture (p. 32) and the "standardised system of emotional attitudes" (p. 119). Although Lebra's use of *ethos* does not stress the emotional aspect, the choice of the term is excellent because the term fits the Japanese cultural matrix, where emotion rather than reason or cognition serves as the cultural binder.

In the former section, the center of gravity of Japanese culture was identified as spiritual or psychological, and was summarized around the concept of *kami*. The example used to illustrate the application of the center of gravity, the safety study at a Japanese plant, omitted the emphasis in Japanese culture of others besides the actor. Lebra refers to this orientation as social preoccupation (1976, 2-6). The commitment is profound to the point where the Japanese are unable to locate prime movers or causes because they are so sensitive to influences flowing between the actor and other. This phenomenon Lebra calls *interactional relativism* (1976, 6-9). The combination of social preoccupation and interactional relativism yields the Japanese ethos of social relativism (Lebra 1976, 9). The concept suggests the definition of the self in Japanese society as a part of the social nexus (Nakamura 1964), guiding behavior along lines of conformity and of imitation of suitable models. This view, of course, neglects the center of gravity in the spirit, but both the idea of *kami* and of social relativism can be combined in the concept of *jen*, the Confucian value of human-heartedness (Kawashima 1967, 265). Adopted as *jin* by the Japanese, the concept carries the meaning of psychic love (Hsu 1966, 62). Although *jin* refers to a cosmic principle among the Chinese, and conveys for the Japanese an abstract idea of relationship resembling the abstraction of *kami*, the Japanese *jin* implies the concrete recognition of others as human beings identical with the self. The individual is conceived to be a member of a group, institution, or society as a whole and to occupy an appropriate place fulfilling all social obligations attached to the position. (The term best illustrating this social orientation is *bun*, and even the term for self is a *bun*—compound noun, *jibun*.) The

concepts from the West of personality, ego, and even of self do not
have the same meaning in Japan (Hasmaguchi 1980, 67). *Jen*
replaces these concepts as more suitable for coalescing human
experience around human relationships.

Although the network of human relationships represents ab-
stractions, Japanese culture avoids empty categories, and thus
the relationships are seen in particularistic settings. Actual contacts are important in Japanese culture; without them, relationships wither. The Japanese also find it difficult to identify with
abstract organizations, thus leading us to conclude that the *jen*
refers to the network of relationships within the perceptual grasp
of the individual, that the self reflections take the form of relationships but invariably these relationships are filled with the self
and others too. All writers agree that *jen* refers to interpersonal
relationships, with most writers tracing the concept to the
Chinese characters that represent it: a person between persons
(人 = jin a person; 間 = kan-between: 人間)

Jen as discussed above summarizes a difficult but critical
aspect of Japanese culture that has played a major role in the
modernization of Japan. By means of *jen*, the social binder or the
primal bonds that hold together Japanese groups, including companies, has been suggested. The loyalty, the dedication, and even
the sense of identity that Japanese managers and workers derive
from their workplace traces to the social relativism exemplified in
jen, which has been mobilized in Japan to form the substructure
of industry.

Japanese Management

Japanese management provides a useful subject for examining
the influence of deep culture in the modernization of Japan. Resembling American management in some ways, but differing from it
in others, Japanese management will be contrasted with American
to heighten the understanding of the *cultural interface* in Japanese industry.

In their study of Japanese management, Pascale and Athos
(1981) identify seven factors in a framework that can be used to
organize information about management. We shall depart from
their approach by assigning a separate section to *structure*, the
organization of firms. We disagree somewhat with their conclu-

sion that the ensemble of "hard" factors, *strategies*, *structures*, and *systems*, are the same in the hands of both Japanese and American managers. It is generally true, however, that the culture of Japan, *kami*, fusion with nature, and *jen* predictably encourage the cultivation of the soft ensemble, *staff*, *style*, skills, and *superordinate goals*. Americans, admiring the tough, decisive, objective, and *macho* executive, assign lower priority, if not neglect, to the same soft factors (Pascale and Athos 1981, 204).

Strategy

Strategy refers to the plans and procedures used by the firm to allocate service resources and to attain success. At least two major but subtle differences exist between American and Japanese strategies, reflecting emphases rather than discrete differences. Both cultures have been described as stressing process rather than structure, how to get things done rather than things themselves, but the Japanese attunement to persistently flowing processes is remarkable. Lebra discusses the high value placed on the steady flow of physical or mental energy (1976, 163). Japanese culture also values repetition and imitation in learning and in performance. These values of deep culture may well surface in the organization of supplies and raw resources in Japanese industry, which more than American industry stresses the constant flow of input to the assembly line, minimizing stockpiling. Although the explanations for the two emphases invite reasons of space and facility, the process emphasis seems natural to all areas of Japanese life. Discussion groups, committees, and plans lack clear beginnings and endings, flowing and proceeding interminably.

The second major but subtle difference categorized under strategy refers to the debate of profit versus market. Profit as an objective carries negative implications in Japan that can be traced to earlier periods in history. Also, the Japanese orientation of social relativism leads us to expect that strategy in business will give priority to the development of human relationships, and will give attention to markets before pushing products and profit. Of even greater interest is the cultural expectation that domestic systems of distribution will be stubbornly defended, and that customers and their networks will receive concentrated attention. These strategies in business reflect cultural factors, particularly social relativism, and *jen*.

Structure

Structure refers to the characterization of the organization of the firm, such as features of centralization and functions. Because structure is discussed below under the heading "Japanese Social Systems," it suffices to mention the vertical organization in Japanese groups built around the *frame*, which is the particular, localized working situation (Nakane 1970). The primal bonds among members of the groups—including the distinctive Japanese form of reciprocal dependence (*amae*), and concentrated energy, derived from both internal cohesiveness and external hostility—on which Japanese modernization has been founded, introduce an intractable aspect of Japanese business. The unity and identity of the people of Japan, constantly reinforced by primordial bonds of language, ethnicity, race, religion, region, and custom, provide an idealized cohesiveness inside Japan that is unmatched elsewhere in the world.

Systems

Systems are defined as the procedural reports and routinized processes used to move information around, and, in an organization, to make decisions and to implement change (Pascale and Athos 1981, 35-36, 81). This American category breaks down when it is applied to Japanese culture because it assumes a universal definition of information, a similar function for communication, and independence between the system of flow and the nature of the information that the system moves. Americans differentiate more than do other people among data, images, impressions, facts, gossip, and other forms of what can be called information, in the technical sense of interpreted or "meaningful" facts. The Japanese do not make similar distinctions but insist that all forms of "information" must be collected. And perhaps more than anyone else, the Japanese believe that quantity of "information" is good, and that no clear distinction exists between common sense "information" and the technical meaning of information, verified and interpreted as facts.

The Japanese cultural orientation toward information raises significant issues on the role of communication in Japanese management. Two points should be mentioned. One, the Japanese language is best suited for hierarchical communication that conveys emotional tones and social feelings. The language itself is ambiguous, leaving understanding open to interpretation. Two, the oral message in Japanese relies on nonoral aspects of communication to a degree seldom appreciated by the English speaker. In short, oral communication is inseparable from nonoral communication and from Japanese experience. The ambiguity and vagueness of the style of communication that in its uncertainty still refrains from developing a posture of adversary relationship places the burden of understanding on the receiver of communication—unlike American communication, which puts responsibility on the sender as well as the receiver. The Japanese way compels the receiver to concentrate on the meaning presumably conveyed, and the sender, bound by indirection and vagueness, becomes equally attentive to the receiver. Communication improves if all communicators know each other well and can anticipate what each will say or do. Thus, the ambiguity and vagueness of communication contribute to team work and group cohesiveness.

Communication in the field of technology raises the additional problem of probability thinking and of coping with uncertainty. Because the subject apparently has seldom been treated from the point of view of deep culture, it is possible to raise questions, to speculate, but to give few answers.

Despite the wide use of statistical control in industry and business, Japanese managers do not readily derive ideas or conclusions from statistical analyses. They prefer a more intuitive process beginning with a general idea, as we will see below. The use of objective probabilities are difficult anywhere, but in Japanese culture there appears to be a greater preference for categorical predictions, i.e., classification of an issue.[1] Japanese managers seem reluctant to make calculated estimates relying on probability, avoiding doing so if possible. In dealing with uncertainty, the Japanese show what can be compared to a craftsperson's criteria: accuracy of measurement, inclusion of all variables, and perfect performance rather than anticipation of consequences. Along with these observations, perhaps more in the nature of speculations, we should mention the Japanese preference for adapting to and adopting existing conditions. In Japanese culture, there exists strong precedent for accepting the phenomenal world in all of its imperfections and impermanence. This orientation seldom leads to inquiries about causes, which at the level of communication avoids asking why, attending instead to what. In compensation for the acceptance of imperfection, the Japanese manager is open to suggestions and accepts the objective of endless improvement. Although the manager has the *kami*-faith, ultimate trust is placed in personnel rather than in ideas or analysis.

Staff

The subject of staff is tangential to the subject of modernization of Japan. The subject is more appropriate for an understanding of technical functioning of companies, so treatment of staff will be confined to three general remarks.

Japanese industry since the Meiji Restoration has accepted the Confucian value of practical knowledge, with the result that Japanese managers drew abreast, by 1928, of the educational attainments of European businesspeople today (Clark 1979, 36). Professional training, however, was done by companies and not by the universities, with the result that attaining the status of member of the company, of citizen, and of professional person became part of the same process of belonging to the company. Education of the employee is carried out in part by moving the employee to various positions within the same company, resulting in a manager who becomes a specialist within the company but at the same time does not develop specialization in finance, marketing, or some other field. The manager consequently becomes more firmly entrenched in the company, and less marketable to other companies. A final point: future managers typically enter the company at the bottom and work their way up. All these factors combine to make a good Japanese company resilient, permitting it to change and adapt to a degree surprising to American management and labor. Because the person in charge of the line may have a degree in engineering, adapting a new process or making a change can be done quickly and efficiently without having to give special training to the work force. The high level of training, and the cohesiveness and dedication of the staff give Japanese companies a strength that would be difficult to export to, and replicate in, countries that prefer adversarial relationships in business and litigation in solving problems.

Style

The factor of *style* furnishes information on the cultural style of Japanese industry. The perspective of deep culture and the psycho-

logical approach to culture imbricate with the definition given by
Pascale and Athos: the characterization of how key managers
behave in achieving the organization's goals (1981, 81). Alhough
the Japanese and American styles of doing business overlap, there
are critical differences. These do not usually represent distinctive
differences, but rather different combinations of values and aspects of patterns of thinking, which combine to produce characteristic points of views and objectives, not to say ways of operating.

In looking at the distinctive features of Japanese deep culture
in business, the Japanese style of making judgments resembles
the American style, but the Japanese is more comparative and
less absolute. Japanese businesspeople display a profoundly comparative judgment that overshadows the highly developed American business judgment, which is also comparative but retains
faint images of absolute judgment. The European judgment, Aus-
trian or German, is a better contrast to the Japanese in the applied area of taking actions. While the European may consider
the appropriateness or the goodness of a course of action, the
Japanese is likely to consider and compare one course of action,
or one person, with another. The European, assuming an ideal
standard, employs an absolute judgment; the Japanese, comparing
like things with each other, employs a comparative judgment. The
style of judgment is a prominent feature of decision making, a
subject of consuming interest in business to which we turn,
reverting to American decision making to supply a contrast to
the Japanese.

American decision making generally relies on a conceptual base
that anticipates future events, usually summarized as objectives
or goals. Thus, American decision making, in its ideal form, is
time bound, reflecting the American vlaue orientation toward the
near future. Americans develop time-binding, as in time-motion
studies, deadlines, objectives, and goals, to a level of managerial
fine art. They use the conceptual base of their decisions to establish definite points of reference in theory, policy, and courses of
action. The process of decision making, particularly for Americans, passes through a mental analysis of positive and negative
factors. Alternatives are carefully weighed and then a decision is
made. The decision maker is an individual or a group, but typically the conceptual nature of the decision and the adversarial
process used in reaching it reveal its major sources. For Amer-

icans, utility is the decision criterion that refers to a future event, not a present one. The employment of the future is the critical aspect of American decision making and perhaps explains the optimistic cast of American decision makers, often presuming greater control over the world than experience gives reason for assuming.

In the East, including Japan, we lack the information for reaching conclusions about similar systematic errors. Managers in Japan are uneasy in accepting any one decision as final or "finalized." Instead, they are likely to perceive a continuously unfolding train of events to which they accommodate (Pascale and Athos 1981, 110). The notion of controlling events in the sense of the American systematic error is much more likely to become an adaptation to the situation and even an avoidance of decision making, allowing events to take their course. Thus, the American desire for closure, for "finalizing," in the Japanese company is more a matter of flowing with events. The differences in decision making follow from the conceptual nature of American decision making, on the one hand, and the organizational aspects of the Japanese company, on the other. Japanese decisions are more like discussions conducted among various people, and lack the formal qualities of alternatives, predictions, and other technical qualities that punctuate American discussions.

Japanese managers are more likely to devote attention and time to building support for a decision than in organizing the conceptual structure of alternatives. Thus, decisions are reached in an organizational or social field in distinction to the conceptual field of the American decision. The Japanese manager feels obligated to include other people on the decision making process. Although individual decisions sometimes occur, group decisions are much more characteristic of a Japanese organization. But the simple comparison obscures the important difference of the patterns of thinking and the nature of judgments that distinguish the two styles of decision making. The Japanese obligation to include others insures that the process of decision making matches the Japanese patterns of self-identity that, unlike the American, are anchored to the group, treated as *jen* or the social nexus (Nakamura 1964). Thus, the process of touching base with many people, redundant to Americans, acculturates the decision and establishes support for its eventuality, which comes after interminable talk. The discussions focus on feasibility, rather than theory, policy, or profit. Each course of action or each alternative is talked through in terms of its "implementational feasibility" (Pascale and Athos 1981, 111). The decision is assumed to require reconciliation of competing interests, all of which would be included to insure a proper balance between substantive options and implementational feasibility. Through a process that may be described as "discussion attrition," the alternative with the best all-around prospect of success emerges as the decision. A formal decision making session often provides a ceremonial consensus to a decision already reached and fully supported by the members of the group.

It is doubtful if the Japanese way of attaining consensus for a purpose qualifies as an example of the social technology of decision making. But a study of the Japanese process throws open to view a perception of Japanese culture. When striving for a consensus, Japanese managers regularly reflect on their own experience, but after withdrawal. In the social context of the workplace, managers are preoccupied with obligations, duties, and protocol surrounding the managerial position. Psychologically, it is essential for managers to escape from the suffocation of the group, to take a fresh look at their own experience, and allow their thinking to percolate through their own emotions without the binding pressures of the work social nexus. Pascale and Athos, discussing the Japanese company Matsushita, describe the need for acceptance time, which gives managers the opportunity to come around to a point of view in their own way.

> Acceptance time is a powerful antidote to conflict in Japanese organizations. The things a person believes in are often more important belongings than physical possessions. People die for their central beliefs as well as for their important possessions. Even less compelling beliefs reach back into a person's past and forward into his future. When new ideas or facts come along, however compelling they may be, it is felt that people need time to let go gradually of the old before they can accept the new. Despite the pressures and intensity, acceptance time is built into the Matsushita way of doing business (Pascale and Athos 1981, 48).

Acceptance time leads to aspects of Japanese deep culture in the areas of identity and learning. Although it is clear that the Japanese self-concept is part of a social nexus, that identity exists in a dialectical relationship with an inner core of the self, emotional and meditative, that is in touch with experience, and with roots leading to Zen, which insists that a person experience the thing in itself, the reality, not the empty abstraction. The central perception of the truth of Zen sees all things as things in themselves and at the same time sees the one in the many and the many in the one. Zen rejects the intellect—verbalization, logic, conceptualization—and accepts intuitive understanding as knowledge that comes from deep within the person's being. Zen is a religion of the will; it is simple, direct, self-reliant, and self-denying. Traditionally linked to the military classes, Zen is now widely dispersed throughout all classes of Japan (Suzuki 1977, 46-49). Withdrawal of the individual to the Zen center of the individual's being, for the purpose of communing with the individual's own experience, is an aspect of the central concept of Zen that has spread throughout Japanese society and deeply influenced strategies of learning and of change. This quality of Zen generates strong internal reserves in its Japanese practitioners, but often leads to serious misunderstanding of the outside world (Aida 1977, 67). The bent of Japanese thought toward experiential self-immolation points to values governing learning that are deeper than those suggested by acceptance time. Withdrawal in time, if not in space, as a condition for learning and accommodating to change refers to *assimilation* rather than acceptance time. The reality of assimilation time and the development of inner reserves do not remove the need for a concrete model that is imitated before it is improved. Education is conducted by means of imitation, which means memorization. The Japanese, in comparison to Americans, are excellent listeners, attentive to the "model" communicated. Furthermore, in Japanese society, emphasis is given to vertical communication, so that the roles of senders and receivers are distinctive, with the receiver assuming the major burden for successful communication.

The factor of style overlaps with the other factors that we are using to organize the review of distinctive aspects of Japanese management. The overlap is particularly apparent with the factor of systems, discussed previously, and the one of *skills*, which follows.

Skills

By *skills*, Pascale and Athos mean the distinctive capabilities of key personnel or of the firm as a whole (1981, 81). The factor of skills is more suitable for comparison of specific companies than for use in reporting the connection between deep culture and modernization. We have preserved the factor merely to bring this paper in closer relationship to existing treatment of Japanese business. The factor of skills serves to draw attention to a distinctive capability of Japanese industry: to improve and perfect a product or a service. This feature can be illustrated with a brief discussion of the Japanese orientation toward technology.

Japanese industry and business have developed and modernized by acquiring technology abroad and then improving and perfecting it in Japan. Generally, Japanese industry has avoided committing too much of its resources to theoretical research that could be used to develop a research-driven technology. Because industry's budget for research and development is likely to be allocated for the improvement of existing products, the best index for gauging the commitment to a research-driven technology is the research and development budget of the government. In 1975, the percentage of research and development financed by the government was 29.7, lower than that of any other major country. Just above Japan was Italy, with 41.4; the United States financed 50.7 percent; and France was the highest, 53.5 percent. Recent figures on patents seem to dispute the assertion that Japanese technology is transfer-driven rather than research-driven technology, but in fact an examination of patents issued confirm the Japanese genius for improving rather than inventing. The controversial figures refer to U.S. patents for inventions issued to foreigners: in 1966 the Japanese received 1,122 patents (8.1 percent); in 1976, 6,542 (25.1 percent). The shift to research-driven technology is not supported by the figures if one accepts the explanation that a team of Japanese technical personnel maintains a close watch for patents nearing expiration, and changes selected patents enough to qualify for a new patent when the old one expires. Keeping track of the situation in the U.S. Patent Office, and moving preemptively seem to be in the mainstream of the Japanese approach to business, and do not indicate a shift to research-driven technology. This quality of Japanese industry is well illustrated by the Matsushita Electric Company.

Pascale and Athos provide an analysis of Matsushita from which we extract the following comments supporting the features of Japanese industry discussed above:

> The third element of Matsushita's strategy is followership. From the outset, Matsushita (the founder and CEO) did not attempt to

pioneer new technology but emphasized quality and price. . . . To
this day, Matsushita rarely originates a product, but always suc-
ceeds in manufacturing it for less and marketing it best. . . . At the
heart of Matshushita's followership strategy is production engineering. An executive from RCA states, "If you watch where Matsushita puts its resources, their success through followership should
come as no surprise. They have 23 production research laboratories
equipped with the latest technology available. Their concept of
"research and development" is to analyze competing products and
figure out how to do it better." (Pascale and Athos 1981, 30-31)

Matsushita is a great Japanese company and therefore not
typical because greatness deviates from normative features of all
companies, but some features we claim are typical in an ideal
sense. The authors point out unusual aspects of the company's
strategy, but with respect to the need for a model, concrete and
operational, which is improved, Matsushita represents the ideal
of a fundamental thrust in Japanese technology.

Superordinate Goals

Superordinate goals include "significant meanings," "shared values," and "spiritual fabric," which function as the guides imbued
in its members by an organization (Pascale and Athos 1981, 81,
177-78). The meaning of *superordinate goals* seems a bit inflated,
and also culturally biased. Placing superordinate goals at the center of the managerial molecule (Pascale and Athos 1981, 202)
raises the operational level of competing objectives to an idealized,
integrated level. The information reflects a decision making style
of thinking in which future events (i.e., goals) serve to organize
the data for the decision maker. Choices made among alternative
courses of action to reach the goal rely on a set of values, including a clear idea of the future, lineal time, and the capacity to
differentiate clearly among alternatives. Conceptual clarity and
logical relations undergrid the decision making process. The formulation aptly reflects American management thought but poses
little resemblance to Japanese ways of thinking. *Superordinate
goals* first refers to a hierarchy of objectives, with the one at the
pinnacle, the superordinate, resolving conflicts among competing
objectives that cannot be treated as instrumental under the guiding influence of the superordinate goal. This rephrasing of the
superordinate goal, with the deliberate exclusion of the temporal
aspect of goals and objectives, lends itself to application to Japanese organizations.

21

The structure of the Japanese organization is hierarchical, with communication and relationships reinforcing vertical rather than horizontal bonds. The Japanese group, bound together by emotional processes, compresses a high potential for splitting into factions and subgroups. Fissions are prevented, or at least contained by the vertical relationship in which allegiance is given upward to only one leader until the top person in the organization is reached. Personal allegiance in a large group extends beyond the span of personal *jen*, hence an extension is needed to encompass all members of an organization. The firm's *belief systems* are described by Pascale and Athos as spiritual values and identified as superordinate goals (1981, 49-52, 81). Belief systems provide concrete examples of what functions as enfolding cognitive and emotional frames for reaching judgments and making decisions. The frames may also be described as deductive thinking in which general and abstract ideas (in the case of the Japanese these are vague and emotionally laden), provide the beginning of a train of thought that moves toward more concrete and particular ideas.

Pascale and Athos use Matsushita, the Japanese company and its founder of the same name, to fill in the abstract ideas posed by superordinate goals because both founder and company are superb examples of the Japanese approach. It is customary for business leaders and government officers in Japan to frame their observations implicitly if not explicitly within a moralistic and ethical frame that provides a deductive but essentially emotional tone to their statements. For Matsushita, people need a way of linking their productive lives with their membership in the larger society. He developed a management philosophy that linked business profits to the social good within a Darwinian paradigm. The concept is very similar to the Protestant ethic in which the saved shall be known by their good works, and therefore success in the secular pursuit of business becomes a sign of grace. For Matsushita, the religious motive existed, but the end is societal and collective rather than individual and sacred.

Profit for Matsushita becomes a vote of confidence from society that what is offered by the firm is valued. When a firm ceases to turn a profit it should be permitted to die because it wastes the resources of the society (Pascale and Athos 1981, 49). The philosophy of the company is implemented in a song, sung each morning, and in a code of values. Employees are exposed to the code and trained in it from the beginning, and conformity to the company's basic principles is strictly required. These principles are general and ethical in quality. The basic business principles commit the employees of the firm to recognize their responsibilities as industrialists. The commitment is made to progress, the general welfare of society, and the development of world culture. The employees' creed approaches a litany of social values of progress, development, combined efforts and cooperation, and continuous improvement of the company. The third aspect is the seven spiritual values: national service through industry, fairness, harmony and cooperation, struggle for betterment, courtesy and humility, adjustment and assimilation, and last, gratitude (Pascale and Athos 1981, 51). These principles provide little guidance for workers on the production line or for decision making by groups discussing technical issues. The power derived from implementing the Matsushita management philosophy resides in the enfolding and centripetal emotional frame established around each member of the company, drawing each to each. The conflict that is present remains latent and competition is sublimated after attaining its goals, to allow for a harmonious community.

The Japanese cultural features of Matsushita can be compared with those of two American firms, IBM and ITT. The appeal of Matsushita was emotional, but that of IBM was cerebral, celebrated by the sign THINK hung in all the factories and offices. During the war PEACE joined THINK, reminding everyone of the war situation and the potential effect for IBM's expanding international business (Pascale and Athos 1981, 180-83). In these practices IBM displayed a pragmatic and rational appeal lacking the emotional bond of the principles of Matsushita that link the company and the society. The beliefs of IBM stress the individual, the customer, and excellence. Fundamental principles place priority first on business and technology, with the people working for IBM, the stockholders, the communities where the facilities are located, and the need to accept responsibility as a corporate citizen of the United States and all the countries in which IBM operates following in that order (Pascale and Athos 1981, 184-85). The American corporation, unlike Matsushita, has commited itself to the cutting edge of research, witnessed by THINK signs.

Another American corporation closely resembles Matsushita: ITT. As a matter of fact it, can be considered the American counterpart of the Japanese firm (Pascale and Athos 1981, 59). ITT has never excelled in basic or applied research, and there are no basic products associated with its name, such as with IBM, Xerox, or Polaroid. Its CEO between 1959 and 1979, Harold Geneen, built a management system based on unshakable facts. An intricate web of checks and balances, a system of rewards and punishments, carefully staged personal confrontations, and an elaborate system of information collection and management permitted Geneen to verify the facts and feed his voracious hunger for facts on which his style of managing relied. The approach permitted him to exercise his superior abilities of reading, recalling, and thinking in the domain of numbers (Pascale and Athos 1981, 70-74). This rational, cold, and impersonal approach, in which negative motivation drove managers to contribute through the mechanism of grinding confrontation, contrasts sharply with Matsushita's emotional envelope constructed to endow the company with meaning.

Japanese Social Systems

By the time of the Meiji Restoration, Japanese visitors to the West confirmed what was already evident: that the strength of a nation lay in its manufacturing industry, and that the means for attaining it was the joint stock company (Clark 1979, 27-29). The challenge was how to start up for modernization. Japan perceived the West to have primed the pump of materialism with individualism and avarice, but this strategy flouted the Confucian ethic and its contempt for material things. But the government and semiofficial entrepreneurs appealed to nationalism and public spirit in an early example of superordinate goal. In the early years of Japanese industrialization, private enterprise was supported by the state, for the government adopted the view that internal motivation was necessary for modernization. This opinion, still current (Cho 1966, 40), aptly describes the Japanese character in the Meiji period and today, with its inner motives for change as well as a spirit of resistance against cultural impact from the West. The piece missing from the puzzle is the social system for business and commerce.

The Japanese merchants during the Meiji period relied on the institution of the family to form their businesses. The family in Tokugawa Japan consisted essentially of a group called a "house" (*ie*). The word refers to a physical entity and to the people associated with it (Clark 1979, 14). Japanese group consciousness goes back to the concept of household. In the words of Nakane:

> The essence of this firmly rooted, latent group consciousness in Japanese society is expressed in the traditional and ubiquitous concept of *ie*, the household, a concept which penetrates every nook and cranny of Japanese society. The Japanese usage *uchi-no* referring to one's work place indeed derives from the basic concept of *ie*. The term *ie* also has implications beyond those to be found in the English words "household" or "family." (Nakane 1970, 4)

One of the implications suggested by Nakane is developed by Clark, which is that the institution of *ie* endowed the Japanese company with two of its ideal values: employees should stay with one organization for life, and their relations within the company should in some sense resemble those within a family (Clark 1979, 17). The process by which a new employee is "adopted" into the company illuminates the critical relationship between a member of the company and the company itself. Facets of the process of introduction have been described by Rohlen (1978), who participated in a training program for new recruits to Uedagin Bank (a fictitious name for a regional bank in Japan).

The high point of the men's four-month training program was a twenty-five-mile marathon walk scheduled as the last special event. The entire group of more than a hundred walked the first nine miles together. The stroll began in the cool of the morning and was pleasant. The recruits talked and joked before breaking into squads to cover the second nine miles. Competition insinuated its influence as some groups quickened their pace. Heat, fatigue, blisters, and stiff muscles began to take their toll. Young men from the bank tempted the walkers with cold drinks, which the recruits had been forbidden to take. Some recruits sank down by the wayside sucking salt tablets as noon approached and the "park baked under the heat of a June sun" (Rohlen 1978, 27). The training staff, walking the course in the opposite direction, instructed men to complete the last seven miles single file and in silence. "Soon a long line of slowly moving trainees stretched along the circumference of the course. Having already covered 18 miles, the last nine at a grueling pace, we found the excitement and clamor of competition gone. We pushed forward, each individual alone in a quiet world, confronted with the sweep of his own thoughts and feelings" (Rohlen 1978, 27).

25

The episode provides a remarkable symbolization of Japanese psychology. Walking the first nine miles all together symbolizes the group affiliation that is the centerpiece of Japanese identity. The second squad phase stands for the specialized work unit that generates hard work and fierce competition. Learning from harsh experience and reflecting on it was the third phase, each individual walking alone and locked in silence. About a third of the way through the program the recruits had received Zen training, learning to meditate and experiencing the spartan rigor of Zen. Other parts of the program emphasized the values of the company, associating its superordinate goals with the welfare of Japan. The training provided the resources for the ordeal of the hike, what the Japanese call spiritual strength (Rohlen 1978, 28). The program overall can be considered as a rite of passage for the recruits, and consistent with the initiation rites that promote internal unity in communities throughout the world (Rohlen 1978, 29-30).

The extensive company training described by Rohlen is not a customary part of Japanese business. It represents a traditional Japanese reflexive reaction that attempts to neutralize cultural changes brought about by the imposed educational reforms of the postwar U.S. occupation and the Westernization of popular culture. The cultural contradictions created by the foreign influences, which were needed but not entirely held at bay from nonessential areas of Japanese society requiring their use, have created schisms such as the one separating the world of business and the world of universities and intellectuals, which have grown apart and become hostile to each other (Rohlen 1978, 29). The gap between the two sectors has not been planned, for the Japanese, infused by the Confucian valuation of knowledge of how things are done, accepted as early as 1871 curricula established by the Ministry of Education for industry and commerce. As a result, the proportion of Japanese managers with college degrees rose from 8 percent in 1900 to 55 percent in 1928, a rate comparable to European industry today (Clark 1979, 36).

The schism between industry and education in Japan suggests that the pattern of industrial organization has characteristic tendencies. Clark identifies four of these. The first one and perhaps the most important is that the company in Japan tends to be "an elementary unit, a clearly defined cell of industrial or commercial activity, rather than merely one of a number of industrial organizations whose memberships overlap" (Clark 1979, 49).

The Japanese company serves as the elementary unit of Japanese industry, and at the same time provides the social nexus of membership and even identity for its employees. The second characteristic is a tendency for the company to be narrowly specialized and engage in one line of business or perhaps a few closely connected ventures.

The third tendency deserves elaboration. Japanese companies are graded, and arranged in a hierarchy in which the bigger the company the better its standing. Large firms engage in capital-intensive modern industries, achieve high productivity, and pay high wages. Small firms, sometimes in traditional industries, use less capital, achieve lower productivity, and pay lower wages. The differences between large and small firms have been called "industrial dualism" and "dual economy."

The fourth tendency is for the company to be associated with other companies in some form of group. This and the preceding three tendencies descry a society of industry, in which a company takes its place according to what it does, whether it is dominant in its particular line of business, how it is allied with prestigious companies, and so on. The society of industry influences the inner workings of each company, and the company has an effect on the wider community of industrial society (Clark 1979, 44-50). The same principle of reciprocal fusion that exists between the individual and the individual's social nexus is repeated among companies and groups of companies. Furthermore, the government assumes a major role with private industry, sometimes blurring the distinction between the public and private sectors. Indicative planning, as it is done in Japan between government and private industry, gives a brief glimpse of their relationship. The functional aspect of uniting government and private industry provides an abstract parallel to the training of recruits for a company. Whereas the physical training of the long march symbolized the transformation of the recruits into members of the company, indicative planning abstractly shows the union of government and industry for the economy of Japan.

Indicative planning in Japan is associated with the actions of Morozumi Yoshihiko, who was one of MITI's first officers to be assigned abroad after the war. In the Japanese embassy in Paris, he became acquainted with the planning in which the French were engaged as a condition of Marshall Plan aid. He returned to Tokyo to urge MITI to adopt indicative planning, described by him with terms such as "consent economy" and "mutually de-termined national targets" (Hadley 1975, 9). Japan did adopt in-dicative planning, which "has been a significant factor in the economy's extraordinarily [good] postwar performance" (ibid., 1).

The governments of all major economies today provide some direction to the economy by employing the tools of monetary and fiscal policy. In indicative planning, these tools are used but in addition the planning process addresses itself to resource alloca-tion for the economy as a whole. Indicative planning supplements market forces—it does not supplant them—by fusing explicitly enunciated goals with reliance on market mechanisms. Unlike central planning, which substitutes market mechanisms with plan-ning, "indicative planning uses market signals, the lure of profit, or market share, to pull resources from where they are in the market into areas where it is believed there will be greater long-run advantage for the nation" (ibid., 4).

When the government planners sit down with industry, they have the economy as a whole in mind as they use input-output analysis for tracing through the resource allocation consequences of changed investment patterns. Industry is neither ordered nor commanded to comply with the plans of the government; instead, the message is "it will be to your advantage to follow this course." When industry does not see the advantage, it does not follow the advice. Incentives offered by the government have taken the form of differential tax treatment, credit at preferential rates, credit availability, facilitated imports of technology, bars against manu-facturing, and bars against the marketing of foreign imports in Japan. When a company reached the export stage, additional benefits were provided but conditional on export performance: the stronger the performance, the larger the benefit (ibid., 14-15).

Hadley attributes the long-time frame of the Japanese planning to the tradition of dynamic economics instead of static economics of the Anglo-American school (p. 9). This assumption of economics as well as the features of indicative planning seem to fit Japanese deep culture. The integration of private industry and of govern-ment has contributed significantly to Japanese modernization. At the same time, indicative planning and the preferential treat-ment given to strong performance tend to concentrate exports in a few products; with Japan these have been cars, transport equip-ment, electric goods, steel, and chemicals (Clark 1979, 246). The resentment created among Japan's trading partners has weakened Japan's position in the world and made the economy vulnerable to structural conditions, political or economic, that will change the favorable economic picture of exports.

Prospects for the Future

The rise of petroleum prices in 1973 precipitated a severe recession in Japan. The response of the economy gave revealing glimpses of the culture and of the future of Japan. During the recession, Japan's real growth rate of 10 percent in 1973 plummeted to -0.3 percent in 1974, then rose to 1.4 percent in 1975, and 6.5 percent in 1976 (Matsuoka 1980, 5). The operating capacity of firms dropped from about 90 percent in 1973 to about 70 percent during the winter months of 1974-75 (Clark 1979, 244-45). Company profits of large firms fell from 3.76 percent of their turnover in 1973 to 0.84 percent in 1975. In fiscal 1973, 9,349 firms went bankrupt; two years later, 13,000, and the debts involved had doubled to more than 2,000 billion yen. Official sources reported that unemployment rose from 440,000 during 1973 to 740,000 during 1976. Certain types of industries were severely hit. Shipbuilding suffered. Companies responded to the crisis by realigning exports, which rose from 12,126 billion yen in 1973, to 23,838 billion yen in 1976, the rise covering the increased cost of oil and other imports. Japan penetrated foreign markets successfully with a few commodities, but the success caused resentment among its trading partners, who are often its competitors. To protect its position, Japan has tried to reduce exports and encourage imports by revaluation of the yen against other currencies. As the yen has appreciated against the U.S. dollar since 1975, the effects on trade have been uneven, and a large number of smaller companies have gone bankrupt, unable to compete on world markets.

> The older and less educated people who worked in these smaller firms could be said to have contributed twice to the Japanese export effort: once in that the low wages they received when they were in employment enabled bigger firms to export fine goods at low prices; and once more in that by losing their jobs they have borne the brunt of the effects of revaluation that the export drive made necessary. (Clark 1979, 246)

Although domestic economic privations were endured, the in-

29

tent was to minimize them. Japan's economy may have an international outlook but the value of its 1977-79 foreign trade was the equivalent of U.S. $815 million, which for 1978, provided a degree of dependence on exports in foreign trade of 10.0 percent. These statistics are higher than those for the United States at 6.7 percent exports, but lower than for European countries and Canada, which depend more on foreign trade than Japan. The Federal Republic of Germany's degree of dependence on exports for 1978 was 22.1 percent; the United Kingdom's, 23.0 percent; and the Netherlands', 38.3 percent. Japan's export drive following the rise of the price of petroleum, excepting only the United States, penetrated markets more dependent on foreign trade than Japan itself. Thus, the resentment caused is understandable from the perspective of foreign trade, again excepting the United States, which was mired in its own problem of unproductivity and hence reacted strongly to the Japanese exports, notably motor vehicles. Japan's concentration on a few commodities, partly a perverse result of indicative planning, gave its industry a predatory image, with an export figure of U.S. $103,032 million for 1979 that did not match West Germany's (U.S. $171,887), which had a cooperative image, nor that of the United States ($181,640) (Matsuoka 1980, 17).

The recourse to exports, taken by Japan to avoid domestic problems, compounded them. In 1973, Japanese companies could cut back on overtime and dismiss temporary workers but not permanent employees; the resilience that would allow an appreciable reduction in labor expenses was lacking. Nor were the companies able to diminish the cost of their capital; most ran on funds borrowed from banks, which also served as a stock exchange. Banks' interest rates were fixed and there were no dividends to stockholders that could be reduced. Facing these intractable structural conditions, the companies increased exports, partly to keep production lines busy and partly to improve cash flow; exports usually were paid for more quickly than sales to domestic customers (Clark 1979, 244). Throughout the crisis, the Japanese companies displaced resolution of their domestic problems to foreign exports. Recovery has been slow and uneven as the pressures on the Japanese economy continued.

The international attitude of Japan regarding exports is reversed regarding imports. Nearly impenetrable bars are in place to stem the flow of foreign products into Japan. The business

orientation of Japan, which relies less on exports than either
Germany or the United Kingdom, and Japan's use of exports to
resolve internal problems in industry, projects a symbolic meaning
to the *foreign factor* that transcends the economic sector and
implicates deep culture.

The contemporary exploitation of the foreign factor resembles
symbolically the use made of foreign influences since early times
in Japanese culture. Japanese society developed slowly and peace-
fully, based on peasants living in small villages and cultivating
rice. The energy and destructiveness of the human condition was
contained within the highly disciplined social forms of the vertical
group, so that primordial bonds associated with race, language,
religion, custom, ethnicity, or region did not create contending
groups that took recourse to war or economic competition. The
need for a universal religion to defend or unite contending parties,
or of a supreme God to be defended and to justify the human
being's efforts to conquer others, did not arise. The low key *kami*
provided the heart of the culture, assimilating the essence of
spirit, giving life to material things, and representing good, evil,
awe, excellence, terror—all with equanimity. Each part of Japanese
culture and society seemed self-contained and at the same time
seemed to represent all other parts of the culture. Indeed the cultural core of the society has persisted to this day in somewhat
the same holographic relationship of all of its parts.

The mosaic of the culture was first brought together and organized as a universal centralized state by Prince Shotoku, prince
regent for thirty years, 592-622 A.D., who used the foreign factors
of Buddhism as a universal teaching that everyone should follow
(Nakamura 1964, 394).

> Prince Shotoku, the real founder of the centralized state of Japan,
> proclaimed the Seventeen Article Constitution in 604 A.D. This was
> the first legislation in Japan—the characteristic expression of the
> original and creative development of the Japanese in those days,
> adopting to a great extent the civilizations and thoughts of China
> and India, chiefly based upon the spirit of Buddhism. (Ibid., 17)

The last part of the quotation deserves emphasis, the reference
to what I am calling the foreign factor. The original religion of
Japan, Shinto, did not produce universal or absolute concepts of
God or of law. Thus, Prince Shotoku founded the country on a

human ethic compatible with the spirit of *kami*. In the absence of an indigenous philosophy, or of an ascendant figure in the arts or in politics, Prince Shotoku himself never attained the rule of Japan in name, remaining prince regent. Japanese culture and society turned to the resolving power of foreign factors to bring Japanese culture and society into focus.

I offer the hypothesis that the foreign factor has been a necessary and useful resolution for Japanese culture since early times, and that the foreign factor is a distinctive aspect of Japanese culture in the same sense that gods or abstract themes function as accoutrements in other cultures. In Japan the foreign factor functions as the resolving light for a holographic culture. Using the hologram as a technical metaphor, the foreign factor is both part of the culture, resolving it, and yet not part of it. I propose a cultural structure with a *kami* based core, layered upon by developments and foreign intrusions. Traditionally, Japan has developed means and ways of modifying and adapting foreign intrusions, usually containing the foreign factor so that it does not influence mainstream Japanese life and continues to function as a resolving light cast upon the mosaic of Japanese culture. Historically, as with Buddhism, foreign factors have been assimilated into Japanese culture, however, in much modified form to harmonize with the spirit of *kami*. The Japanese scholar Nakamura in his magisterial work has shown how Buddhism was changed when it was introduced in Japan (Nakamura, 1964). The holographic culture changes somewhat, but the new form can still be peeled back to display the original core. The danger is that the limited certainty and predictability developed by the *kami*-faith and modified Buddhism now confronts a foreign factor of awesome dimensions, laying down a direct challenge to the heart and core of Japanese deep culture: a causal-technical analysis of the world providing the core of science and technology.

I cannot elaborate this theme because it lies beyond the scope of this paper. I am convinced that many Japanese sense the danger and are alarmed by the difficulty of containing the foreign factor and preserving Japanese *kami*-faith, the core of Japanese success. I believe that the remarkable resilience of Japanese culture and the inaccessibility of its writing and speaking systems to the Western way will eventually contain the foreign factor in its role of resolution. I believe that the nature of the containment will proceed as a qualitative approach to information, a development of cognitive theory to circumscribe the foreign factor, while the holographic culture preserves its own prized, embedded, and layered cultural mosaics. I believe that Japanese culture functions on a different logical principle, which I have attempted to sketch using the hologram as a metaphor, and that predictions of the future in Japan should incorporate in projections the holographic principle, with the foreign factor offering the resolution.

The future prospect of Japanese modernization will be tracked nearer the surface of the culture, in the history and events of group responses to the pressures exerted by the economy and modernization. Since the Meiji Restoration, various groups have borne the major burden for progress in Japan. In the Meiji period, the peasants carried the heaviest load; since World War II, the private citizen has been most heavily hit. Since the recession, the older and less-educated people have for the second time sacrificed for the nation. Pressure from these groups, such as increasing retirement age to sixty-five, will make labor more expensive because earnings rise with age and experience. When Japan made its mark on the economies of the world during the 1960s, its labor force was young and in its prime. Now that it is older, under pressure to raise the age of retirement, the Japanese economy faces restricted foreign markets and increased vigor in the competition from abroad as Japan's special niche in the economies of the world begins to crumble. The second source of pressure on the economy of Japan is likely to be more indirect, affecting the educational and political systems.

The less educated and those who fail to make their way through the rough and competitive system of Japanese examinations are likely to exert pressure by mounting a movement or exerting political pressures on the government and indirectly on the economy. Because the world of education is separated from the economic institutions, the pressures on the companies will be indirect. They have already taken measures to counteract the influences of individualism and Westernization that they consider detrimental to their interest. Perhaps their hostility toward educational enterprises contributes to the economy because they conduct their own professional training, which consists of creating a citizen in the company's image from the new recruit. The schools and universities have done their job by selecting students through the examination system and providing them with a general education. The rest is in the hands of the companies.

The cultural arrangement proved resilient and survived the jolt of the 1973-75 recession, but Japan, like the United States, will most likely lose its special economic niche in the world as its economy slows down, the cost of labor increases, the competition from the established industrial powers improves, and newcomers such as Korea display their economic mettle. Japanese companies appear to have used the period since the recession for assimilation time. A number of changes appear to be in process for some of the large companies. Still, it will be difficult to satisfy the growing demand for an easier life (particularly from the families of hard-working men), time for more leisure, and a lessening of the fierce competition and selfishness that has brought the Japanese economy so far (Clark 1979, 257-61).

From the point of view of deep culture, we have seen that the structure of the economy and of the company have made an exquisite match with traditional Japanese deep culture. For the future, foreign factors can be expected to grow, increasing the problem of containment. Changes in the field of communication, growth of the media, and lessening significance of informal and interpersonal communication represents a frontal attack on the traditional forms of ambiguity and vagueness of communication. These developments represent a threat to traditional Japanese deep culture, and whether they will be contained in their relevant places of application or will spread to other sectors and areas of Japan remains to be seen.

Japan, in the way of a crustacean, will probably be compelled to shed its outer skeleton of heavy industry, which drains its wealth while supplying plants with raw materials and energy. The natural area for Japan to meet its need for developing its own technology, now that it has achieved parity with the most industrialized nations, is in communications. Application would stress the Japanese intelligence, hard work, and dedication to craftsmanship. It would also put a premium on the demonstrated Japanese emphasis on quality, in distinction to quantity, in the field of communication.

The years ahead promise difficult times as the economy and the culture adjust to emerging realities in the twenty-first century. Relying on its core deep culture, Japan will travel a rocky path, and its future will probably depend on the Japanese ability to mobilize its *maki*-faith and effectively communicate its meaning to the world for the purpose of maintaining foreign factors as resolutions rather than determinants of its way of life.

Note:

This entire chapter is from the Proceedings of the ICUS, 1981, Seoul, Korea, Volume II, 891-929.
1. In the aftermath of the Three Mile Island nuclear accident in the United States, the writer conducted a study of the managing of nuclear power during a crisis in the United States, Korea, Japan, and Germany, and concluded that cultural differences exist in thinking about and "managing" risk, uncertainty, and probabilities. Subjective prediction (i.e., categorical predictions) seems more compatible with the Japanese way than objective probabilities. However, the writer is familiar with development work conducted by a Japanese company that goes beyond the specifications of the U.S. manufacturer in using computer simulations to estimate the probability of malfunctions in its hardware technology. The Japanese engineers have introduced variables not used by the U.S. manufacturer in creative computer simulations of the performance of their technology.

References

Aida, Yuji. "Anatomy of the Japanese Consciousness." In *Guides to Japanese Culture*, ed. Murakami Hyol and Edward G. Seidensticker. Tokyo: Japan Culture Institute, 1977.

Bateson, Gregory, *Naven*. 2d ed. Stanford: Stanford University Press, 1958.

Bloom, Irene. "Japanese Conception of Nature" (letter). *Science* 184 (1974): 850.

Campbell, Louise, "Science in Japan." *Science* 143 (1964): 776-82.

Cho, Koyoki T. "Japanese Ideologies and Cross-Cultural Understandings." *Business and Government Review* (University of Missouri). 1966.

Clark, Rodney. *The Japanese Company*. New Haven: Yale University Press, 1979.

Hadley, Eleanor M. "Japanese Indicative Planning." Paper presented at Southeast Region Conference, Association for Asian Studies, 23-25 January 1975.

Hamaguchi, Eshun. "Basic Problem in the Study of Anthropology." *Personality* 8 (1980).

Herbert, Jean. *Shinto: The Fountainhead of Japan*. New York: Stein & Day, 1967.

Hsu, F. C. K. *Confucianism*. Pondicherry, India: Sri Aurobindo International Center of Education, 1966.

Keane, John. *The Kami Concept: A Basis for Understanding and Dialogue*. Oriental Studies, No. 16. Tokyo: Orient Institute for Religious Research, 1980.

Lebra, Takie Sugiyama. *Japanese Patterns of Behavior*. Honolulu: University Press of Hawaii, 1976.

Lerner, Daniel. *The Passing of Traditional Society*. New York: Free Press, 1958.

Lockwood, William W. *The Economic Development of Japan*. Princeton: Princeton University Press, 1968.

Maruyama, Masao. "The Intellectual Tradition in Japan." In *Guides to Japanese Culture*, ed. Murakami Hyol and Edward G. Seidensticker. Tokyo: Japanese Culture Institute, 1977.

Matsuoka, Toshio, ed. *Japan 1980.* Tokyo: Keizai Koho Center, 1980.

Nakamura, Hajime. *The Ideal of World Community.* Madras: University of Madras, Dr. S. Radhakrishnan Institute for Advanced Study in Philosophy, 1981.

————. *A History of the Development of Japanese Thought.* Tokyo.

————. *Ways of Thinking of Eastern Peoples: India-China-Tibet-Japan.* Honolulu: East-West Center Press, 1964.

Nakane, Chie. *Japanese Society.* New York: Penguin Books, 1970.

Pascale, Richard T., and Athos, Anthony G. *The Art of Japanese Management.* New York: Simon & Schuster, 1981.

Rohlen, Thomas P. "The Education of a Japanese Banker." *Human Nature* (January 1978): 22-30.

Stewart, Edward C. "Adapting to Deep Structure of Business in Japan." Paper presented at the 20th International Congress of Applied Psychology, International Association of Applied Psychology, Edinburgh, July 1982.

————. "Deep Culture in Technical-Industrial Society." Unpublished paper.

————. "American Techology and Deep Culture." Unpublished paper.

Suzuki, Daisetse. "Zen and Japanese Culture." In *Guides to Japanese Culture.* ed. Murakami Hyol and Edward G. Seidensticker. Tokyo: Japan Culture Institute, 1977.

Vogel, Ezra F. *Japan as Number One.* Cambridge: Harvard University Press, 1979.

Watanabe, Masao. "The Concept of Nature in Japanese Culture." *Science* 183 (1974): 279- 82.

2.

Economic Development in South Korea

Paul W. Kuznets

I. Introduction

South Korea is one of the four East Asian "miracle economies" (the others are Taiwan, Singapore, and Hong Kong) whose speed and quality of economic development distinguish the group from the rest of the developing world.[1] Korea's gross national product increased at an average annual rate of almost 10 percent from the mid-1960s to 1973 and, despite oil shocks and worldwide economic recession, rose by more than 7 percent a year during the 1973-82 period. ("Korea" and "Korean" are substituted for "South Korea" and "South Korean" when possible in what follows.) One result of this rapid growth or development (the terms are used synonymously here) is that the average person's income tripled in two decades, so that the typical Korean is now much better off than twenty years ago. Standard welfare surrogates for food and housing consumption, access to medical services, and so forth all confirm the increase in individual economic well-being during the period. Also, the averages do not conceal wide disparities, as is often the case. Income inequality has increased somewhat since the mid-1960s, but it is still low by international standards. Though Korea's "miracle" status is not unique—it is shared with three other East Asian economies—it is nonetheless particularly impressive because Korea is much larger than the others, and consequently has had to overcome larger problems, including the devastation of the Korean War.

Rapid output growth, relatively even income distribution, and widespread welfare gains are perhaps the main characteristics of Korea's recent development, but there are others also worth mentioning. In particular, development has altered the country's industrial structure and, with it, people's working lives. Growth has centered in the industrial sector, especially manufacturing for export, and because manufacturing has been concentrated in urban areas, not only to benefit from agglomeration but also to make use of access to ports and to the government, new employment has also been concentrated there. What was mainly a rural and agrarian economy only two decades ago is therefore now a predominantly urban and industrial economy. The speed of the transformation is noteworthy because the same changes in structure (and urbanization) took place over much longer periods in today's developed countries. The rapidity of Korea's growth has probably contributed to crowding, to pollution, and to inefficiency (this last because supply is less elastic in the short run than in the long run). Even if slower growth would not have reduced the diseconomies or negative by-products of development, it might have lessened their impact. On the other hand, the rapidity of Korea's growth has created an expansionary psychology, inspired business confidence, and induced receptivity to change. Without these, the alternative to rapid growth might not have been moderate growth but possibly little or no growth.

Though the welfare consequences of Korea's rapid development are necessarily a matter for speculation, the dimensions of this development are well documented. In particular, we know that development was slow and unsatisfactory from the end of the Korean War until the mid-1960s, when growth accelerated. It has remained unusually rapid during most of the period since then. The acceleration raises the question of why development was slow before the mid-1960s and fast afterward. Possible reasons are examined in the following section, which suggests that although policy changes were needed for more rapid growth, acceleration could not have occurred without favorable external conditions and the previous accumulation of (unexploited) productive potential.

Reasons for acceleration are significant because they account for Korea's economic success. Success, in turn, has aroused interest in Korea as a development model. However, it is not at all clear that Korea's experience is transferable, and it is quite possible that the model may prove misleading. One reason for skepticism is that economic results have social, cultural, political, and institutional causes as well as economic causes. Some of Korea's noneconomic attributes, such as the Confucian tradition, may be found elsewhere (most notably among the other East Asian miracle economies), but many are not. This does not necessarily mean that Korea's success is *sui generis* but that the Korean model may be more or less applicable according to local circumstances and the particular characteristic being considered.[2] For instance, two characteristics that appear to be especially significant in Korea's development are examined in subsequent sections. One of these is the active role played by the government in economic affairs. Because the government's activism has cultural and political as well as economic causes, this is one instance where the Korean model is not generally applicable. The second significant characteristic discussed here is the government's heavy emphasis on export expansion. This is an aspect of the Korean model that should be applicable elsewhere.

Though the public sector's share of economic activity is masked in Korea by accounting difficulties, it is probably not very different from public-sector shares in other developing countries. It is therefore not so much the size of government output or expenditure as the government's influence on the private sector that makes the economic role of government significant. Neither the Park nor the Chun government has hesitated to intervene in markets or to guide the invisible hand as policy has dictated. Possible reasons for activism are assessed and several features of the policy-implementation process—planning and credit allocation—are discussed in Part III, "The Government and the Economy." Korea's reasons for choosing an export expansion strategy and the economic effects of expansion are examined in Part IV. Recent changes and possible future developments in the economic roles of government and of exports are considered in Part V.

II. The Record

Though Korea has a long and distinguished history, South Korea's development experience dates back only to 1948. Even in the relatively short period since then, development was interrupted by the Korean War (1950-53). Development can of course be traced to earlier years when Korea was a colony in the Japanese empire (1905-45) or to the Yi Dynasty (1392-1905), but in the first instance Korea was an economic and political satellite, not an independent country, and in both cases South Korea was only part of a unified Korea. These differences in circumstances, I believe, make comparison of South Korea's experience before 1948 with what followed of questionable value in explaining subsequent development, particularly because the South Koreans were unable to control their own economic and political fate.[3] This was also true of the years 1945-48 when, though occupying the same territory as South Korea now does, the southern part of the Korean peninsula was ruled by a U.S. military government. Only with the establishment of the Republic of Korea under President Syngman Rhee in 1948 did South Korea (hereafter simply "Korea") acquire the independence needed to control its own development experience.

Political independence may cloak economic and military (strategic) dependence, and this was true of Korea before the mid-1960s. The modest economic progress achieved after 1945 with the help of U.S. emergency relief and economic assistance was wiped out in the Korean War, and the war itself confirmed U.S. responsibility to assist Korean reconstruction and subsequent development. Korea was clearly a client state during the reconstruction era (reconstruction was pretty much complete by 1958) and into the mid-1960s, when assistance was still sufficiently large to permit U.S. aid officials to influence Korea's economic policies, most notably the decision to adopt a liberalization program that would free the economy of restrictions, or what has been termed "the second postwar restructuring."[4] Since the mid-1960s grants have been replaced by loans, surplus agricultural (PL 480) commodity shipments have been phased out, and total economic assistance has been greatly reduced.[5] Military assistance has dropped too, particularly since the establishment of a domestic armaments industry. The decline in assistance, combined with Korea's own economic successes, means that Korea is no longer the U.S. client state that it once was.[6]

The consistent statistics needed to explain Korea's economic growth or development are available only for the period since 1953. They show quite unimpressive performance from the end of the Korean War through the student uprising in 1960 that unseated the Rhee regime, the short-lived successor government of Chang Myŏn, the military coup led by Park Chung-hee, and the ill-considered currency reform adopted in 1962 by the new military government under General Park. GNP rose at an average annual rate of 3.7 percent. From 1962 to 1973, however, GNP increased at an annual rate of 9.6 percent and has continued to grow only somewhat less rapidly since then (7.1 percent a year from 1973 to 1982) despite the oil shocks of the 1970s and the domestic political turmoil of the early 1980s.[7]

Basic indicators of Korea's economic development and those for Korea's World Bank reference group of sixty-one middle-income countries are given in table 2.1. The indicators and the acceleration in the pace of Korea's development raise questions of why development was so slow before the mid-1960s, and of what happened to raise the pace since then, either when compared with

Table 2.1.

Basic Economic Indicators for Korea, and for Average of Sixty-One Middle-Income Countries, 1960 and 1980

	Korea	Middle-Income Countries
Per capita GNP (U.S. $), 1980	1,520	1,400
GDP growth rate (annual average)		
1960-1970	8.6	5.9
1970-1980	9.5	5.6

	1960	1980	1960	1980
Distribution of GDP (%)				
Agriculture	37	16	24	15
Industry	20	41	30	40
Services	43	43	46	45
Expenditure of GDP (%)				
Public consumption	15	13	11	14
Private consumption	84	64	70	64
Gross domestic investment	11	31	20	27
Gross domestic saving	1	23	19	25
Exports [1]	3	37	16	25
Resource balance [2]	-10	-8	-1	-2

1 - Goods plus nonfactor services.
2 - Difference between exports and imports of goods and nonfactor services.

Source: World Bank, World Development Report, 1982 (New York: Oxford University Press, 1982), Indicator Tables 1, 2, 3, and 5.

Korea's earlier experience or the contemporary experience of other middle-income countries.

There are a number of possible reasons that development was slow from 1953 to 1963. One was the prior division of the peninsula, which separated two complementary parts of a single economy: rice production and light industry in the South; heavy industry, electric power generation, and wheat in the North. This was in addition to the breakup of the Japanese empire, in which Korea's specialized role no longer existed. (Korea supplied rice to Japan, for example, and imported finished consumer goods). Also, there were immediate problems of liberation, including a shortage of administrators and professionals (high-level personnel had been Japanese), hyperinflation as the Japanese monetized their assets on departure, and a misoriented transport system. Coal was plentiful in the Northeast, for example, but there were no rail connections to bring it to Seoul. The process of transforming a fragmented economy into a functioning whole and of rebuilding after the Korean War was necessarily time consuming.

Another reason for slow growth was the Rhee government's preoccupation with political problems at the expense of the country's economic needs. There was no overall economic strategy, possibly because such a strategy would be inconsistent with the political goal of reuniting the two Koreas. Also, the economy was hampered by inflation, the overvalued exchange rates used to maximize U.S. aid receipts, heavy trade deficits, unrealistically low bank interest rates, and inadequate tax collection. In short, Korea displayed all the characteristics of inept policy and weak implementation found in many developing countries. In addition, exports lagged while emphasis on import substitution created the usual web of controls that perverted entrepreneurial incentives by making avoidance of controls rather than increased productivity the main source of profit. Furthermore, substitution was becoming increasingly difficult as the opportunities were exhausted for the sort of easy substitution that suited domestic factor proportions (abundant labor, scarce capital) and employed simple technology. It is hardly surprising that growth slowed during the mid-1950s and then came to a halt in 1959-62 when political upheaval and the new military government's initial fumbling upset everyday economic activities.

Development accelerated during the mid-1960s and the economy expanded very rapidly during most of the period until 1979.

One reason was a policy shift under the new Park government (Park was elected president in 1963) from emphasis on import substitution to promotion of exports. The shift was probably as much a result of the evident failure of import substitution and widespread public demand for better economic performance as it was due to pressure from U.S. advisers and the imminent decline in U.S. assistance. Whatever the reason, the new strategy included a series of liberalization measures during the mid-1960s that encouraged entrepreneurs to expand output for export. The result was a spectacular increase in exports from U.S. $100 million in 1964 to $1 billion in 1971 and $21 billion by 1981. Rapid industrialization followed, for these exports have included an increasingly varied range of manufactures. Table 2.1 documents this process during the 1960-80 period: Korea's industrial and export shares both rose from less than to more than the middle-income country average. It shows, in short, that Korea is a good example of what is meant by "export-led" growth.

The shift in strategy may have been a necessary condition for acceleration in the pace of development but it was not sufficient in itself. Korea's exports have soared since the mid-1960s because world markets were expanding rapidly, particularly those in the United States and Japan, Korea's main trading partners. On the supply side, Korea, the epitome of a labor-surplus economy, had unexploited comparative advantage in its hard-working and relatively well-educated workers. There was also an ample stock of entrepreneurial talent, no significant opposition to the new export strategy, and a regime with sufficient control of the bureaucratic process to implement its economic policies. A number of these elements, such as the well-educated labor force or absence of opposition, can be traced to land reform or generalization of education that predate the strategy shift by many years. The new strategy was therefore only one of many elements responsible for the acceleration of the mid-1960s.

Although exploitation of favorable export opportunities can explain rapid development through 1973, it does not explain the rapid development after 1973 when the first oil shock and subsequent worldwide inflation and contraction limited export opportunities. Development after 1973 was rapid because the Koreans employed a risky strategy to maintain growth. Instead of adopting restrictive policies to offset the inflationary impact of the oil shock, as did most countries, the government increased foreign borrowing, used the proceeds to expand industrial capacity, and the new industrial capacity to generate more exports.[8] This strategy might have succeeded if it had not been combined with an obsessive drive to expand the heavy and chemical industries. The drive contributed to inflation, and the inflation, when combined with the second oil shock, the political unrest following President Park's assassination, and a disastrous harvest, led in 1980 to the first downturn in Korea's GNP growth since 1956.[9] Inflation has been curbed since then by the new government of General (now President) Chun Doo-hwan, but the economy suffered from excess capacity and underemployment in 1981-82 before recovery began in 1983.

III. The Government and the Economy

The influence of the political leadership ("regime," here) on Korea's or any other country's economic development should depend on the size of the public sector, the capacity of the regime to implement policy, the priority attached to economic goals, the ease or difficulty of governing, and so forth.[10] These are all difficult to specify and depend, in turn, on such disparate factors as Korea's geopolitical position and Confucian ethic as well as on the regime's characteristics and economic institutions—which, in Korea's case, are mainly the market mechanism and private property rights rather than central planning and state ownership. Economic response to regime stimulus is likely to differ among countries or between regimes in the same country because of these intervening factors. We know, for example, that a change in required reserves alters the money supply and eventually affects prices. We know little about the size and speed of response, however, because these depend among other things upon how the bureaucracy responds to political directives. It is hardly surprising, therefore, given the complexity of relationships and the obvious influence of institutional and cultural factors, that economists treat "government" as exogenous and that neither economists nor political scientists have a paradigm that can satisfactorily explain how the regime or government influences economic development.

One factor that ought to determine the impact of government

actions on the economy is the relative size of the public sector, on the grounds that the larger the public sector's share of the economic activity, the more ways the regime can affect the economy.[11] Possible measures of the size or relative importance of the public sector include the government's share in total expenditures (budget ÷ GNP), the proportion of gross domestic product that originates in the public sector, or the revenue ratio (government revenues ÷ GNP), the government's share of total claims on resources. In 1980, for instance, the revenue ratio was 22 percent, the government's share of total expenditures (the public consumption shown in table 2.1 plus public investment) was 20 percent. There are no meaningful statistics on the proportion of GNP originating in the public sector. Any of these measures is misleading, however, because they understate the size of Korea's public sector. One reason is that accounts of public and quasi-public enterprises, such as the tobacco monopoly and the Korea Electric Power Company, are included with the private sector not, as is the practice elsewhere, with the public sector. Also, U.S. military assistance to Korea is omitted from government budgets, the national accounts, and balance-of-payments statements. Published *won* defense expenditure accounted for 30 percent of central government budget outlays in 1980, or 6-7 percent of GNP. U.S. military assistance, though substantial in the past ($7.3 billion from 1953 to 1978), has been equivalent to only 5 percent of budgeted defense expenditures in the past few years.

If it is impossible to calculate the size of Korea's public sector, or compare it with public sectors of other middle-income countries, something can be said of the pattern of the government's economic activities and of trends in revenues and expenditures. Infrastructure requirements during early stages of development typically generate heavy government investment; demand for social expenditures increases government consumption at later stages. Government investment does not decline as a proportion of GNP in Korea, however, and government consumption remained a fairly steady 8-10 percent of GNP since 1953 before rising to 11-12 percent in the early 1980s. Revenues, in turn, typically rise more than proportionally with GNP as an economy develops. Growth of per capita income accounts only for absolute increase; the additional, relative increase is associated with other concomitants of development that increase tax capacity, such as growing monetization and expansion of foreign trade.[12] Korea's experience has been typical as revenue ratios increased from 14-16 percent during the early 1960s to 20-22 percent in 1979-81. The increase can be attributed partly to supply-side factorslike monetization and reform of tax administration (since 1964), and partly to demand-side considerations like the high-income elasticity of demand for education and other publicly provided services.

Though revenue ratios and public-expenditure shares tend to rise with per capita income, they differ markedly among countries with the same per capita income. This suggests that the government's share in the economy is influenced by political preferences as well as by demand considerations or the government's revenue-raising capacity. The increase in expenditures (and therefore revenues) has been limited in Korea both by historical accident and by political preference. At the end of the Korean War the country inherited a swollen bureaucracy and defense establishment that needed little expansion as the economy grew. Also, there has been a continued "production-first" philosophy that, like Japan's, has directed resources to increasing output rather than to social ends. This can be seen in Korea's recent government budgets, in which less than 10 percent of total outlays has been allocated to social-expenditure categories, such as social security, welfare, housing, and community services.

What is unexpected in Korea is the large role of public enterprise in an otherwise free-enterprise economy. Jones and Sakong show that in 1972, for instance, public enterprises produced two-thirds of the country's electric, gas, and water supplies; 30 percent of transport and communications services; 15 percent of manufacturing; 30 percent of mining output; and an unusual 80-90 percent of financial services.[13] While many public enterprises originated in Japanese concerns whose ownership was vested in the government after liberation, public-enterprise production is important (9 percent of domestic product in 1972; possibly more now) less because of inheritance than because of above-average growth in enterprise output during recent decades. The growth probably reflects increased demand for the sorts of goods and services suited to public production; a cost-efficient enterprise record rather than a history of drain on the public fisc, as in many developing countries; and a pragmatic rather than an ideological approach to issues of public *versus* private ownership.[14]

The Korean government may influence the economy more in other ways than by its fiscal activity or direct production, for the private sector accounts for roughly three-quarters of national output and expenditure. Whether a government is active in economic affairs or not should depend on the priority accorded to economic goals, the regime's ability to control the bureaucracy, the ease or difficulty of governing the country, and possibly the earlier success achieved by assuming an active role. In each case the situation in Korea permits the government to exert great influence in economic matters, which perhaps explains why both the Park and Chun regimes have played an active, even interventionist, role in the economy.

One possible reason for the economic activism of Korean governments is that they have been led since the early 1960s by authoritarian regimes, perhaps best described as military, bureaucratic-authoritarian regimes. They are "bureaucratic" because the military rules more as an institution than through the personal rule of a military strongman; "authoritarian" because obedience to government dictates is required of individuals.[15] There is no reason, however, that authoritarian regimes should be more active in economic affairs than democratic regimes except, perhaps, that without the same need for prior consultation and widespread agreement, they can act faster. Rather, the activism of Korea's authoritarian regimes has probably resulted from their success, not their authoritarianism, because successful action should foster further action, whereas unsuccessful action would not. Another logical possibility, that authoritarian governments are successful because they are authoritarian, is contradicted by evidence that there is no correlation between successful economic activism and type of regime, though countries with "authoritarian forms of government [tend to] perform either very well or very poorly."[16]

Other than success as a possible cause of activism, action is promoted by the factors that ease the tasks of government in Korea. One of these is the hierarchic and authoritarian Confucian tradition of family and political relationships. Though the Park and Chun regimes may not have received the Mandate of Heaven, they have had at least the tacit support of the population. Consistent with this tradition has been a history of highly centralized government; regions and localities have never had much autonomy and do not now. Also, population, geography, and economic size are all favorable. Korea's land area (98,000 square kilometers) is compact, unlike that of Indonesia and the Philippines, and its smaller population (39 million) is easier to administer than the enormous populations of countries like India and China. Market size (population times per capita income; now about U.S. $60 billion) is large enough to permit economies of scale. Though it may not be sufficient to support adequately a domestic auto industry, it is large enough to permit a much wider range of specialization than can be attained in small markets like Singapore's or Hong Kong's. Also, the population is unusually homogeneous; there are no linguistic or ethnic minorities with separatist tendencies or demands for special treatment. Furthermore, the threat of attack from the North has had a powerful unifying effect. Although the threat is sometimes used by the regime in a cynical fashion to stifle dissent, it also provides a sense of national economic purpose because economic strength is seen as a defense prerequisite. Finally, little evidence exists to indicate the social malaise associated with wide income disparities and multigenerational poverty. In fact, inequality of income distribution is unusually low, and there seems to be a fairly high degree of social and economic mobility.[17]

Another reason for the government's active role in the economy, besides success with activism and the ease of governing, has been effective administration. It is effective because the state apparatus can be used to transmit and enforce the regime's policy directives either by compulsion or by administrative discretion. Myrdal has characterized the "soft states" of South Asia as ones where "policies decided on are often not enforced" and where "the authorities. . .are reluctant to place obligations on people".[18] A "hard state" can be specified by contrast: one that is ready to place obligations on people and to enforce them if necessary. Korea is definitely a "hard state" in that the regime has been effective in obtaining compliance with government directives, either by direct command or by discretionary controls. The efficacy of direct command under an authoritarian regime is self-evident, but the success of discretionary controls deserves mention. Such controls work well in Korea because the leadership's commitment to economic development is passed down through the hierarchical command structure to the lowest administrative levels so that no official can afford to act in ways that obstruct development.[19] Both types of control are widely used in Korea because the government has not hesitated to intervene in the economy, and because the approach to policy implementation has been highly pragmatic. If one type of intervention proves ineffective, another is tried.

A final reason for the government's economic activism has been the high priority attached to economic goals. Insofar as media coverage reflects public priorities, then the unusual emphasis by the media on economic matters can be taken as evidence in point. The overall economic goal, typically the improvement of living standards for the population (i.e., mass welfare), is only one of several major regime goals in most countries, and Korea is no exception. Other possible goals, such as the preservation of political power or the maintenance of national security, are important too and may shape economic policies. These three are probably the major goals in Korea and are competitive as well as complementary, which explains why policies to achieve self-sufficiency in food production or to foster heavy industry may appear irrational to economists but make perfect sense to policymakers.[20] Since the early 1960s, the economic goal has perhaps been emphasized more in Korea than in most other developing countries because the economic failures of the Rhee government made economic improvement the overriding national objective, and because good economic performance has been the main means of achieving legitimacy for new military regimes.

Evidence is plentiful that the Park and Chun regimes have played active roles in economic affairs. For example, the list of items eligible for import, the terms of export financing, and tax-rate maxima are often changed. Besides the usual repertoire of monetary, fiscal, and commercial policy instruments, Korean governments have used other means to achieve economic ends, including direct market intervention. After the second oil shock and disastrous harvest of 1980, for instance, the Chun regime used wage and price controls to curb inflation; both the Park and Chun regimes have employed a "two-price" policy to increase farmers' incomes and reduce urban rice costs. Of particular interest, however, are planning, credit allocation, and export promotion. Planning, perhaps the leading symbol of government intervention, is of interest because the function of planning is controversial in Korea. Credit allocation is noteworthy because it is the major single instrument of government control.

The possible relation of planning to Korea's economic success has inspired a literature that, at one extreme, comes close to attributing accelerated growth to planning and, at the other, to viewing the plans mainly as a means for improving market functions. The plans themselves, which date back to the Rhee regime, have not always been adopted and vary widely according to the econometric sophistication with which they are constructed. Planning is probably more prescriptive than in Japan, for example, because the government tends to intervene more in the economy than does the Japanese government, and because it has more power to allocate credit. Still, there is a large, market-oriented private sector that is not bound by the plans. Also, because actual growth has typically been well above plan targets, the plan itself, despite annual adjustments, tends to become increasingly irrelevant with time. In addition, the plans do not specify the means or policies that will be needed to reach plan targets, and it is evident that some targets are included without providing the means to achieve them, possibly because the planners must cater to political as well as economic imperatives.[21] Given such limitations, it is possible to adopt a minimalist position in assessing the function of Korea's plans: they serve to sustain market functions by reducing risk and uncertainty, minimizing information costs, and generating an expansionary psychology.[22] If plans do more than this, that is, if they have a role independent of improving market functions, then it may be to establish priorities and to insure that public-sector activities are feasible and coordinated. To assert, however, that "public sector policies derived from the planning function were indispensable to the economic growth of the last 10-15 years [before 1977]" is to overstate the case.[23] Because other developing countries have employed planning without achieving Korea's economic success, what may be significant in Korea is not planning itself but the combination of planning and sophisticated policy implementation.[24]

Credit allocation and control of access to foreign exchange are perhaps the main means of achieving the government's economic goals in Korea. The typical enterprise is highly leveraged and therefore especially vulnerable to reduction or withdrawal of credit. Loanable funds are scarce and lending rates are limited by statute so that the organized money market (i.e., the banking system) cannot fully satisfy credit requirements. The government directs and supervises special-purpose banks, such as the Korea Exchange Bank or the National Agricultural Cooperatives Federation, and controls commercial banks both through the Monetary

Board, which supervises commercial bank activities, and until recently through stock ownership as the major shareholder in four of the five nationwide commercial banks. Access to foreign credit is also controlled because foreign loans are guaranteed by the Exchange Bank. The unorganized money market (curb market) is the one credit source not controlled by the government.[25] Excess demand for credit can usually be satisfied in the curb market, but only at a cost of roughly three to six times going rates at banks. Because the government probably controls three-quarters to four-fifths of the supply, and excess demand requires rationing, it is not surprising that credit is allocated in ways that are consistent with the government's economic goals to firms that promise to perform satisfactorily.[26] In recent years allocation has favored export activity, heavy and chemical industry projects, and the *chaebŏl*, or large conglomerate enterprises.

IV. Exports: Key to Korea's High-Growth Strategy

Export expansion has been the main theme of Korean economic policy since the mid-1960s. A wide range of incentives, particularly preferential loans, has been used to promote exports and, as indicated earlier, exports have responded by growing phenomenally.[27] The immediate reasons for new emphasis on exports were mainly negative, in that earlier import-substitution policies had failed and could not be continued, and exports would provide the foreign exchange needed to offset the expected decline in foreign assistance. There are also conventional economic reasons for export promotion, if only to offset the distortions created by foreign-exchange controls and the tariffs used to protect import-substitute industries. Positive reasons are provided by the standard comparative-advantage argument (in Korea's case, advantage in labor-intensive and possibly skill-intensive products) and the argument that competition in world markets makes output for export necessarily efficient. More recently, though, it has become apparent that export expansion is also the key to Korea's high-growth strategy. Growth is maximized by allocating a very large proportion of total expenditure to investment, and Korea's investment ratios (investment ÷ GNP) of 25 to 35 percent in recent years have been among the world's highest. The investment is partly financed by foreign borrowing, which not only provides foreign exchange to pay for the imported equipment and other

51

foreign goods and services needed for investment purposes but also makes up for insufficient domestic saving. Foreign borrowing (saving) has, in fact, financed about a third of investment in recent years. Exports are important because they generate the foreign exchange needed to repay loans from foreign lenders. Continued export expansion is also important because it encourages foreign lenders to extend loans to Korean firms since expansion promises to generate the foreign exchange that will be needed to repay debts (of around U.S. $40 billion at the end of 1983) when they come due.

The three strategy alternatives that might, conceivably, have been adopted by the new Park government in the early 1960s included the continuation of earlier import-substitution policies; expansion of agricultural production for export; or reorientation of manufacturing from output for the domestic market to output for export. Import substitution usually follows a logical pattern in which the first or easy phase is devoted mainly to types of output for which there is an established market (i.e., consumer goods) and that can be produced using simple, labor-intensive technology. Textiles, apparel, footwear, and processed foods are typical first-phase import substitutes. Korea had already entered the second phase of substitution by the early 1960s, however, a phase in which substitution shifts to intermediate goods or materials— such as cement and rubber products—that are produced by more complex, capital intensive technology, often in large plants to benefit from economies of scale. Because these products were not well suited to existing factor endowments while domestic markets were too small to permit scale economies, production of second-phase products proved inefficient and the economy suffered from overcapacity and a decline in the rate of output growth. Continued emphasis on import substitution clearly offered little promise for renewing growth, and neither did agricultural exports. Though Korea had been a major source of rice for Japan during the colonial era, this market was now cut off. Also, high-value rice exports had been offset by low-value millet and barley imports (hence the term *starvation exports*), and the potential for expanding agricultural output, given Korea's limited supply of arable land, was distinctly limited. This left the export of labor-intensive manufactures, many of which were already being produced domestically, as the only feasible alternative. To bring this about required export-promotion measures, devaluation, and the other elements of a liberalization program that would encourage entrepreneurs to produce for export rather than substitute for imports. This was all accomplished, with U.S. backing, in the mid-1960s.[28]

An ample labor supply was not in itself sufficient to establish Korea's comparative advantage in labor-intensive manufactures. Labor had to be available, which it was, because there was a surplus of underemployed workers who could be transferred to the new industries (without significant loss of output) from agriculture and the services.[29] Labor had to be cheap, which it was, because there were no effective unions or other barriers to low wages, such as the high-cost of wage goods. Labor also had to be productive, for competitiveness depends on unit labor costs, a function of both wages and productivity. Productivity was fairly high because Korean entrepreneurs are adept at organizing production and workers are relatively well educated, skilled, and hard working. Finally, the so-called strong-factor hypothesis had to hold, so that what was produced by labor-intensive methods in Korea could not be undersold by employing capital-intensive methods elsewhere. Cross-national comparisons show that this hypothesis is, in fact, correct, and that what is produced by labor-intensive means in one country is produced by the same means elsewhere.[30] The hypothesis, incidentally, only requires similar ordering of industries by factor intensity; all production can be more labor intensive in Korea than in capital-abundant economies like the United States. Figures for Korea's exports in 1972 and in 1981 are given in table 2.2 and grouped according to whether they are products of L-industry (labor-intensive industry) or H-industry (capital-intensive industry) groups. Table 2.2 shows, not surprisingly, that Korea's export mix, particularly in earlier years, has been consistent with comparative advantage in labor-intensive manufactures.[31]

The main economic advantage of concentration in labor-intensive exports for a country like Korea is that products of cheap, abundant labor can be exchanged for capital-intensive or natural resource-intensive products that are either expensive or impossible to produce locally. Evidence for this can be found in data for the 1960s, which show that Korea's imports were much more capital intensive than its exports.[32] Another advantage is that export expansion provides productive employment for people who would otherwise be underemployed. (Underemployment, not unemployment, is the most likely alternative to employment where, as in Korea, tightly knit families absorb the otherwise unemployed in family business, and self-employment rather than work for wages predominates). Several studies indicate that export expansion made a major contribution to employment during the 1960s, both in the export industries themselves, and indirectly in the industries that supply export producers.[33] Also, the growing importance of exports in Korea's output mix has undoubtedly increased overall economic efficiency. Exporters face worldwide competition and cannot hide behind tariff barriers as can producers for the domestic market. Subsidies provided by export-promotion measures, furthermore, have been too low to protect inefficient producers. Finally, exposure to new markets and the need to keep up with

Table 2.2

Korea's Changing Export Structure and Factor-Endowment Categories

	1972		1981	
	$ million	%	$ million	%
L - industries[1]	645	40	7,681	36
H - industries[2]	180	11	5,057	24
All commodities[3]	1,624	100	21,254	100

Note: L-industries or labor-intensive industries are those with particularly low value added per worker, whereas H-industries or capital-intensive industries (both human and physical capital) are those with especially high value added per worker.

1. Includes textiles (Standard International Trade Classification [SITC] 65), travel goods (83), clothing (84), and footwear (85).

2. Includes machinery and transport equipment (SITC 7) and instruments (86).

3. Also includes exports of intermediate industries, or those that are neither very labor intensive nor capital intensive.

new technology should have diversified the economy's output and increased productive capacity more than if production had been mainly devoted to supplying domestic markets.

Products that Korea exports are usually products that are already being produced for domestic markets. Though there are notable exceptions, such as the offshore assembly of electronic components for U.S. firms, previous production experience is typically needed to reduce costs and raise quality. In the same way, production for domestic markets often substitutes for earlier imports. In fact, Akamatsu found that the sequence beginning with imports, then import substitution to supply domestic markets, and finally output for export described Japan's industrial development.[34] The same sequence, Akamatsu's "Wild-Flying Geese" pattern of growth, also fits much of Korea's industrial growth. When import substitution becomes sufficiently competitive to generate exports, as in Akamatsu's sequence, the import-substitution and export-promotion strategies are not necessarily competitive. What Korea exports is explained, at least in part, by prior import substitution. Exports are also determined by changes in comparative advantage, both in Korea and elsewhere.

Heavy investment in education and in plant and equipment since the mid-1960s had substantially expanded Korea's capital stock by the early 1980s.[35] The expansion, marked by the growing importance of physical and human capital in Korea's factor endowments, was one reason for the shift away from L-intensive toward H-intensive exports shown in table 2.2. Another reason is that just as exports of labor-intensive products like plywood, textiles, and apparel from Korea, Taiwan, and other low-wage, newly industrialized countries reduced Japan's world-market share of labor-intensive manufactures, growing competition from China, the Philippines, and other even lower wage countries has had the same effect on Korea's more labor-intensive exports in recent years. The Park regime's push to develop the heavy and chemical industries during the middle and late 1970s may have been partly designed to expand Korea's military capabilities, but it was also a response to this increase in competition from below. More recently the Chun regime's industrial policy has focused on expanding electronics, machinery, and other skill-intensive, high-value-added types of production. Policy in both instances continues the shift in export composition from L-intensive to H-intensive products, and in each case the policy has been consistent with changes in Korea's comparative advantage.

Demand considerations, price changes, and financial developments have affected Korea's high-growth strategy as well as the supply factors that determine comparative advantage. The *won* exchange rate has been tied to the U.S. dollar, for example, so that Korean exports have suffered from *won* overvaluation in recent years despite a series of modest devaluations to raise the *won*/dollar rate. More substantial devaluation would aid export competitiveness, but it would also contribute to inflation (via higher import prices) and increase the burden of servicing dollar-denominated foreign debt. This debt places Korea among the top four developing-country international borrowers, but the debt-service ratio (interest plus amortization ÷ current-account receipts), now around 15 percent, is not considered dangerously high. Korea's debt jumped with widening balance-of-payments deficits after each oil shock, and Korea, along with other oil-importing countries, has suffered from deterioration in the terms of trade as oil prices escalated and export prices did not. Perhaps more significant than adverse price movements, however, has been the impact of restrictive policy measures adopted elsewhere to restrain the inflation ignited by oil shocks. Such measures contributed to worldwide recession in the early 1980s and to rising protectionism as well, both of which have reduced demand for Korea's exports.

V. Recent, Current, and Future Developments

Korea's export growth centered on textiles, apparel, and other labor-intensive manufactures before capacity was developed in the late 1970s to produce more capital-intensive products. Exports, particularly of labor-intensive products, have been restricted by tariffs, quotas, and other protectionist devices used in advanced industrial economies, particularly the Multi-Fibre Arrangement (MFA) quotas on textiles employed during the past decade and the "orderly marketing" arrangement limiting footwear imports to the United States. These restraints, along with increased competition from lower-wage competitors and changes in Korea's own factor endowments, encouraged the government to expand the heavy and chemical industries in the 1970s and are now a factor behind recent efforts to promote the development of more skill-intensive products. Current industrial policy, designed to exploit Korea's growing comparative advantage in human-capital-intensive production, is to be implemented by investment in a set of national research projects (to develop semiconductor, bioengineering, and other technologies), liberalization of technology imports, establishment of industry research institutes, and upgrading of technology in small and medium enterprises. Intra-industry rather than inter-industry specialization will be encouraged to avoid protectionist barriers to skill-intensive exports.

New policies and the sort of restructuring they require reveal weaknesses in Korea's industrial structure and problems that will have to be met in shifting to more skill-intensive exports. One weakness, for instance, is the increasing concentration of industrial output in a small set of *chaebŏl* or giant conglomerates that dominate export activity. Concentration has been encouraged by allocation or preferential loans to firms whose previous records promise good performance, namely the *chaebol*. Small credit-starved firms, in consequence, have been unable to purchase equipment embodying new technology and have therefore been confined mainly to the local market because they cannot compete in world markets. Measures to support small enterprises and to establish industry research institutes should help to arrest, if not reverse, growing concentration. The major problem facing current industrial policy is not concentration, however, but a problem that is inherent in the production and transfer of new technology. Because new technology is developed in only a few advanced industrial countries, it has to be imported either by nonmarket means (education and training) or by licensing, royalty payments, joint ventures, turnkey plants, foreign investment, and other market arrangements. These arrangements typically do not provide state-of-the-art technology and often prohibit export by purchasers. Purchases are thus restricted by proprietary rights and are expensive because markets are dominated by monopolistic or oligopolistic sellers, and because the purchasing process entails high information costs for buyers. Producers of new (for Korea) skill-intensive products must therefore overcome comparative disadvantages before output is exportable, and output is likely to be confined to mid-life-cycle products for which comparative advantage has already been established elsewhere.

The government's new industrial policies may alter output structure and comparative advantage, but Korea's high-growth strategy still requires rapid export expansion. Export growth was greatly diminished, however, by the recent worldwide recession. When world trade registered zero growth in 1982, for instance, Korea's exports grew by only 5 percent in real terms as unit prices fell by 2.5 percent. Because export production accounts for 30 percent of total production, overall economic growth was well below average in 1981-82. This slowdown raised doubts in Korea about the feasibility of a strategy tied to continued export expansion and has renewed interest in more traditional import-substitution policies. The slowdown also reawakened a much wider controversy involving the "liberalizers," who favor greater reliance on the market mechanism, and the "traditionalists," who are reluctant to drop the controls that have been associated with past economic success. Because export expansion is associated with more liberal views, the future of Korea's high-growth strategy is tied to the outcome of the liberalizer-traditionalist controversy as well as to world economic recovery.

The main arena for the liberalizer-traditionalist controversy is not trade strategy but the proper role of the government in economic affairs. The source of current differences was a series of crises during the early 1970s, particularly the one-third reduction by the Nixon administration of U.S. troop levels in Korea, growing protectionism after the breakdown of the fixed exchange-rate system, and import inflation with the commodity boom of 1972-73 and the first oil shock in 1973-74. The government met these crises by accelerating development of heavy industry with military potential, diversifying trade (especially by encouraging construction activity in the Middle East), and by increasing domestic food-grains production. These moves signaled a retreat from earlier, more liberal or outward-looking policies, and served either to increase import substitution or, in the case of trade diversification, to generate skill shortages and wage inflation. Inflation was compounded by overexpansion of the money supply to finance heavy industry and by consumer-goods shortages as investment in light industry was restricted to favor heavy industry. Inflation was met with price controls rather than by devaluation and import liberalization so that an overvalued *won* and rising wage costs limited export competitiveness. The structural causes of rising inflation were recognized in an essentially liberal stabilization program adopted in early 1979, but the program was overwhelmed by the second oil shock, the assassination of President Park, and subsequent political upheaval. It was not until 1981-82 that the stabilization program was reinstituted and some of the more market-oriented policies of the liberalizers adopted. Since then, evidence has been accumulating of a general swing toward liberal views and, possibly, of a fundamental reorientation in economic strategy.

When the Economic Planning Board (EPB) released the final version of Korea's Fifth Five-Year Plan (1982- 86) in August 1981, an EPB plan summary (undated) noted that the "major strategy adopted. . .is to change the overall management of the economy from one that makes extensive use of government controls to one which relies heavily on the operation of the market mechanism." President Chun later announced in his January 1982 state-of-the-nation address that "institutional reforms will be continued to strengthen the functioning of the market mechanism." Since then, the government has sold its equity in commercial banks, is removing import restrictions, and is planning to abolish technology import licenses, end limitations on foreign investors' equity in Korean firms, and phase out high agricultural price supports. This is all evidence that the Chun regime may be adopting a new, more market-oriented strategy or, to use earlier terminology, evidence that Korea may now be in the early stages of a third restructuring.

There are a number of plausible reasons for restructuring, including the new regime's desire to establish its own economic strategy, attribution of inflation and structural problems after the investment boom of 1977-1978 to "excessive government intervention in the private sector. . .[because resource allocation was] not. . .guided by the market mechanism but, rather, subject to priorities established by the government," and the growing complexity of the economy that makes it more difficult to allocate resources efficiently through highly centralized decision making.[36] Whatever the reasons, what is significant is the possibility that the Chun regime will employ a less activist economic strategy than its predecessor. What is also significant is the slowness and hesitance involved in reducing government intervention and increasing reliance on the market mechanism. The liberalizer-traditionalist controversy has clearly not yet been settled in favor of the liberalizers, nor has the present regime abdicated in favor of

Adam Smith's invisible hand. In the face of present uncertainty, only one conclusion seems justified, and this is that the ebb and flow of the liberalizer-traditionalist controversy should strongly influence the course of Korea's future economic development.

Notes

1. The four most successful developing economies (here "miracle economies") or, simply, the "Four," was the term used by Little in discussing Taiwan's growth in a comparative context. See Ian M.D. Little, "An Economic Reconnaissance," in *Economic Growth and Structural Change in Taiwan*, ed. Walter Galenson (Ithaca, N.Y.: Cornell University Press, 1979), pp. 448-49.

2. See David I. Steinber, "Development Lessons from the Korean Experience: A Review Article," *Journal of Asian Studies* 42 (November 1982): 91-104.

3. The issue of what constitutes worthwhile comparison is raised here because South Korea's development is sometimes analyzed by comparing the economic situation before and after independence. We know that South Korea's agricultural production fell from 1940 to 1953, for example, but cannot explain this simply as a consequence of disruption during World War II and the Korean War because South Korea also lost rice markets with the dissolution of the Japanese empire and the separation of the peninsula into North and South. The land, the climate, and even the people may be the same, but analysis is confounded because the comparison involves otherwise totally dissimilar units.

4. *First* and *second restructurings* are terms used to denote the economic strategy of import-substituting industrialization adopted by most newly independent nations after World War II (the first restructuring) and the new, more market-oriented export-promotion strategy initiated by many developing countries during the 1960s (the second restructuring). See Benjamin I. Cohen and Gustav Ranis, "The Second Restructuring," in *Government and Economic Development*, ed. Gustav Ranis (New Haven: Yale University Press, 1971), pp. 43-69.

5. See Edward S. Mason et al., *The Economic and Social Modernization of the Republic of Korea* (Cambridge: Harvard University Council on East Asian Studies, 1980), chap. 6.

6. Nor is Korea any more dependent than other peripheral states, as the term *dependent* has been used by *dependencia* theorists to describe exploitative economic relationships between center and peripheral states. A major element of this exploitation, for example, is the heavy penetration of foreign capital. Multinational corporations (MNCs) have a very small presence in Korea, while cumulated foreign direct investment of around $1 billion (end of 1982) was insignificant relative to

foreign borrowing (debt) of $36 billion. Heavy penetration of foreign capital may of course occur in forms other than direct investment or local activities of MNCs, and exploitation is not limited to heavy penetration of foreign capital but may be manifested in unequal exchange, "marginalization" or increasing inequality of income distribution, and so on. There is little if any evidence of these other features that necessarily distinguish center from periphery, or explain the economic backwardness of the periphery. See Sanjaya Lal, "Is 'Dependence' a Useful Concept in Analyzing Underdevelopment?" *World Development* 3 (December 1975): 799-810.

7. The shift from one economic phase to the next is much less precise than is implied by the single-year bounds used here. They are used, however, for the sake of convenience.

8. See Bela Balassa, "The Newly-Industrialized Countries after the Oil Crisis," *World Bank Staff Working Paper No. 437* (October 1980), pp. 24-25; the author's "Response to External Shocks: The Experience of Four Countries in 1973-80," *Economic Notes*, no. 2 (1982): 137.

9. See the author's "The Dramatic Reversal of 1979-80: Contemporary Economic Development in Korea," *Journal of Northeast Asian Studies*, 1 (September 1982): 71-87.

10. The material in this section is taken in large part from one of the author's earlier works, "The Korean Economy in the 1980s: The Roles of Government, Restructuring, and Take-Off," scheduled for publication in *Sino-Soviet Affairs*.

11. For example, industrialization failed in nineteenth-century China, it is argued, because the Ch'ing government's share of GNP was so low (an estimated 1-2 percent) that it did not have the resources needed to support industrialization. See Dwight Perkins, "Government as an Obstacle to Modernization: The Case of Nineteenth Century China," *Journal of Economic History* 27 (December 1967): 478-92.

12. Determinants of tax capacity are analyzed by Joergen R. Lotz and Elliott R. Morss in "A Theory of Tax-Level Determinants for Developing Countries," *Economic Development and Cultural Change* 18 (April 1970): 328-41.

13. Leroy Jones and Il Sakong, *Government, Business, and Entrepreneurship in Economic Development: The Case of Korea* (Cambridge: Harvard University Council on East Asian Studies, 1980), p. 150.

14. Ibid., pp. 151-55. Issues of Korean public-enterprise pricing and efficiency are discussed in Gilbert T. Brown, *Korean Pricing Policies and Economic Development in the 1960s* (Baltimore: Johns Hopkins University Press, 1973).

15. Though the analogy is imperfect, the Park and Chun regimes are similar in significant ways to contemporary military regimes in Brazil and Argentina. See F. Cardoso, "Characterization of Authoritarian Regimes," *The New Authoritarianism in Latin America*, ed. David Collier (Princeton: Princeton University Press, 1979), pp. 33-57.

16. G. William Dick, "Authoritarian versus Nonauthoritarian Approaches to Economic Development," *Journal of Political Economy* 82 (July-August 1974): 819. The presumed economic benefits of authoritarian regimes, such as political stability, firm purpose of direction, and shielding of decision making from popular demands or pressures of economic interest groups, are probably offset by the greater individual participation, benefits of nonconformity, and increased effectiveness of criticism associated with democratic or more competitive regimes.

17. Low income inequality should follow from land reform in the late 1940s and the 1950s, asset destruction during the Korean War and asset confiscation by the military government in 1961, and widespread generalization of education. A World Bank-Institute of Development Studies report shows an unusually low degree of income inequality for Korea, and an annex to the report (by Irma Adelman) suggests that the overall degree of income inequality has remained unchanged. See Hollis Chenery et al., *Redistribution with Growth* (New York: Oxford University Press, 1974). The validity of the evidence used to establish Korea's distribution has been questioned. See Bai Moo-ki, "Examining Adleman's View on Relative Income Quality in Korea: With Focus on Her Studies Outlines in the World Bank Report," *Social Science Journal* (Korean Social Science Research Council-Korean National Commission for UNESCO) 5, no. 1 (1978): 85-99. The recent Fifth Five-Year Economic and Social Development Plan indicates that inequality has in fact increased from 1965 to 1980. See Government of the Republic of Korea, *The Fifth Five-Year Economic and Social Development Plan* (English version; Seoul: 1982), p. 9.

18. Gunnar Myrdal, *Asian Drama: An Inquiry into the Poverty of Nations* (New York: Twentieth Century Fund, 1968), vol. 1, p. 66; vol. 2, pp. 895-900.

19. Jones and Sakong, *Government, Business and Entrepreneurship in Economic Development*, p. 139. This leaves the question of why the Rhee regime, unlike the Park and Chun regimes, was ineffective in enforcing economic policies. One possible reason is that the Rhee regime was ineffective because it was not authoritarian. A more persuasive reason is that it was ineffective because President Rhee gave priority to political rather than to economic problems, and was therefore not committed to economic development, as was President Park or as is President Chun.

20. See B.R. Nayar, "Political Mainsprings of Economic Planning in New Nations," *Comparative Politics* 6 (April 1974): 341-66.

21. See the author's "Korea's Five-Year Plans," in *Practical Approaches to Development Planning: Korea's Second Five-Year Plan*, ed. Irma Adelman (Baltimore: Johns Hopkins University Press, 1969), pp. 40, 44-45.

22. See Youngil Lim, *Government Policy and Private Enterprise: Korean Experience in Industrialization*, Korea Research Monograph No. 6 (Berkeley: University of California, Institute of East Asian Studies, Center for Korean Studies, 1981), pp. 11-18.

23. L.L. Wade and B.S. Kim, *Economic Development of South Korea* (New York: Praeger, 1978), p. 196.

24. For example, "the government developed effective planning procedures" and "it was. . .in the implementation of policy that the Park regime particularly distinguished itself from governments in most less-developed countries." See Mason et al., *The Economic and Social Modernization. . . of Korea*, p. 293.

25. Comprehensive descriptions of the organized and unorganized money markets are given by David C. Cole and Yung Chul Park in *Financial Development in Korea: 1945-1978* (Cambridge: Harvard University Council on East Asian Studies, 1983), chaps. 3, 4.

26. The extent to which the government controls the credit supply is necessarily conjectural. Curb-market activity is illegal, so little is known about the volume of curb-market lending. See the author's *Economic Growth and Structure in the Republic of Korea* (New Haven: Yale University Press, 1977), pp. 188-89.

27. Promotion measures are surveyed and effective exchange rates analyzed in Larry E. Westphal, "The Republic of Korea's Experience with Export-Led Industrial Development," *World Development* 6 (March 1978): 347-82.

28. Possible roles of U.S. aid in restructuring are discussed by Ranis. See Gustav Ranis, "Why Foreign Aid?" *Venture Magazine* (Yale University Graduate School) 8 (February 1968): 22-30. Effective subsidy rates for export and domestic sales are estimated in Charles R. Frank, Jr., Kwang Suk Kim, and Larry E. Westphal, *Foreign Trade Regimes and Economic Development: South Korea*, vol. 7, Special Conference Series on Foreign Trade Regimes and Economic Development (New York: National Bureau of Economic Research-Columbia University Press, 1975), pp. 197-200.

29. Korea in the 1960s was, in short, the epitome of the sort of economy described by Arthur Lewis in "Economic Development with Unlimited Supplies of Labour," *Manchester School of Economic and Social Studies* 22, no. 2 (1954): 139-91.

30. See Hal B. Larry, *Imports of Manufactures from Less Developed Countries*, (New York: National Bureau of Economic Research-Columbia University Press, 1968), chap. 3.

31. Labor intensity is measured, by convention, according to value added per worker. Where value added is high, it is assumed that inputs other than raw or unskilled labor, such as physical capital or human capital (i.e., workers who are paid more than unskilled wages) are high. The formulation here derives from Seev Hirsch, "Capital or Technology? Confronting the Neo-Factor Proportions and Neo-Technology Accounts of International Trade," *Weltwirtschaftliches Archiv*, Band 110, Heft 4 (1974): 543-44.

32. Relative factor intensities of exports and imports depend upon whether imports are competitive or noncompetitive with goods produced in Korea, and on a number of assumptions that have to be made if non-

competitive imports (i.e., bananas) are replaced with domestic production. See Wontack Hong, "Capital Accumulation, Factor Substitution, and Changing Factor Intensity of Trade: The Case of Korea (1966-72)," in *Trade and Development in Korea*, ed. Wontack Hong and Anne O. Krueger (Seoul: Korea Development Institute, 1975), pp. 65-87.

33. See David C. Cole and Larry E. Westphal, "The Contribution of Exports to Employment in Korea," in *Trade and Development in Korea*, ed. W. Hong and A.O. Krueger, pp. 89-102.

34. Kaname Akamatsu, "A Historical Pattern of Economic Growth in Developing Countries," *Developing Economies*, preliminary issue no. 1 (March-August 1962): 3-25.

35. The value of investment in human capital in 1960 was estimated by C.Y. Jung to be somewhat larger than that in physical capital, and to have grown more rapidly during the 1960s. A reference to Jung's estimates can be found in Youngil Lim, "Korea's Trade with Japan and the U.S.: Issues and Implications," in *The Korean Economy: Issues of Development*, Korea Research Monograph No. 1 (Berkeley: University of California, Institute of East Asian Studies, Center for Korean Studies, 1980), pp. 44-45.

36. Jong-seok Seo, "Fifth Five-Year Economic and Social Development Plan," *Monthly Review* (Korea Exchange Bank) 15 (October 1981): 2.

Comments on "Economic Development in South Korea"

Ung Soo Kim

The author's observations and evaluations of the process of South Korea's economic development from the end of the Korean War through four five-year economic development plans (1961-81) and the current fifth five-year plan, which started in 1982, are very comprehensive and cautious. The essence of his observations is that "rapid output growth, relatively even income distribution, and widespread welfare gains," an active and efficient government role, and an export-led growth policy have greatly contributed to this achievement. Three stages of restructuring the economy are: (1) its structural change from an agrarian economy to urban-centered labor-intensive manufacturing industry up to 1973; (2) an ambitious attempt to deepen capital investment in the heavy and chemical industry complex up to the end of 1979; and (3) the last painful structural adjustment, which has been going on since 1980, in the midst of world recession, based on unsettled controversies between liberalizer and traditionalist ideologies. I have some reservations regarding income distribution and will comment on this later.

The author rightly states that the transferability of the Korean development process to other economies may prove misleading because the "economic results have social, cultural, political, and institutional causes as well as economic causes." Interestingly enough, the four successful Asian developing economies mentioned in this paper all share relative political stability, a relatively highly educated and thus industrious population with a deep-rooted Confucian culture. Their success has given hope for the Third World's future and probably has been a stimulus in shaping the new liberal development policy of the post-Mao People's Republic of China.

In my comments I will identify the important positive aspects of this paper with respect to Korean economic development and also point out what I believe are the negative factors that have not been properly treated in this paper. A relatively heavy investment in education during Rhee's administration was subject to constant American criticism. However, almost all economists agree that the investment has paid off during the development process. Recent statistics show that over 30 percent of high school graduates are admitted to college, and over ten thousand graduate students are at institutions of higher learning abroad. Along with the impact of education on the Korean economy, the impact of war and the military establishment must not be overlooked. The war brought not only destruction but also new vitality to the Korean people and helped in changing traditional attitudes and accepting innovations. Mass military participation has elevated the general education of the public, accelerated social mobility, and furnished the experience of organizational behavior and basic professional skills required for industrial development. A big military establishment and the presence of U.S. forces provided a substantial market.

The government's active role, especially through direct investment, was cited as proof of government efficiency. This is an overstatement. Many industries previously under direct government control have become privately owned because of revealed inefficiency. Industries that are still under government control are characterized as lacking in efficiency.

Positive Aspects and Results of the Active Government Role

Capital Formation

The government's role in raising revenues and creating national capital for direct investment in social structures and in some industries, in channeling capital through the banking system (most

of which is under government control), and in guaranteeing repayment of foreign loans to private industries has accelerated the
formation of national capital. This might not have been possible
if left to private initiatives.

Open Economic Policy

The government's open economic policy has contributed to bringing in joint ventures, e.g. Gulf Oil, external financing, and technology transfer. The port of Masan has been opened for bonded
industries, and the government provides guarantees to foreign
lenders. The export of educated technocrats to the Third World
and construction activities in the Middle East are results of
economic policy outreach.

One unique characteristic of the Korean development process
is heavy external financing that exceeded $37 billion by the end
of 1982, and amounted to approximately 55 percent of Korea's
GNP. External financing hastened Korean development but it also
is a Korean weakness. The debt service ratio exceeds 20 percent if
short-term loans are included. Under the Japanese occupation,
most heavy industry, such as electric power, steel, and fertilizer,
was located in the northern part of Korea. The more rapid growth
of the South Korean economy, with its advanced technology, as
opposed to the closed economic system of North Korea, can be
attributed to the open policy of the South.

Geopolitical Contribution

The division of Korea into two parts is regrettable for both political and economic reasons, but the geopolitical environment of
South Korea and its contribution to economic development is
unique. The creation of the nation of South Korea by United
Nations resolution and the strong will of the United States in
defending South Korea have fostered both political and economic
stability during the development process. United States military
and economic aid, and credit extension for the purchase of food
grain and raw material for textile industry are very significant.
The U.S. and Japanese efforts have encouraged other Western
countries to do the same. Japanese compensation for its Korean
occupation was equivalent to half the foreign currency requirement during the second five-year economic plan. The recent

agreement of Japan to make a $4 billion commercial loan to Korea will help during the current, fifth five-year economic plan.

Some Key Negative Aspects of the Active Government Role

Inefficient Resource Allocation

Most banks in South Korea are under government control, and bank rates are never equal to curb-market rates. Credit is controlled by the government, and in the early phase of development, loans to industries whose outputs were in the national interest were subsidized by much lower rates than the going bank rates. Considering the high rate of inflation (never below 30 percent before 1981), excess demand and political favoritism became natural in the course of operation. Government guarantees of foreign loans further encouraged borrowing. Simply getting such a loan itself meant success. Naturally, exaggerated market demand resulted in excess capacity in various industries: cement, fertilizer, textiles, automobiles, machinery, and chemicals. Loans were made for purely speculative purposes and continuous borrowing became more important than improvement in productivity. Many industries have defaulted or have been taken over by the government because it was liable for the major portion of the debt, including the foreign debt. The government carries more risk than do the entrepreneurs.

Resource concentration since 1974 in the heavy and chemical industries, including military hardware, can be partially explained by economic policy, which changed from international comparative advantage to self-sufficiency after the Vietnam war and reduction of U.S. forces in Korea. It can also be explained by the built-in inefficiency in the use of scarce national resources.

Weak Financial Position

The easy availability of credit has made the financial position of industry very weak. Statistics show that the equity ratio of manufacturing is not more than 17 percent in Korea, compared to 38 percent in Taiwan. Such a financial structure creates pressure for higher production costs and brings on the risk of defaulting unless there is continuous low-rate borrowing. To maintain an international comparative advantage, improved productivity is an imperative.

Concentration of Capital and Market Structure

The government activities just described and imbalanced credit allocation have created big conglomerates (*Jaebols*) within a short time span. The conglomerates are products of the requirement of economies of scale to survive international competition and inefficient resource allocation through direct government intervention. About 50 percent of the total manufacturing output is produced by industries belonging to *Jaebols* and 90 percent of them have a monopolistic market structure. It is therefore natural that they maintain a discriminatory price structure that limits the domestic market, and hence export industries must rely heavily on government subsidy to compete in the world market. An increase in protectionism and slow recovery of the world economy necessitate an expansion of the domestic South Korean market to offset limited expansion in the export market. Recent policy changes liberalizing importing are designed to force technological improvement and expand the domestic market potential.

Due to rapid growth policy and inefficient resource allocation, the increase in the wage rate through inflation is higher in South Korea than in its four neighbor countries. The overconcentration of loans to big business deprives small labor-intensive businesses of the opportunity to improve their productivity, thus setting off rising costs in wages. Small business is at the present time the main producer of labor-intensive exports. Because natural resources are scarce, Korea will require a comparative advantage in labor-intensive products for some time to come.

Distribution

The author's opinion that there is relatively even income distribution is not entirely so. The first problem is the concentration of wealth in the few *Jaebols*, through government credit allocation, a policy skewed against small businesses. The second is that heavier investment along the southeastern corridor of the country (Pusan-Taegu) has regionally imbalanced growth. The locations of new industries are not necessarily based on economic consideration.

Koreans became rich only through land ownership during the Japanese occupation. Land reform was completed just before the Korean War, but realizing capital from it became impossible for former owners immediately after the war because the compensation was in government bonds, which were rendered almost worthless by inflation. Added to the destruction of the entire country during the war, it brought about a fairly even distribution of income. The high level of education and sudden growth of wealth with skewed distribution of capital resources to the few *Jaebols*, and the regional imbalance through government power are causes of social discontent and political instability.

Connected with the distribution problem is the relationship between the *Jaebols* and political power. The soundness of big corporations is always a public concern, but in Korea's case, the *Jaebols* look to the state-controlled banks for major capital. This means pressure on the government for survival is crucial, and that should they default on their loans the situation would be very serious. This tends to constrict the government's policy choices.

In summary, if both the strengths and weaknesses of Korean economic development policies and government power politics are explained, it is easier to understand recent issues: the stabilization policy, market function, productivity improvement through technological change, integration of heavy and chemical industries, the liberal import policy, and the increasing trend in social welfare spending.

Because exports constitute more than 30 percent of Korea's GNP, the Korean economy is affected heavily by the world economy. Hence, continuation of Korean economic development depends on the success of the future policies for (a) the maintenance of price stability, (b) technical innovation to maintain existing comparative advantage in labor-intensive export products, (c) expansion of domestic markets, and (d) success in comparative advantage in technology-intensive industry.

3.

The Economic Development of Taiwan, 1950-1980

John C. H. Fei

From a historical perspective, the economic development of contemporary developing countries (DCs) during the post-World War II period (1950-80) represents a transition process from pre-war agrarian colonialism (1850-1950) to what was referred to by Simon Kuznets as the epoch of modern economic growth based on science and technology. From a worldwide perspective, the epoch of modern economic growth was ushered in by the industrial revolution in England during the last quarter of the eighteenth century, and then spread to Western Europe and the United States (early nineteenth century); Germany, Canada, and Japan (late nineteenth century); Eastern Europe and the Soviet Union (early twentieth century); and later to other parts of the less-developed world.

It is now apparent that modern economic growth has been particularly successful and rapid in the Far East. Taiwan, South Korea, Singapore, and Hong Kong are becoming known as the newly industrialized countries in Asia (NICAs), or the "Far Eastern Gang of Four." In just thirty years these countries (especially Taiwan and South Korea) have come from an agrarian colonialism to join the family of industrialized nations.

The characterization of the economic development of these countries as transition growth immediately suggests that it should be viewed as an evolutionary process. In the case of Taiwan, three phases of the process can be identified:

- import-substitution phase (1950-63)
- external-orientation phase (1963-80)
- technology-sensitive, external-orientation phase (1980-)

Any attempt to analyze the development experience of Taiwan faces two tasks: identifying the distinct mode of operation of the economy during each phase; and explaining why one phase ended and the next began—a key matter in any evolutionary thesis.

The movement of Taiwan through the three phases was to a certain extent determined by particular economic, geographic, and political characteristics. The economic characteristics are generally recognized to be those of a *small, labor-surplus dualistic economy* (i.e., consisting of an agricultural sector and a nonagricultural or industrial sector) endowed with relatively *good human resources* (i.e., an educated labor force and commercial entrepreneurs). To a certain extent these related economic, geographic, and political characteristics are also present in Taiwan and South Korea, which accounts for their having moved through strikingly similar phases during the same period. The successful experiences of the NICAs suggest that the economic characteristics they have in common are conducive to modern economic growth.

In respect to political characteristics, we should be aware that in the transition process the DCs were imbued with a newfound sense of nationalism. Dedication to national economic construction was often associated with socialism, broadly interpreted as a preference for mutual concern. As a result, the form of economic organization that emerged was a *mixed one* involving government intervention in the marketing institutions that were evolving. In the mixed economy of Taiwan, the intervention (e.g., public enterprises, land redistribution, and efforts toward equality in income distribution) were rationalized by the doctrines of Sun Yat-sen, the founding father of the Republic of China.

Compared with other noncommunist DCs, Taiwan perhaps has had a stronger need for political indoctrination because of its sensitivity to national security. However, actual government economic intervention through the exercise of various policy instruments (e.g., monetary, fiscal, exchange rates) has always been carried out in a spirit of nondoctrinal pragmatism. Indeed, the teachings of Sun Yat-sen are broad enough to accommodate different shades of interpretation that could be explored experimentally. In the course of the past thirty years the organizational arrangement was gradually oriented toward the free market as the economy became increasingly complex.

Due to its relatively small population and limited resources, Taiwan's interaction with the outside world through trade and/or capital movement has been a crucial aspect of its development. Hence, Taiwan is often labeled as a case of the development of a labor-surplus, resource-poor, *open dualistic economy*.

As an open economy, Taiwan was influenced by certain major exogenous events. First, the early postwar period (1950-70) was a prosperous time for the industrially advanced countries that were, and still are, the major trading partners of Taiwan. The prosperity was unprecedented in the entire history of capitalism, and conducive to the expansion of world trade. The early termination of import-substitution growth (for Taiwan and Korea) and the external orientation of the NICAs were no doubt facilitated by the free-trade thinking and practices of this period. The adverse effects of the slowdown in growth and the oil crisis in the 1970s that have blemished the records of practically every country were absorbed with relative ease by the NICAs.

Another exogenous factor that influenced the postwar development of the DCs was the emergence of the new institutions of long-term capital movement after the war. During this period, a type of profit-seeking, commercial long-run capital movement (especially direct investments by multinational firms) gradually replaced the humanitarian, politically motivated resources-transfer system of foreign aid, which itself was a new, postwar phenomenon. In the case of Taiwan, foreign aid was one aspect of economic development during the import-substitution phase. However, the importance of the role of foreign aid has been exaggerated. Foreign—mainly U.S.—aid during this period was not a persistent and steady stream of resources for economic development; rather, it is more appropriately viewed as political-stabilization aid that alleviated pressures on the government budget (and budget-induced inflation) stemming from limitation of the taxing capacity and the demand for national defense expenditures. Given the fact that an unusually large portion of all resources were then devoted to defense, whether foreign aid fully compensated for the "defense drain" is debatable. In any case, as Taiwan entered its external-orientation phase, foreign aid terminated quickly. International resources transfer into Taiwan was replaced by direct investment by foreigners and overseas Chinese. In recent years Taiwan has even developed an export surplus, indicating a persistent pattern of net resources outflows. While one may argue that the net capital export was premature for Taiwan from the economic standpoint, the phenomenon is consistent with its defense sensitivity, for it allowed the government to build up a substantial stock of foreign exchange, a reserve for political and economic security.

The ideas of the transition to modern economic growth, the exogenous worldwide influences, and the typological character-istics that determined the evolution through the import-sub-stitution (I-S) phase, the external-orientation (E-O) phase, and the technology-sensitive (T-S) phase are shown in the upper part of figure 3.1. In analyzing the economic development of Taiwan, or any other country, we can with historical hindsight identify the *cumulation of accomplishments* as well as the *cumulation of problems* shown in the bottom part of the figure. The former refers to the economic progress or achievements (e.g., the ac-cumulation of capital, the development of human resources, the building up of new institutions); the latter refers to the develop-ment-bottleneck factors that stood in the way of progress. Usually these problems constituted the focal point of economic policies. In particular, major policy revisions usually occurred when one growth phase gave way to another, that is, around *1962* and *1980*. An Evolutionary thesis stresses that the emergence of a new growth phase can be traced to a cumulation of accomplish-ments and to problems overcome by accommodative policy changes.

In this paper we shall develop an evolutionary thesis—based essentially on the typological characteristics of Taiwan—to show why accomplishments and problems of particular types surfaced. We shall refer to the accomplishments and the problems identified in figure 3.1, and the key element of why a growth phase comes into being will be made clear.

Almost everything we say in this paper is statistically verifiable through the use of aggregate economic data regarding such things as population growth and the allocation of labor between agriculture and the nonagricultural sector; GNP agricultural and industrial outputs; imports and exports; savings and investment finance; government expenditures and revenues; and prices, wage rates, interest rates, and foreign exchange rates. An evolutionary thesis is essentially a formulation of ideas regarding these quantifiable elements into a related system. However, here we convey only a sense of this approach typical of economists. The use of actual data to substantiate or refute the theoretical notions is beyond the scope of this paper.

Import-Substitution Phase

Colonial Agrarian Heritage

In the broadest and most abstract sense, an agrarian-colonial economy is a primary-product export (E_a) economy based on specific natural resources, such as mineral and/or agricultural resources. The foreign exchange earnings of the exports are used to import manufactured consumer goods (M_c), textiles being the most important, for the domestic market, in which the purchasing power consists mainly of income (V_a, or value added) generated by primary-product production (see fig. 3.2). A sizable manufacturing sector is not present.

Overt and covert colonialism has existed in various parts of the Third World for periods of differing duration; in Taiwan it lasted from 1900 to 1950. As a result of colonialism DCs acquired both a land-based export capacity and a domestic market for products such as textiles, the production of which required modern science and technology, and the consumption of which implied product familiarity in the income-receiving masses. As a starting point for transition to modern economic growth after World War II, most contemporary DCs shared these basic characteristics of the colonial-agrarian status.

Import-Substitution Growth

Import substitution (I-S) is a growth type involving a particular mode of operation of the economy (depicted in figure 3.3). For this traditional growth type, primary product export earnings (E_a) are diverted from the import of manufactured consumer goods (M_c) to the import of producer goods (M_i; capital equipment and raw materials) to build up the domestic import-substituting industries, the output of which (D_c) gradually replaces the traditional imports in the domestic market. As a direct result, the labor force is gradually allocated from the agricultural sector to the industrial sector.

It is quite obvious that the I-S growth type came out of colonial agrarianism in at least two senses. First, the growth-promotion force was the expansion of the markets for primary products. Second, domestic entrepreneurs directed their attention to the domestic market that already existed; there was no need to cultivate the consumer taste that would have been required by introduction of new products. The I-S growth type also represented technological complementarity between the DCs and the industrially advanced countries that fostered production of the imported producer goods (M_i). By this avenue modern science and technology were first transmitted to the DCs. The I-S growth type is the most popular growth type for contemporary DCs because it is the most natural.

Role of the Agricultural Sector

The agricultural sector (the primary-product producing sector) plays a particularly crucial role in the I-S phase by providing foreign exchange; the labor force; a savings fund; and the market. In the case of Taiwan, the agricultural sector performed these functions extremely well; indeed, this is what distinguished Taiwan from almost all contemporary DCs, including South Korea, during the I-S process.

During the I-S phase, the industrial sector gradually gained the capacity to produce some investment goods (I), financed by two types of savings funds originating in the agricultural sector (S_a) and industrial sector (S_i), respectively (see fig. 3.3). Because the investment goods output (I) was destined for capital accumulation mainly for the industrial sector, S_a is *intersectorial* financing (the use of agricultural savings to finance capital accumulation in the industrial sector), and S_i is *intrasectorial* financing (essentially a reinvestment of entrepreneurial profit within the industrial sector). Intersectorial financing was quantitatively more important because the new industrial sector was not able to meet its own investment requirements until some time later.

The fact that the agricultural sector provided a market for the products of the import-substituting industries offered an opportunity for exploitation of the farmers by the urban industrial entrepreneurial class. This came about when the domestic import-substituting industries were protected so that the farmers had to pay higher prices to buy domestically produced products of inferior quality.

Several factors account for the agricultural sector's having done extremely well in the early I-S phase in Taiwan. First, as a former colony of Japan, a food-deficient country, Taiwan had received a good investment in rural infrastructure, e.g., irrigation, and associations of farmers had been set up. Second, the modernization of the agricultural sector was carried out through the use of chemical fertilizers and new seed varieties. The government was primarily responsible for the organization of these modern inputs (e.g., fertilizer factories; agricultural experiment stations), but the dissemination of the inputs was channeled through the extension services of the farmer associations.

A third factor in the early success of agricultural modernization was the high population density of the island, which supported spatially dispersed small cities, where nonagricultural productive activities were conducted. Because of the daily contacts between the farmers and city dwellers, the farmers readily acquired favorable attitudes toward profit making that were transferable to their own livelihoods. The attitude transformation was furthered by the land-reform programs, started early in the I-S phase by the government, that contributed to the molding of traditional farmers into profit-seeking entrepreneurs with a high propensity to use new production methods.

Import-Substitution Strategy

The transformation from agrarian colonialism to import-substitution growth was initiated by awareness of backwardness, of being underdeveloped. It generated social favorability toward government intervention to promote import-substituting industries, a manifestation of a demand for national economic independence following naturally upon the colonial experience. An import-substitution strategy was adopted by almost all DCs soon after World War II, but the untried skills of the domestic entrepreneurs and their fear of foreign competition were the actual reasons that called for political action. The general principle of an import-substitution strategy is an *artificial augmentation of the profits of the domestic entrepreneurial class by the government.* The augmentation can be brought about only by the *transfer of income* from other classes of producers that bear the burden of the transfer strategy. The classes so exploited were naturally the farmers and the consumers, i.e., the workers who had no choice but to spend their money income in the domestic market (see fig. 3.3). Typically a host of policy instruments were employed, in particular ways, to implement the import-substitution strategy; foreign exchange rates, interest rates, and tariff protection were the major import-substitution policy instruments.

Low-Interest Policy

The channelization of savings (S_i and S_a) to finance investment (I) determines a natural rate of interest that clears the market (i.e., equates the supply and demand for loanable funds) in an ideal fashion. However, because of market imperfections, government intervenes to assist the import-substituting entrepreneurs with an interest rate much lower than that which prevails in the free or black markets. This can be done, and usually was, by expanding the money supply through the government controlled commercial banks to augment voluntary savings (S_a and S_i). When governments resort to printing-press money to solve economic problems, it is quite obvious that inflation is inevitable, and this was experienced by almost all import-substituting countries. It should be emphasized that a low-interest policy combined with inflation provides one of the most "classical" methods of income transfer that can be resorted to by a government. The consequence of inflation is not only to lower the repayment burden of the borrowing entrepreneurs but also to add the burden of higher prices to the consuming public.

In the case of Taiwan during the I-S phase, the low interest rate was revised upward intermittently to dampen inflation. The arrival of the external-orientation phase around 1962 was preceded by the government's effort to bring inflation under control through a high-interest-rate policy, for an upward revision of the interest rate can attract the flow of savings to the banking system and thus obviate the necessity for monetary expansion to meet the demand for investment funds. The Republic of China was the first country to experiment with controlling inflation by a high-interest policy. (The same policy is only now being experimented with by the United States.) The ROC's success in inflation control during the latter part of the I-S phase is a major transferable experience that should be explored carefully by DCs facing serious inflation problems; Latin American countries come to mind in this respect.

High-Tariff Protection

To prevent foreign competition in the Taiwan domestic market, a high tariff wall was erected to protect domestic producers. On the one hand, the importation of manufactured consumer goods was discouraged by high tariff rates, or even prohibited outright; on the other hand, low tariff rates were applied to imported producer goods. Thus, the domestic entrepreneurial profits were augmented by higher prices and lower costs, but the creation of artificial profits by political means did not hide the fact that the consumers were bearing the burden of the implied income-transfer policy.

One should also be aware that because of the point specificity of tariff collection, that is, at ports of entry, the method entails fewer demands on administrative capacity than do other forms of taxation. Hence, when a new national government is established, tariff revenues are usually the lion's share of government income. Resorting to a protection policy, then, serves two purposes: it helps domestic entrepreneurs and it helps the government. Evolution of an economy in a free-market direction necessitates the lowering of tariffs, which can be achieved only when alternative sources of revenues can be found. In the case of Taiwan, the institution of an income tax during the external-orientation phase was an essential precondition for market liberalization in the 1970s, for the tariff revenues as a proportion of government income declined consistently in the later years of the decade.

Overvalued Foreign Exchange Rate

During the Taiwan I-S phase, because primary-product export provided the basic growth-promotion force, an effective method to execute the income-transfer strategy was adoption of an official exchange rate under which the domestic currency, the Taiwan NT, was overvalued at a rate of U.S. $1 equaling 10 NT, when U.S. $1 equaled 20 NT in the black market. The primary-product producers, the farmers, as exporters were forced to exchange their foreign earnings at the official rate, and thus acquired fewer units of domestic currency in return than they would have acquired "on the street." The industrial entrepreneurs, contrariwise, were favored by the official rate as importers—another instance of income transfer.

After World War II almost all primary-product exporting DCs adopted an overvalued exchange rate. Such an income-transfer policy was politically convenient because the transfer mechanism was implicit or covert. With the exception of professional economists, very few people can work their way through the intricacies of the relatedness of the foreign exchange rate and comparative international price levels. The farmers were not sufficiently knowledgeable to be suspicious of the transfer mechanism of which they were the victims.

Under continued inflation, the official exchange rate had to be devalued periodically, but the pace of devaluation always lagged behind the inflation. Because the shortage of foreign exchange was keenly felt, overvaluation was combined with a multiple-exchange-rate system to give some encouragement for the expansion of a narrowly selected subset of exportable products. In the I-S phase Taiwan as well as many other contemporary DCs resorted to control measures to bring about industrialization.

Operation of a Mixed Economy

The exercise by the Taiwan government of all the major policy instruments described above implies government intervention in the free market in one form or another. I-S growth is thus a process manipulated to a large extent by the government. The profit created for the entrepreneurs took on a windfall coloration, for it was incommensurate with entrepreneurial task efficiency, that is, with management and risk taking. Indeed, I-S growth was dedicated to a visible nationalistic accomplishment rather than oriented toward production efficiency.

In addition to its role as economic director, the Taiwan government also took a direct part in production. It spent heavily in three areas: infrastructure; public enterprises; and national defense. Because the tax base was limited in the I-S phase, the insufficiency of government revenues was relieved by monetary expansion, adding much to inflation. Inflation was a common phenomenon for DCs in the I-S phase. This was so because governments found it irresistibly convenient to "solve" real social and economic problems by manufacturing purchasing power. The coming together of the interests of the government and the entrepreneurial class in this regard is similar to what happened in regard to tariffs. U.S. aid to Taiwan in this period was primarily aimed at stabilizing the government in its fight against inflation. Taiwan was successful and others were not because there was a strong will to stand firm against inflation in the first place.

As a direct result of I-S growth for some twelve to fourteen years, Taiwan achieved certain economic ends (see figure 3.1). For the industrial sector, the building up of the visible import-substituting industries implied the formation of both a new urban labor force and an industrial entrepreneurial class. The development of these human resources was largely a learning-by-doing experience. Land reform and the modernization of the agricultural sector led to the creation of the commercialized farming sector. All this took place concurrently with the development of new government machinery and a new financial system. The foundation was laid for the external-orientation phase.

Certain socioeconomic problems surfaced conspicuously during the I-S phase, and government attention was directed toward them. Among the most important policy-related issues were unemployment, the shortage of foreign exchange, the government deficit, price inflation, and the infancy of the domestic entrepreneurship. To a certain extent, all the DCs faced the same set of problems. Unemployment calls for further elaboration.

Unemployment in a Labor-Surplus Economy

One of the basic demographic phenomena in the transition of a traditional society is the acceleration of population growth. The population explosion, which resulted in a surplus of labor, was keenly felt by all DCs in their early I-S phase. There were two dimensions to the unemployment problem. One, the migration of rural dwellers to the urban centers, which in many contemporary DCs has created slums. Two, the inability of the cities to provide employment opportunities for the newcomers.

When we examine the unemployment experience in the I-S phase from a worldwide perspective, the urban open or hidden unemployment was not as serious in Taiwan as in other countries. Its urban slums were not on a scale comparable to those of other DCs, due primarily to the fact that it had inherited an agricultural sector from the colonial past that could absorb additional people with relative ease. Further, because of well-dispersed cities, members of farming families could find jobs in nearby small centers. A distinguishing characteristic of the Taiwan agricultural sector is that the agricultural household can earn a substantial portion of its income in nonagricultural pursuits. To illustrate, soon after the close of the I-S phase, rural families were receiving nearly 40 percent of their income from off the farm.

Nevertheless, even in Taiwan unemployment was a dominant social concern during the I-S phase. The problem persisted because the import-substituting industries were not developing at a pace that matched the numbers being added to the laboring-age pool. Capital accumulation, that is, investment, was limited by savings capacity. As a result, the population structure, in other words, the percentages employed in the agricultural and non-agricultural sectors, remained for the most part unchanged during the I-S phase.

In this regard we should add that per capita income is generally thought to be the most important index of economic performance. However, for a DC in transition, population structure is an even more reliable performance index. (For example, the proportion of the population employed in the agricultural sector currently accounts for a mere 3 to 5 percent in some of the advanced industrialized countries.) There has been no significant change in the population structure of the People's Republic of China during the past thirty years, indicating the absence of substantial economic progress. In the case of Taiwan, a static population structure during the I-S phase was replaced by a structure with a declining agricultural component during the external-orientation phase. The drop of the agricultural segment from 65 percent to 28 percent of the Taiwan population between 1963 and 1980 was an indication that something quite new and dramatic was happening in the economy.

External-Orientation Phase, 1963-1980

External-Orientation Growth

The central phenomenon of the external-orientation (E-O) phase was the emergence of the export of manufactured goods to the world market, which became the dominant growth-promotion force of this period. The exports of the I-S phase had been land-based primary products; thus, E-O growth can be described alternatively as export-substitution growth (the supplanting of primary products by manufactured goods in the export commodity structure). The success of Taiwan and the other NICAs can be explained primarily by this single factor.

During the E-O phase, exports were labor-intensive manufactured products. From a static viewpoint, it was often said that the comparative advantage of Taiwan had its source in low-paid abundant labor. More significantly, from a dynamic, or development, perspective, it should be emphasized that Taiwan for the first time had discovered a way to employ its hitherto surplus labor fully; foreign markets provided the vent. The labor force could earn valuable and much-needed imported goods embodying modern science and technology on a much larger scale than was possible during the I-S phase. It was that exchange that was the secret of success for all four NICAs during the past twenty years. It should be noted that the NICAs traded overwhelmingly with the industrially advanced countries and relatively little with one another or with the other LDCs.

During the E-O phase, the domestic entrepreneurs became externally oriented in outlook. They developed a world perspective and a sensitivity to the demands and technological potential of the industrially advanced countries. And because the four NICAs were selling in the same marketplace, they became competitive and thereby efficiency conscious. Freed of the government controls that had operated in the I-S phase, they developed a sense of self-reliance and individuality. The learning-by-doing process elevated entrepreneurship to a much higher level.

From the Import-Substitution Phase
to the Export-Orientation Phase

Most contemporary LDCs entered the post-World War II period with I-S growth; Taiwan and South Korea remained in that phase only ten to fifteen years, while some others—Latin American countries, for example—still linger there. What accounts for Taiwan's and Korea's move into the E-O phase? And why was it not duplicated elsewhere? The answer is basically a typological one. Taiwan and South Korea are characterized by an abundance of educated, surplus labor and scanty natural resources. For such countries, quick termination of the I-S phase is a necessity. The growth-promotion force of the I-S phase is continuous expansion of primary-product exports, something beyond the reach of resource-poor countries.

The termination of the I-S phase can be seen in an examination of the long-run output trend for the production and export of primary products that earn foreign exchange. When nearly all foreign exchange earnings are allocated for producer-goods imports and when the domestic market for manufactured consumer goods is supplied nearly completely by domestic outputs, the inability to expand the production of primary products implies that the import-substitution process is completed. A continuation of the import-substitution strategy, as we discussed, cannot rectify the shortage of foreign exchange, and it thereby increases urban unemployment and slows growth. It is the worsening of these socioeconomic problems that forces a government to abandon the import-substitution strategy and experiment with alternatives.

Ironically, countries with a shortage of natural resources (e.g., the NICAs) did considerably better in the transition growth process than those with an abundance of natural resources (e.g., Latin American countries and some countries in the Middle East). Normally this contrast would suggest a "desperation thesis": countries made desperate by few resources have to act and in doing so fare better. But the NICAs turned instead to their human resources—their labor force and entrepreneurs. The NICAs have been more successful because modernization is based on the development of technologically competent human resources.

External-Orientation Strategy

As we mentioned earlier, the heart of the import-substitution strategy is a politically enforced income-transfer mechanism to augment artificially the profits of entrepreneurs oriented toward the domestic market. This changes in the E-O phase. The heart of the export-orientation strategy is liberalization, i.e., a lessening of government controls to allow entrepreneurs oriented toward the foreign market to explore fully the absolute advantages of export based on the availability of low-wage labor. Major policy innovations in the E-O phase in Taiwan consisted of an export-manufacture zone; a tariff-rebate system; tax-concession schemes; and a price-stabilization policy.

Export-Manufacture Zone

The establishment of an export-manufacture zone located near a major harbor enabled foreign and domestic entrepreneurs to manufacture export products, e.g., textiles, there. It also allowed them to import whatever manufacturing inputs were required (such as raw cotton and machinery) duty free and without inspection. Two properties of such a zone should be noted: (1) in addition to entrepreneurship, the major domestic input is the commuting labor force, and (2) the products cannot be sold in the domestic market.

The primary purpose of the export-manufacture zone was to enhance the competitive position of the country in the world market. Because producers in the free port of Hong Kong can import the most suitable inports duty free from anywhere, Taiwan's zone puts the country's manufacturers on a par with manufacturers in Hong Kong in the world market. Foreign manufacturers were encouraged to build factories in the zone, and their help was enlisted. The foreigners supplied financing, technological know-how, and marketing skills that were indispensable. The zone permitted utilization of the labor force while Taiwan's own stock of entrepreneurship was still somewhat deficient.

Because products of the zone were not allowed to be sold in the domestic market, the domestic consumers were still bearing the burden of the duties on the imported manufacturing-input goods and were still being exploited. (A Taiwan housewife buying the same product as a U.S. housewife would have to pay a much higher price.) Thus a "free island," the zone, in an otherwise protected sea really amounted to a partial liberalization—a heritage of the I-S phase.

Tariff Rebates

A factory outside the zone had the option to sell its product either in the domestic market at higher prices (because of the burden of import duties) or in the world market at lower prices. In the latter instance, the manufacturer would not be able to compete with the Hong Kong manufacturer or the manufacturer inside the zone because of duties previously paid on imported raw materials. The tariff-rebate system that came into being was a device by which the duties were rebated to the extent that the product was exported. Essentially, the domestic consumers were still carrying the burden of import duties. As far as the promotion of the labor-intensive export is concerned, the tariff-rebate system and the export-manufacture zone are basically the same: both lessen government interference with the market mechanism.

Tax Concessions

After the establishment of the income tax in the E-O phase, a tax-concession scheme was devised to exempt corporations from paying income taxes; there were tax holidays for new firms or new investment projects. From the viewpoint of the evolving free-market economy, the scheme was a mixed blessing. On the positive side, the provisions diminished government control. On the negative side, the scheme added to government discretion in that government decided which firms and investment projects would receive privileged status.

The tax-concession scheme was cumbersome because the criteria to establish preference were difficult to formulate but even more difficult to apply. What, exactly, served to "promote export," "enhance technology," "increase value added"? What would stimulate enterprenuerial risk taking? The tax-concession scheme had to reflect a certain amount of government arbitrariness. It is next to impossible to assess the investment-stimulating effect of the scheme. As the economy became more complex, the workability and value of the scheme came increasingly under doubt.

Price Stabilization

The initial period of the E-O phase (1963-70) coincided with a period of worldwide prosperity, with considerable price stability in the industrially advanced countries (see figure 3.1). Given the favorable external environment, Taiwan enjoyed rapid externally oriented growth with remarkable price stability, which is a condition essential to rational calculation in the functioning of a free-market economy. Two factors were basic to price stability. First, no externally originated inflation entered the domestic economy. Second, because of the demand for Taiwan's exports, production was booming, and there was no need to stimulate investment by means of low interest rates through monetary expansion. In the later part of the external-orientation phase

(1970-80), growth slowed because of rampaging inflation in the industrially advanced countries. Taiwan, as well as many other DCs, experienced inflation problems that were more serious than during the 1960s.

In addition to the oil crisis and the generalized international inflation, inflation in Taiwan was accounted for by two other factors. First, when growth slowed, the government attempted to stimulate recovery by expansionary monetary policies. In this regard, we might say that the Taiwan experience duplicated that of the United States: printing money did not bring recovery but, rather, inflation. Second, the larger export capacity meant export surpluses when demand slackened, a circumstance that encouraged the government's expansion of the money supply. The export surplus had been at least partly encouraged by the government through its maintaining of an undervalued currency, which allowed the government to build up its foreign exchange reserves for political national security reasons.

Operation of the Partially Free Economy

An externally oriented economy between 1962 and 1980 was Taiwan's success story. Some of the major accomplishments are summarized in figure 3.1. In the industrial sector, the new industries were run by outward-looking, competitive, and efficiency-conscious entrepreneurs, and were the employers of laborers who were more and more skilled. For the first time unemployment was virtually nonexistent. The full utilization of the formerly surplus labor—Taiwan's most important asset—has led to a high GNP. The labor shortage has manifested itself in a sustained rise in real wages—in the final analysis the surest way to bring about equality in income distribution, which occurred in Taiwan in this period. The higher per capita income has led not only to a higher standard of living but also to a consciousness of a measurable quality of life. The experience of Taiwan has shown that full and productive employment is a sure cure for almost all major social maladies, and, moreover, that externally oriented growth is one avenue to full employment.

The enlargement of export capacity contributed to the early termination of foreign aid during the I-S phase, replacing it with investment from abroad. It should be added that foreign capital was attracted mainly by the very externally oriented growth

87

process because most foreign firms were in manufacturing (e.g., electronics). Because such enterprises earned foreign exchange, the problems of capital and/or profit repatriation that involved the use of foreign exchange were minimized.

When increasing real wages and a labor shortage adversely affected the rural sector, the focus of agricultural modernization changed from the biochemical innovations that characterized the I-S phase to mechanization. This led to a demand for a second round of land reform to negate the "land-to-the-tiller" spirit of land reform in the I-S phase. Small family farms cannot use large pieces of equipment efficiently. The trend in agriculture now is toward the combined operation of family farms, an organizational innovation.

During the E-O phase, the Taiwan government managed a balanced budget as a result of the enlargement of the tax base and the initiation of the income tax. A substantial part of the revenues raised was used for infrastructure expenditures (e.g., harbors, roads, railways, electricity) and for investing in public enterprises (e.g., shipbuilding, iron, steel). Toward the end of the E-O phase there was a movement to reexamine the issue of public enterprises in regard to cost and efficiency.

Taiwan's accomplishments were achieved even as the problems that surfaced in this period were being dealt with (see figure 3.1). In addition to the basic externally oriented strategy discussed above, labor policy received further attention. First, with workers in short supply, there was heightened awareness of the importance of skill and ability. Professional education and training became major policy issues. Moreover, as real wages began to increase, the country sensed the gradual disappearance of its competitive advantage based on labor-intensive manufactured exports. This set the stage for the next phase.

Technology-Sensitive, External-Orientation Phase

Taiwan and Korea are expected to be in a technology-sensitive, externally-oriented phase during the rest of this century, representing, perhaps, the ending of the transitional stage toward modern economic growth. Crucial in this phase will be issues related to research and development and to the transfer of foreign technology into the domestic sphere. As new problems appear, the Taiwan government will be taking policy actions in at least three major areas.

Role of Foreigners in Technology Transfer

Direct investment by foreigners in a DC provides a package of services: technology, savings, and management. It is expected that in the technology-sensitive phase, foreigners will play a much larger role in Taiwan than heretofore. Now there is resistance to foreign investment oriented toward the domestic market—a policy that needs to be reexamined. It is also desirable that Taiwan study its patent regulations, including those governing royalty payments on patents. Government interest in foreign investment currently centers on the jointly owned company (e.g., the automobile factory owned by Japan and a combination of Taiwan private and government capital) that must market some of its products (e.g., passenger cars) domestically. Such ventures are innovations that it is anticipated will spread to other enterprises.

Domestic Research and Development

Taiwan manufacturers and industries now collectively spend a very small fraction of the GNP on research and development. To induce greater expenditure by private entrepreneurs is certainly going to be a major task in the near future. In this regard we can distinguish between a direct-intervention approach and a free-market approach. In the former, government makes discretionary decisions to aid the research and development activities of selected strategic industries through tax concessions and/or lending practices. In the latter approach, the government eliminates the various control measures (e.g., tariff protection, restrictions on foreign investment) that have served their original purposes so as to build a free-market economy. Research and development activities are expected to grow in direct consequence of vigorous competition because they are known to be a necessary condition for the very survival of the firms and industries.

Financial Institutions

In the ideal free-market economy, private commercial banks and entrepreneurs are primarily responsible for the allocation of investment funds for industries that undertake research and development activities. At the present time in Taiwan the non-competitive commercial banking system is controlled by the government through the Central Bank, which serves the financial

Figure 3.1

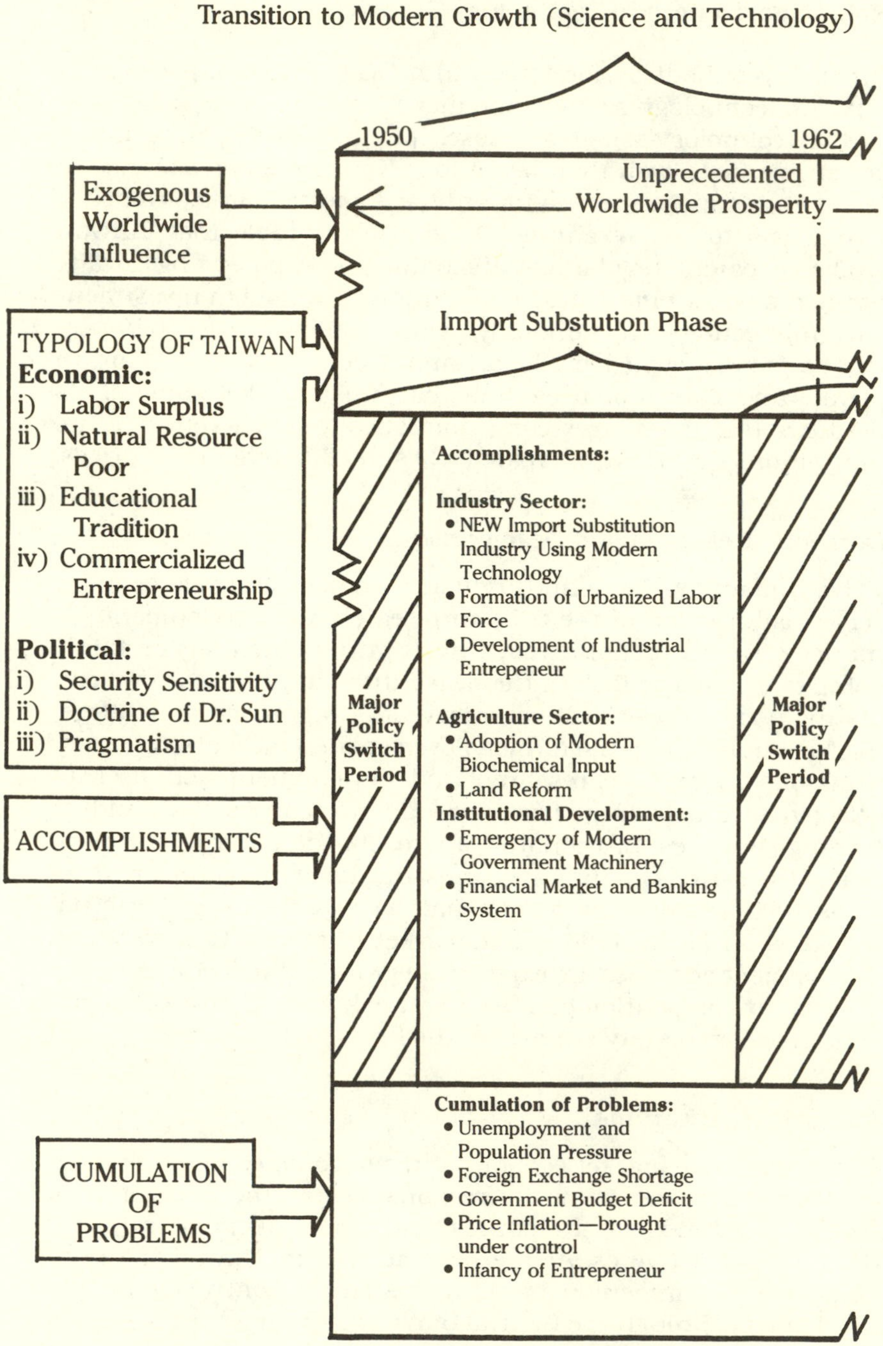

Transition to Modern Growth (Science and Technology)

1950   1962

Exogenous Worldwide Influence

Unprecedented Worldwide Prosperity

Import Substution Phase

TYPOLOGY OF TAIWAN

Economic:
i) Labor Surplus
ii) Natural Resource Poor
iii) Educational Tradition
iv) Commercialized Entrepreneurship

Political:
i) Security Sensitivity
ii) Doctrine of Dr. Sun
iii) Pragmatism

ACCOMPLISHMENTS

Accomplishments:

Industry Sector:
• NEW Import Substitution Industry Using Modern Technology
• Formation of Urbanized Labor Force
• Development of Industrial Entrepeneur

Agriculture Sector:
• Adoption of Modern Biochemical Input
• Land Reform

Institutional Development:
• Emergency of Modern Government Machinery
• Financial Market and Banking System

Major Policy Switch Period

Major Policy Switch Period

CUMULATION OF PROBLEMS

Cumulation of Problems:
• Unemployment and Population Pressure
• Foreign Exchange Shortage
• Government Budget Deficit
• Price Inflation—brought under control
• Infancy of Entrepreneur

Transition to Modern Growth (Science and Technology)
(continued)

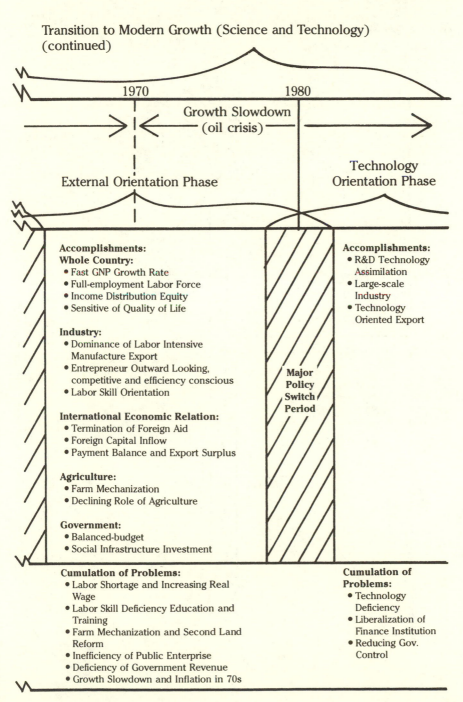

1970

1980

Growth Slowdown
(oil crisis)

External Orientation Phase

Technology
Orientation Phase

Accomplishments:
Whole Country:
- Fast GNP Growth Rate
- Full-employment Labor Force
- Income Distribution Equity
- Sensitive of Quality of Life

Industry:
- Dominance of Labor Intensive
  Manufacture Export
- Entrepreneur Outward Looking,
  competitive and efficiency conscious
- Labor Skill Orientation

International Economic Relation:
- Termination of Foreign Aid
- Foreign Capital Inflow
- Payment Balance and Export Surplus

Agriculture:
- Farm Mechanization
- Declining Role of Agriculture

Government:
- Balanced-budget
- Social Infrastructure Investment

**Major
Policy
Switch
Period**

Accomplishments:
- R&D Technology
  Assimilation
- Large-scale
  Industry
- Technology
  Oriented Export

Cumulation of Problems:
- Labor Shortage and Increasing Real
  Wage
- Labor Skill Deficiency Education and
  Training
- Farm Mechanization and Second Land
  Reform
- Inefficiency of Public Enterprise
- Deficiency of Government Revenue
- Growth Slowdown and Inflation in 70s

**Cumulation of
Problems:**
- Technology
  Deficiency
- Liberalization of
  Finance Institution
- Reducing Gov.
  Control

Figure 3.2. Colonial Economic Heritage

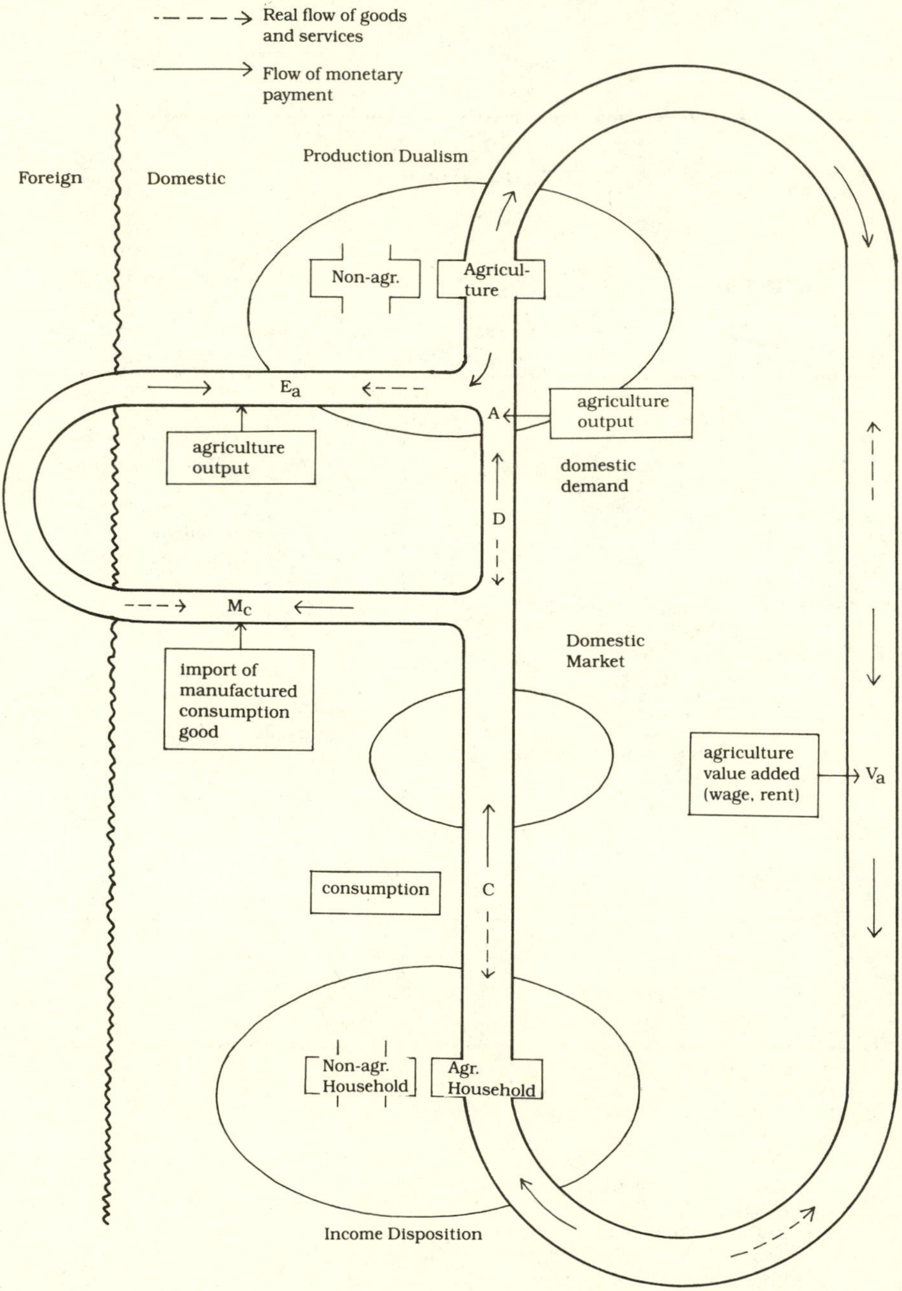

- - - → Real flow of goods and services

───────→ Flow of monetary payment

Production Dualism

Foreign   Domestic

Non-agr.   Agricul-ture

E_a

agriculture output

A

agriculture output

domestic demand

D

M_c

import of manufactured consumption good

Domestic Market

consumption   C

agriculture value added (wage, rent) V_a

Non-agr. Household   Agr. Household

Income Disposition

Figure 3.3   Import Substitution growth   (1950-1963)

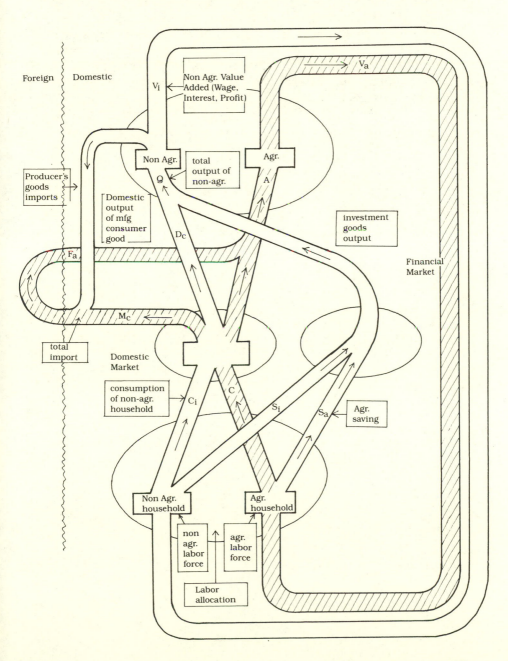

needs of a narrow spectrum of large industries. Technology-sensitive development is expected to be undertaken in this phase by a multitude of new-generation, medium and small-sized entrepreneurs; their financial needs must be taken care of by a new system of intermediation that does not operate like a central bank nor like the informal free market. The devising of such an institution should be a top priority for the technology-oriented growth phase in the years ahead.

4.

Economic Development in Hong Kong and Singapore

Sidney Klein

Introduction

In the post-World War II years, the economies of the United States, the USSR, the People's Republic of China, India, and Japan have been in the world's limelight; the economies of each of the first four nations because of their land areas and populations, and that of Japan in spite of it.[1] It has all too often been accepted that Japan is an exception to the rule that economic growth requires large supplies of domestically available raw materials and a large population to use them. Although economic progress in South Korea and other medium-size nations has, in recent years, invalidated that thesis, the best evidence that it is not so lies in the economic performance of Hong Kong and Singapore. These two entities can best be described as economic microchips, extremely small but increasingly more powerful and impressive in performance. Their combined population is about one-third that of the state of California, and in terms of land area they are individually smaller than a number of counties in the United States, much less the states. Rhode Island's land area of 1,214 square miles and population of 947,000 (1980) is perhaps the closest we come to an approximation of these two political entities among the fifty states. The function of this paper is to sketch the rapid economic development of Hong Kong and Singapore in the post-World War II period and to contrast the different solutions to the problem of economic development adopted by their governments.

Hong Kong and Singapore: The Similarities

There are numerous similarities between Hong Kong and Singapore. Both are noted for their harbors and shipping. Because they lie in major shipping lanes, until recently, when manufacturing became dominant, commerce was their economic mainstay. Both are among the largest and busiest ports in the world. Thousands of oceangoing ships, coastal steamers, junks, and mechanized vessels of all sorts populate their harbors. Both were colonized by Great Britain in the nineteenth century. Leased from Holland in 1819 because of its location in the strategically important Strait of Malacca and its excellent harbor, Singapore was purchased outright by Great Britain in 1824. Great Britain's acquisition of Hong Kong required three phases. In 1842, under the Treaty of Nanking, which settled the Opium War of 1840-42, China gave Hong Kong Island to Great Britain. In 1860, after another war, China ceded the tip of the Kowloon Peninsula. In 1898, Britain leased the New Territories from China for ninety nine years. These today constitute the British Crown Colony of Hong Kong; however, with respect to economic policies, it is independent of Great Britain and is treated as such. In the nineteenth and twentieth centuries, the British invested heavily in port facilities in both colonies and created the two leading entrepots in Southeast Asia. Free trade, an honest, efficient colonial administration, and personal and business security attracted many thousands of merchants and financial houses from elsewhere in Asia where bureaucracy and corruption were endemic. Mainly Chinese, these immigrants brought skills in trade, accounting, finance, and management that contributed to the tremendous economic vitality of both countries, an economic vitality that overcame the incredible lack of natural resources in each country.[2] Table 4.1 reflects the lack of natural resources and the extent to which it was overcome by the 1980s.

Aside from the two sets of data expressed in absolute terms, i.e., area and population size, and aside from the presence of different minor natural resources, the basic data are substantially similar. In relative terms, they are virtually twin economies, yet Hong Kong and Singapore have radically different attitudes about the role of government in economic development plans. Although both are essentially free-market economies in which the private sector is predominant, Hong Kong has a laissez-faire, supply-side approach to the private sector, and in Singapore there is a great deal of government regulation of business and the heavier taxation needed to fund that regulation. Let us consider their individual recent national economic experiences in some detail and then

Table 4.1.

Comparative Data for Hong Kong and Singapore

Measure	Hong Kong	Singapore
Land area (sq. mi.)	415	241
Major natural resources	None	None
Minor natural resources	fish, clay	rubber, coconuts
Population (in millions)	5.2 (1982)	2.4 (1980)
Population rate of growth	1.2% (1980)	1.2% (1980)
GDP (U.S. $, billions)	28.3 (1982)	12.5 (1981-est)
GDP per capita (U.S. $)	$5,411 (1982)	$5,119 (1980)
Birth rate/1000	16.9 (1981)	17.1 (1980)
Death rate/1000	4.8 (1981)	5.2 (1980)
Infant mortality (per 1,000) live births)	9.8 (1981)	12 (1981)
Life expectancy: males	72 (1982)	67 (1980)
females	78 (1982)	71(1980)

Sources: GDP per capita from Federal Reserve Bank of San Francisco, *Pacific Basin Economic Indicators* (December 1982), p. 2; other data from Census and Statistic Department, Hong Kong, various publications, and from Ministry of Trade and Industry, Republic of Singapore, various publications; 1981 estimate of Singapore GDP calculated from Singapore Government, Ministry of Culture, Information Division, *Singapore Facts and Pictures, 1982*, pp. 50-51.

take up the issue of the laissez-faire approach versus government regulation.[3]

Economic Development in Hong Kong

World War II buffeted Hong Kong severely. During the Japanese occupation Hong Kong lost over one million of its residents—over

Table 4.2

Growth in Hong Kong Gross Domestic Product, 1961-1975 (average annual rate, %)

	GDP		Per Capita GDP	
	At Current Market Prices	At Constant Market Prices	At Current Market Prices	At Constant Market Prices
1961-65	14.8	12.1	11.2	8.5
1965-70	12.2	7.8	10.0	5.8
1970-75	14.5	5.8	12.3	3.7
1961-67	12.7	10.5	9.7	7.6
1967-73	16.2	8.0	14.1	6.0

Source: Hong Kong Government, *Two Decades of Economic Achievement,* (February 1977), table 4.

60 percent of the total population—through emigration. At war's end they returned, and, in addition, large numbers of refugees from the civil war in China, 1946-49, sought permanent refuge there as well. Many of the immigrants were educated and skilled and brought with them entire factories, including machinery and equipment, from Shanghai, Canton, and other industrial cities. Their entrepreneurship and energy over the next third of a century helped transform Hong Kong from a small entrepot into a manufacturing and trading nation of considerable importance. That rapid transformation is indicated by the growth of its gross domestic product (tables 4.2, 4.3).

In constant market prices, in each five-year segment between 1961 and 1975, the average annual rate of growth of GDP ranged between 5.8 percent and 12.1 percent (table 4.2). If the period used is 1961-1973 and two seven-year segments are established, the average annual rate of growth ranged from 8.0 percent to 10.5 percent. These are extremely impressive figures. They are reflected in per capita GDP data at constant market prices in increases that range between 3.7 percent for 1970-75 (which includes the devastating world "oil-price shock" of 1973-74) and 8.5 percent for 1961-65. Even allowing for the relatively low base against which the increases were measured, the increases in GDP

Table 4.3

Growth in Hong Kong Gross Domestic Product, 1976-1982 (% increase over previous year)

Year	GPD in Current Market Prices	Per Capita GDP at Current Market Prices	GPD in Constant 1973 Market Prices	Per Capita GDP in Constant 1973 Market Prices
1976	28.1	26.7	18.8	17.5
1977	14.7	13.0	10.2	8.6
1978	16.7	14.5	10.3	8.2
1979	28.6	21.2	12.8	6.2
1980	26.3	22.3	11.7	8.1
1981	21.6	18.9	10.9	8.4
1982	14.5	12.8	2.4	0.8

Source: Data for 1976-1981 from Hong Kong Department of Industry, table A of unidentified study; data for 1982 from Hong Kong Census and Statistics Department, *Hong Kong in Figures, 1983.*

and GDP per capita for 1961-65 are particularly impressive.

As table 4.3 indicates, Hong Kong's progress has continued until the present. For the years 1976-82, the increases in GDP in constant market prices ranged between 2.4 percent for the world depression-ridden year of 1982 to 18.8 percent for 1976. However, except for 1982, all of the average annual increases were 10.2 percent or greater in constant market prices. For per capita GDP, the increases ranged from 0.8 percent for 1982 to 17.5 percent for 1976, with values generally in the 6.2 percent to 8.6 percent range. It is difficult to escape the conclusion that the economic progress of Hong Kong was unusually rapid overall 1961 through 1982.

The increases in GDP and per capita GDP came from several sources, of which the two most important are manufacturing and trade, areas of economic activity closely linked to each other in Hong Kong. In the immediate post-World War II period, Hong Kong was still dependent on the entrepot trade. Between 1947 and 1951, the total value of the trade grew at an annual average rate of 35 percent.[4] However, in 1951, the United Nations placed an embargo on trade with the People's Republic of China, Hong Kong's most important market for reexports, and Hong Kong's entrepot trade dropped sharply. Within one year the China trade had decreased by two-thirds, and by 1961 it was down to 6 percent of its 1951 level.[5]

In response to the need for its population, then about three million people, to earn a livelihood, Hong Kong developed a manufacturing capability based on the skills and capital of its population and a rising world demand for manufactured goods. In the 1950s world trade was increasing at an annual average rate of about 6 percent. By 1962 Hong Kong had a flourishing manufacturing sector, and the level of its exports had recovered to the 1951 preembargo level.

The textile and clothing industries were and are the core of Hong Kong's new industrial growth. In 1951 clothing exports constituted only 5 percent of exports. By 1962 they had grown at an annual average rate of 17 percent and then constituted 26 percent of total exports and 35 percent to 40 percent of total domestic exports. By 1981, of about 905,000 workers in Hong Kong employed in some 47,000 factories, the textile and clothing industries accounted for about 40 percent of the total industrial labor force and were accounting for about 42 percent of the value of Hong Kong's total domestic exports.[6] That of course was neither surprising nor unusual, for the textiles and clothing industries have always been in the forefront of the industrial revolution.

In Great Britain in the late eighteenth century; in Germany, France, Russia, the United States, and Japan in the nineteenth century; and in South Korea and other nations in the twentieth century, the textile and clothing industries provided employment for large numbers of women and children, and in addition for men who otherwise would have been unemployed or underemployed in rural areas. The new textile and clothing factories required a relatively simple technology and only small amounts of capital to build and manage. Over time, they generated profits that were used to finance larger, more complex, and more costly industrial enterprises. Reinvestment of profits made possible the employment and further training of still more skilled, industrial, commercial, and professional employees. Over time the production process became more elaborate, complex, and roundabout, and the final product frequently became more complex, more efficient, and lower priced. The textile and clothing industries and other light industries in the nations cited above made possible the transformation of primarily agricultural economies into heavy industrial nations. They made import substitution and export promotion possible on the part of those nations. By that, of course, it is meant that as nations developed their own industries, they imported less of their needs from other nations, and ultimately began to export in successively larger quantities those light and heavy goods and the services associated with them that they had formerly imported. By then they had not only become industrialized but urbanized as well. Where there were villages, there developed cities and large towns. Such rural areas as remained shrunk until they were of relatively minor consequence.

That, of course, was the pattern in Hong Kong. By 1981, Hong Kong was broadly industrialized, very much urbanized, and extremely densely populated. As noted above, the textile and clothing industries were Hong Kong's largest. The electronics industry was also firmly established, with some 89,000 employees in 1,150 factories, creating products for export valued at more than $1.8 billion. They included transistor radios, computer memory systems, electronic calculators, transistors, integrated circuits, semiconductors, prepackaged electronic modules, television games, electronic burglar alarm systems, smoke detectors, integrated circuit wafer chips, and microcomputers.[7]

Another important new industry was watches, clocks, and accessories, the domestic exports of which were valued at over $1.3 billion in 1981. A third new industry was plastics, which in 1981 accounted for over $750 million in domestic exports; these included injection molding and extrusion machines, dies and molds, toys and dolls. Still other new industries were the light metal products industry, which includes household utensils, locks and keys, cookery implements, key chains, and metal tops; the machinery and machine tools industry, which makes injection molding and extrusion machines, power presses, lathes, shapers, drilling machines, and polishing machines; the shipbuilding and ship repair industry; and the aircraft engineering industry, which involves the complete overhaul of airplanes and engines of many types of aircraft.[8] These industries underscore the high degree of technical and administrative skill required of management to organize and operate such enterprises; and the high degree of technical skill required of the labor force to do the work.

As Hong Kong's manufacturing sector expanded, so too did its exports, both domestic and reexport (table 4.4). Since the years

Table 4.4

Growth of Hong Kong Trade, 1950-1982 (average annual rate, %)

Period/Year	Imports	Domestic	Reexports	Total Exports
1950-55	-0.4	N.A.	N.A.	-7.4
1955-60	9.5	N.A.	N.A.	9.2
1960-65	8.9	11.9	7.0	10.7
1965-70	14.5	19.7	14.0	18.5
1970-75	13.7	13.1	19.2	14.4
1976	29.3	42.7	28.0	39.3
1977	12.5	7.3	10.1	7.9
1978	29.5	16.3	34.3	20.2
1979	36.1	37.3	51.7	40.9
1980	30.1	21.9	50.2	29.4
1981	23.9	18.0	38.8	24.3
1982	3.3	3.2	6.3	4.3

Source: Data for 1950 to 1975 inclusive from Hong Kong Government, *Two Decades of Economic Achievement*, (1977), table 3 opposite 6; data for 1976 to 1982 from Hong Kong Census and Statistics Department, *Hong Kong in Figures*, various issues, 1977 to 1983. Data for total exports, 1977 to 1979, calculated by author; others reproduced as is.

1950-55, when the impact of the embargo on the China trade led by the United States was most severe, Hong Kong's total exports have increased annually between 1955 and 1982 at rates between 4.3 percent and 39.3 percent. The annual rate of increase of domestic exports, 1960-82, ranged between 3.2 percent and 42.7 percent, and the annual rate of increase of reexports ranged between 6.3 percent and 28.0 percent. From 1955 to 1982, the average annual rate of growth of imports ranged between 3.3 percent for the world-depression year of 1982 to 30.1 percent for the world-inflation year of 1980.[9]

Hong Kong's main imports in 1981 were manufactured goods (29 percent), machinery and transport equipment (23.3 percent), foodstuffs (10.1 percent), mineral fuels, lubricants, and related equipment (7.9 percent), and chemicals (6.5 percent). Over time Hong Kong undoubtedly will produce more of the manufactured goods and machinery and transport equipment it currently imports and its dependence on imports in these areas will decline.

Table 4.5

Hong Kong Birth and Death Rates, 1971-1981

Year	Estimated Population (Midyear)	Birth Rate (Per 1,000 Population)	Death Rate (Per 1,000 Population)	Infant Mortality Rate (Per 1,000 Live Births)
1971	4,045,300	19.7	5.0	17.7
1972	4,115,700	19.5	5.2	17.4
1973	4,212,600	19.5	5.0	16.4
1974	4,319,600	19.3	5.1	16.8
1975	4,395,800	18.2	4.9	14.9
1976	4,443,800	17.7	5.1	13.8
1977	4,509,800	17.7	5.2	13.5
1978	4,597,000	17.6	5.2	11.8
1979	4,878,600	17.0	5.2	12.3
1980	5,038,500	17.1	5.0	11.2
1981	5,154,100	16.9	4.8	9.8
1982	5,233,000	17.0	5.0	N.A.

Source: *Hong Kong Government, The Facts—Population,* (January 1982), p. 1;
1982 data from Hong Kong Census and Statistics Department, *Hong
Kong in Figures, 1983.*

However, its dependence on imported foodstuffs, mineral fuels, and chemicals seems likely to continue into the foreseeable future.

Much of Hong Kong's economic progress since the end of World War II is attributable not only to the skills and capital transported to Hong Kong by refugees but to the human capital created by the Hong Kong government itself. This was accomplished through major programs in the areas of health, education, and welfare. Unlike Great Britain, Hong Kong does not have a national health service, but it does have a system of low-cost medical and health services. For example, in 1982 it cost only about a dollar a day to stay in a government hospital, with the charge covering treatment, medicine, and specialized examinations. Charges at the outpatient clinic were about sixty cents a visit and included X-rays and drugs. There was one doctor per 1,160 persons and 4.2 hospital beds per 1,000 of population—ratios second only to Japan in Southeast Asia.[10]

The progress of health care in Hong Kong between 1971 and 1981 is reflected in table 4.5. As it indicates, the death rate ranged from a very low 5.2 per 1,000 in 1972 to an even lower 4.8 per

1,000 in 1981; the infant mortality rate dropped in that same decade from 17.7 per 1,000 live births to a remarkably low 9.8 per 1,000 live births in 1981. As maternal and health services improve, the general death rate and infant mortality rate should continue to improve.

Education too has been a major contributing factor in Hong Kong's economic growth. In 1981-82, about one-fourth of Hong Kong's population was in a primary school, secondary school, or kindergarten, and the government spent 13 percent of its budget on education. Some nine years of free compulsory education are provided up to the age of fifteen, and nearly three-fifths of the fifteen-year-olds were receiving subsidized schooling.[11] Only a small percentage of children have to have their education paid for, primarily voluntarily, because they attend schools for expatriates or choose to attend private, fee-charging schools.

The emphasis on education in Hong Kong was reflected in 1981 in the 729 kindergartens providing preschool education for over 200,000 children. Among children aged three to five, over 85 percent attended day schools. Of children aged twelve to fourteen, some 93 percent were in school; for the fifteen-to-sixteen-year category, the percentage was nearly 71 percent.[12] There were sixty eight special educational facilities for the blind, deaf, physically handicapped, maladjusted, deprived, slow learners, and mentally handicapped. Technical education is currently provided in secondary technical schools, prevocational schools, and technical institutes, and at Hong Kong Polytechnic, which offers education of a wide variety of types. The technical education is offered in full-time day classes, short courses, part-time day classes, and evening classes. There are three postsecondary colleges plus three colleges of education and a technical teachers college. Still further, adult education is provided through the Evening Institute, the Evening School of Higher Chinese Studies, the evening department of the technical institutes, and sixteen adult education and recreation centers, and in private institutes that offer postsecondary and adult education courses. Last, but by no means least, there are two universities, Hong Kong University and the Chinese University of Hong Kong. Hong Kong University has five faculties and three schools; the Chinese University consists of three colleges and four faculties. Having taught at Hong Kong University for two years and having had some contact with the Chinese University, this writer can personally attest the high quality of the educational services offered. The statistical data issued by the Hong Kong government are not mere "academic body counts."

The economic development of Hong Kong has also been furthered by an extensive positive social welfare policy. Hong Kong provides social security, family and child care services, group and community work services for the young and elderly, and rehabilitation as well as probation efforts and training for young offenders.[13] These programs have operated to insure that the needy receive sufficient income to survive and have helped create a stable economic and political environment in Hong Kong. They have helped people to overcome all sorts of tragedies and to go on with their lives to become productive members of society within the limits created by their minds and bodies.

A brief summary of the social welfare programs will underscore the extent to which they have contributed to the economic stability of Hong Kong. The public assistance program, introduced in 1971, provides cash grants to bring family income up to the minimum needed to survive. In 1980, a disability supplement was added to aid the partially disabled. In addition, there are special needs allowances for the elderly, the profoundly deaf, and the severely disabled that are paid over and above the minimum needs-based cash grants. Other social security programs provide compensation for people injured or for dependents of those killed in a crime of violence or through the action of a law enforcement officer while carrying out duties. There is also a cash grant paid to traffic accident victims or their dependents regardless of who was at fault in the accident. Last, cash grants, food, and other necessities are given to victims of natural disasters.

Family welfare services constitute a second public welfare program that enables the population of Hong Kong to achieve satisfying standards of health.[14] The services provided deal with interpersonal relationships; problems arising from the neglect, abuse, and ill-treatment of children, including the area of morality; problems that spring from poor mental and physical health, disabilities, and old age; and hardship resulting from unemployment, imprisonment, desertion, illness, and death. A third public welfare service that contributes to the economic welfare of Hong Kong is community and growth services. Some fourteen community halls and sixteen community centers are operated to serve the recreational and cultural needs of people.

The fourth public welfare function is rehabilitation services for the blind, the deaf, the physically handicapped, and former mental patients. These groups are helped in rehabilitation, housing, and welfare centers and clubs. The last provide residential as well as day facilities and workshops so that the disabled may lead a useful working life. A fifth public service function revolves around the treatment and rehabilitation of "offenders"—i.e., criminals. Hong Kong has five residential training institutions to provide academic, prevocational, social, and recreational training for inmates. In addition, there are probation services.

The role of government in provision of social services and the creation of human capital has been a large one; in sharp contrast, its role in the marketplace has been minimal. With respect to taxation and regulation of business, the Hong Kong government has maintained a very low profile. Indeed, it has been and still is the epitome of laissez-faire and is very different from Singapore in this respect. Before contrasting the two nations, let us consider Singapore's economic development to date.

Table 4.6

Growth in Singapore Gross Domestic Product, 1969-1980 (annual rate, %)

Industry	At Current Factor Cost				At 1968 Cost			
	1969-1979	1978	1979	1980(p)	1969-1979	1978	1979	1980(p)
TOTAL	14.7	10.2	11.2	14.0	9.4	8.6	9.3	10.2
Agriculture and fishing	8.6	-3.5	7.7	9.3	2.2	-0.8	3.3	2.6
Quarrying	9.2	-22.0	11.5	80.9	9.1	-13.4	14.3	27.0
Manufacturing	19.7	15.2	18.4	16.6	12.1	11.3	15.0	11.9
Utilities	12.1	16.4	21.7	17.3	10.1	14.0	9.4	8.2
Construction	15.6	-6.8	10.9	15.6	6.9	-7.7	7.0	10.0
Trade	12.7	9.2	9.2	10.4	7.6	6.9	7.1	7.2
Transport and communication	17.1	17.5	5.0	9.7	14.7	15.6	14.4	11.9
Financial and Business services	15.1	10.0	14.8	22.6	10.5	10.0	10.7	16.6
Other services	11.5	9.4	10.7	14.0	6.7	7.8	5.6	6.9

Source: Republic of Singapore, Economic Survey of Singapore, 1980, pp. 72, 73.

Economic Development in Singapore

As was Hong Kong, Singapore was occupied by the Japanese during World War II and was returned to Great Britain in 1945. In 1959, it was granted its independence. In 1963, Singapore merged with Malaya, Sarawak, and Sabah to form the new nation of Malaysia. The union lasted until 1965; Singapore has been an independent nation since then. Its economic progress has been remarkable.

Table 4.6 reflects the rapid growth of Singapore's GDP, 1969-80, by industry. Even with some years in which some industries contracted rather than grew, for the period 1969-79 the various major components of GDP increased in real terms between 2.2 percent and 14.7 percent per annum. The modest rate of 2.2 percent per annum for agriculture is quite respectable, considering the emphasis on industrialization and urbanization by the Singapore government in this period. In current monetary terms,

Table 4.7

Singapore Gross Domestic Fixed Capital Formation, 1969-1980 (annual growth rate, %)

| Industry | At Current Market Prices | | | | At 1968 Market Prices | | | |
	1969-1979	1978	1979	1980	1969-1979	1978	1979	1980
TOTAL	17.9	12.2	16.2	28.7	10.8	10.5	10.4	19.0
Construction and works	16.6	-3.6	14.1	35.1	7.2	-5.4	6.0	17.2
Residential buildings	13.3	-15.0	-0.7	21.3	4.6	-15.8	-6.8	6.6
Nonresidential buildings	22.3	16.8	39.2	37.8	12.1	14.1	29.4	19.2
Other construction and works	15.0	-2.5	5.1	57.8	5.4	-4.5	-2.6	36.5
Transport equipment	26.2	20.2	28.2	15.6	20.1	15.7	19.0	11.8
Machinery and equipment	15.0	29.1	9.7	32.5	9.4	23.6	7.5	26.5

Source: Republic of Singapore, *Economic Survey of Singapore, 1980,* p. 79.

of course, the average annual growth rates of all segments of GDP, agriculture and fishing, were decidedly more impressive. Where, for all industries for 1969-79, the average annual growth rate at 1968 factor costs was 9.4 percent, in current monetary unit terms it was 14.7 percent.

The growth of manufacturing was particularly impressive. Between 1960 and 1980, it increased by about twenty four times in current factor costs and about nine times in 1968 factor costs and became Singapore's leading industry. Trade, which had been the leading industry, had slipped to second place by 1980.

The rapid increase in the pace of economic life is also reflected in table 4.7. Between 1969 and 1980, in current market prices, total gross domestic fixed capital formation experienced average annual growth rates of between 12.2 percent and 28.7 percent. In 1968 market prices, the rates were still in the impressive 10.4 percent to 19.0 percent range. It was that rapid expansion of fixed capital, 1969-80, that led to the explosion of manufacturing facilities, output, and so on in Singapore in that same period (table 4.8).

As a result of the unusually rapid rates of increase (table 4.8), by 1980 the number of manufacturing establishments in Singapore was about six times that which existed in 1960; the number of employees in 1980 was about nine times that of 1960; output in 1980 was about twenty one times that of 1960; and the value of direct exports in 1980 was about seventeen times that of 1960.

Table 4.8

Singapore Principal Statistics of Manufacturing 1969-1980 (annual growth rate, %)

	1969-1979	1978	1979	1980
Establishments	6.1	11.6	5.9	7.1
Employment	9.9	11.0	10.4	6.6
Output	20.0	12.1	29.3	34.1
Input	19.1	10.7	29.0	35.3
Remuneration	20.2	17.0	21.0	24.4
Value added	22.3	15.2	30.6	31.5
Direct exports	24.0	14.7	29.2	37.8

Source: Republic of Singapore, Economic Survey of Singapore, 1980, p. 81

Table 4.9

Singapore Principal Statistics of Manufacturing by Major Industry Group, 1980

Industry	Establishments No.	%	Employment No.	%	Output $ Mil.	%	Value Added $ Mil.	%	Workers Per Establish-ment No.	Value Added Per Worker $000	Ratio of Value Added to Output %
Food and beverages	305	9.1	13,393	4.7	2,091.7	6.1	446.1	5.0	44	33.3	21.3
Textiles	101	3.0	9,755	3.4	507.1	1.5	158.2	1.8	97	16.2	31.2
Wearing apparel	488	14.6	30,176	10.5	895.8	2.6	302.2	3.4	62	10.0	33.7
Wood products	130	3.9	10,997	3.8	795.9	2.3	215.8	2.4	85	19.6	27.1
Furniture	110	3.3	5,886	2.0	175.3	0.5	69.7	0.8	54	11.8	39.8
Paper products and printing	376	11.2	16,058	5.6	787.2	2.3	323.0	3.6	43	20.1	41.0
Chemical products	123	3.7	5,941	2.1	865.6	2.5	405.1	4.6	48	68.2	46.8
Petroleum	10	0.3	3,299	1.1	14,806.5	43.2	1,844.2	20.9	330	559.0	12.5
Rubber and plastic products	232	6.9	10,820	3.8	607.8	1.8	210.0	2.4	47	19.4	34.6
Nonmetallic minerals	86	2.6	4,403	1.5	560.0	1.6	174.9	2.0	51	39.7	31.2
Basic metals	26	0.8	2,237	0.8	510.8	1.5	186.0	2.1	86	83.1	36.4
Fabricated metal products	324	9.7	15,121	5.3	1,037.3	3.0	372.9	4.2	47	24.7	35.9
Machinery and appliances	619	18.5	111,359	38.7	7,529.1	22.0	2,627.3	29.7	180	23.6	34.9
Transport equipment	242	7.2	31,255	10.9	2,306.2	6.7	1,190.9	13.5	129	38.1	51.6
Precision equipment	48	1.4	10,305	3.6	381.9	1.1	173.8	2.0	215	16.9	45.5
Other products	127	3.8	6,309	2.2	426.7	1.3	142.1	1.6	50	22.5	33.3
TOTAL excl. rubber processing	3,347	100.0	287,314	100.0	34,284.9	100.0	8,842.2	100.0	86	30.8	25.8
Rubber processing	14	—	1,840	—	1,205.8	—	85.5	—	—	46.5	7.1
TOTAL incl. rubber processing	3,361	—	289,154	—	35,490.7	—	8,927.7	—	86	30.9	25.2

Note: Refers to establishments engaging ten or more persons.
Source: Republic of Singapore, *Economic Survey of Singapore, 1980*, p. 83.

It is difficult to describe such progress as anything short of impressive.

By 1980 Singapore was a light industrial nation well on the way to becoming not only a more heavily industrialized one but a broadly diversified nation as well (table 4.9). Unlike Hong Kong, Singapore in 1980 was not dependent on the export of light industrial goods such as textiles and apparel but, rather, on its exports of petroleum products, machinery and appliances, transportation equipment, and electronics manufactures. In 1980, in contrast to Hong Kong, its industries were decidedly on the heavy side, capital intensive, and much more diversified. Over three-fifths of the value of its manufacturing output was coming from technologically complex capital-intensive industries and less than two-fifths was coming from technologically relatively simple labor-intensive industries.[15] In Hong Kong, less than one-fifth of the value of its manufacturing output was coming from heavy capital-intensive industries and four-fifths was coming from light, labor-intensive industries.[16] In Singapore in 1980, for example, only 17.6 percent of the manufacturing establishments and 13.9 percent of the employment were in the textile and wearing apparel industries.[17] In Hong Kong, in 1981, 28.5 percent of the manufacturing establishments and 40.5 percent of the employment were in the textile and wearing apparel industries.[18]

In Singapore, laborers in the machinery, appliances, and other heavy industrial plants worked with larger, more complex, more efficient machinery, and in larger more efficient plants than did laborers in the textile, wearing apparel, and other light industrial firms; and consequently the former earned higher incomes than

Table 4.10

Singapore Trade, 1960, 1970, 1979, 1980
(annual change, %)

	1960	1970	1979	1980
Total trade	4.2	20.2	31.7	34.0
Imports	4.8	19.9	29.5	33.9
Exports	3.5	20.6	34.6	34.0
Domestic exports	25.5	26.9	37.6	41.8
Reexports	-0.7	15.3	30.5	22.8

Source: Republic of Singapore, Economic Survey of Singapore, 1980, p. ix.

the latter. The greater values added per worker in the heavy industries of Singapore may explain in part the difference in per capita national income between Singapore and Hong Kong. In 1981 it was U.S. $5,119 for Singapore and U.S. $4,527 for Hong Kong.[19]

In 1980 manufacturing was the largest component of GDP, accounting for nearly 30 percent of the total in terms of current factor costs and nearly 25 percent at 1968 factor costs. A very close second was trade, which accounted for about 25 percent at current factor costs; it was the leading industry when 1968 factor costs were used, weighing in then at over 25 percent of the total GDP.

As with industry, the growth of Singapore's trade was most impressive. By the 1970s the annual rate of growth of Singapore's foreign trade was well into double digits (table 4.10). For 1980 the lowest rate of increase registered for any segment of foreign trade was 22.8 percent for reexports; the highest, 41.8 percent, was for domestic exports. These data mirror the rapid growth of domestic exports as Singapore's manufacturing capacity exploded. Between 1960 and 1980 total foreign trade increased by a factor of over 11, and the domestic exports portion increased by a factor of 118.[20] About one-third of Singapore's total trade was in petroleum, which was imported, processed, and then exported. The main sources of the petroleum were Saudi Arabia and Kuwait, and the principal export markets were Japan, Hong Kong, and West Malaysia. Machinery and transport equipment constituted the second-largest group of commodities traded, accounting for 28 percent of the total. The imports consisted mainly of semiconductors, ships, aircraft, machine parts and components, and switch-gears; the exports consisted of such high-value-added products as motors, pumps, machine parts, and components for data-processing machinery and calculators. In 1980, because of increased interest in oil exploration, ten oil rigs were built and delivered, with six of them going to the United States.[21]

As with Hong Kong, the source of the rapid economic progress in Singapore is the high-quality, work-oriented population. In mid-1980 Singapore had a population of about 2.4 million, of whom about 1.1 million were in the labor force and among whom there was only a 3 percent unemployment rate. In 1982 Hong Kong had a population of 5.2 million, of whom 2.5 million were in the labor force and among whom there was an unemployment rate of 3.8 percent.[22] As in Hong Kong, education is stressed in Singapore. Educational programs and facilities include preschool, primary, secondary, vocational, postsecondary, tertiary adult education, and special education for handicapped children. Specialized professional and other training is available in five institutions of higher learning. In all, over 500,000 students were enrolled in full-time education in 1980. That same year Singapore's output of graduate-level, technical, and skilled manpower was 12,710, with an enrollment of about 33,000 coming up behind them.[23]

Singapore's excellent health facilities are reflected in its medical statistics. In 1982, hospital beds per 1,000 were 3.0 and doctors per 1,000 were 0.9, compared with 6.0 and 2.7 respectively for the United States in 1980, and major hospital development plans were under way. Life expectancy in 1980 was sixty seven years and seventy one years for males and females, respectively.[24] With respect to welfare, the government's policy is to emphasize self-reliance and hard work rather than dependency on government. However, it still provides public assistance funds to those rendered destitute because of age, illness, or disability. The Central Provident Fund requires compulsory contributions from all employers and many employees, and provides some income for workers in their old age and further aids them in the purchase of homes. Some employees can withdraw their contributions to the fund for the purpose of buying apartments built with public funds.[25]

Overall, Hong Kong taxes and regulates lightly, and provides many social services but somewhat fewer assistance programs for business. Singapore, in contrast, taxes and regulates heavily, provides fewer social services but many more assistance programs for business. Let us consider the role government in the economic development of these two ministates.

Government and Economic Development

It is evident that Hong Kong and Singapore have much in common—strategic location, colonial history and legacy, paucity of inanimate resources, hard-working population, and rapid growth of GDP and per capita income—but there is one aspect of economic development about which they clearly differ: the role of government in economic development. Although both preach the virtues of free enterprise and encourage investment and production, Hong Kong is by far the economically freer and less regulated of the two. It has far lower rates of taxation than does Singapore, and has fewer economic controls over its citizens and foreign investors.

The revenue of the government of Hong Kong comes from three sources: direct taxes, which in 1978/79 accounted for 33.4 percent of total revenue; indirect taxes, which in that same period accounted for 27.6 percent; and miscellaneous fees, which accounted for 39 percent of total revenue in 1978/79.[26] The direct taxes include a tax on profits earned in Hong Kong that has graduated rates up to a maximum of 15 percent of total income less allowable donations for individuals and 17 percent for corporations; a "salaries tax" on money and real income (e.g., free living quarters) earned in Hong Kong, with rates of 5 percent to a maximum of 15 percent; an "interest tax" on interest and the interest portion of annuities received in Hong Kong, with rates of 5 percent to a maximum of 15 percent; and a "property tax" of 15 percent levied against 80 percent of the assessable value of land and nonowner-occupied buildings in Hong Kong.[27]

These already low rates have numerous qualifying clauses that result in even lower taxes being paid. With respect to the "profits tax," no tax is applied to income or profits arising abroad even if remitted to Hong Kong. There is limited double-taxation relief when income taxable in Hong Kong has been taxed in another Commonwealth territory (excluding Britain). With respect to the "property tax," if the owner uses the property for business purposes, the "property tax" can be offset against any "profits tax" charged on the business, and where the "property tax" is greater than the "profits tax" he or she can claim a refund of the excess.[28]

Hong Kong does not tax offshore income, alimony, the capital portion of annuities, capital gains, dividends whether from a Hong Kong source or not, or income from a trust. There are no payroll, turnover, sales, value added, or gift taxes.[29] The business depreciation allowances in Hong Kong are similarly generous. For industrial structures, 20 percent of the cost can be deducted in the first year, with 4 percent per year thereafter for twenty years. For expenditures on machinery and plant, the first year's depreciation allowance is 25 percent, with the rates in subsequent years varying from 10 percent to 25 percent per year.

The indirect taxes include a tax on the rental of land and buildings (11 percent to 11.5 percent), excise taxes, royalties and concessions, stamp taxes, and other taxes.[30] There is also a "first-registration tax" on private cars in Hong Kong. The tax rates—unusually high for Hong Kong—range from 35 percent to 45 percent of the value of the vehicle and are intended more to discourage the importation of automobiles into an already over-crowded city-state than to provide revenue. Motorcycles are taxed at 35 percent, and all other vehicles except franchised buses are taxed at 15 percent. More typical are the excise taxes, which are levied against only four groups of commodities: tobacco, alcoholic beverages, hydrocarbons, and methyl alcohol. The rates are low by international standards; for example, less than U.S. $0.10 per liter of motor oil. There are no export duties. There are extremely low business registration fees (U.S. $35); company incorporation fees (U.S. $60 plus U.S. $0.80 per U.S. $200 of nominal capital); stamp duties on documents, which range from 0.25 percent to 2.75 percent; and "trade declaration charges" of U.S. $0.40 plus U.S. $0.10 per U.S. $200 of the value of the goods being declared. There is also an estate tax levied against property of the deceased situated in Hong Kong. Estates of less than H.K. $300,000 (about U.S. $50,000 to $60,000) are exempt, and the rates range from 6 percent to a maximum of 18 percent on estates over H.K. $3 million (about U.S. $500,000 to $600,000).[31]

In spite of its low tax rates, Hong Kong not only has accumulated a large reserve of tax revenue over many years but provides numerous useful services, both positive and passive, to aid private enterprise. With few exceptions, trade is not subject to import and export licensing. There are no customs tariffs and thus no bureaucracy to impede the flow of imports and exports. The few trade controls it has generally deal with health, safety, and security, or enable Hong Kong to meet its international obligations; as for example, in connection with certificates of origin, which are required by many of Hong Kong's trading parties.[32] The Hong Kong government aids rather than restricts business in general by requiring the registration of all enterprises when dangerous trades are involved, where dangerous goods may be handled, where offensive trades and processes may be organized, and where the environment may be threatened by waste disposal practices or by water, air, and noise pollution. Its standards are not onerous and indeed some visitors to Hong Kong, including this writer, believe that they are not high enough with respect to the environment.

Hong Kong has made strong continuing efforts to attract foreign investment. The government makes no distinction between local and foreign companies; both types can hold title to land and both are treated equally with respect to taxation and regulation.[33] In June 1980 there were 441 foreign firms engaged in manufacturing in Hong Kong with foreign (i.e., non-Hong Kong) capital invested of nearly U.S. $500 million. Two-thirds of the money invested was by U.S. and Japanese interests who opened mainly electronic, chemicals, textile, and watch and clock factories, and a broad diversity of other types of manufacturing operations.[34] Their investments created jobs for over 88,000 people.

Singapore, too, strongly encourages foreign investment, but that is perhaps the only major similarity in the policies of Hong Kong and Singapore in the areas of taxation and government regulation of business. Singapore's approach is much more planned and socially oriented. In 1981, of the total revenue of the government of Singapore, tax revenues accounted for 73.7 percent and other revenues accounted for 26.3 percent.[35] The main sources of tax revenues were direct taxes on income and property, primarily the former. The indirect taxes included import duties, excise duties, motor vehicle taxes and fees, and stamp duties.

The income tax rates on individuals and companies are high; they reach a maximum rate of 40 percent. However, to offset the disincentive effects on hard work, the government in the 1980s increased the depreciation rates of plants and machinery. It gave specific tax incentives for research and development activities.[36] On the other hand, because of government policy springing from noneconomic considerations, i.e., health, the excise duty on cigarettes manufactured in Singapore was increased and a duty was placed on locally grown tobacco. To restrain the growth of privately owned automobiles in a densely populated country, Singapore imposed heavier road taxes, vehicle registration fees, and license fees. Light truck registration fees were also increased. To foster greater use of buses, the motor taxes on buses were reduced to encourage the installation of heavier engines. Import duties on buses and commercial vehicles were abolished and the registration fee was reduced.[37]

115

With respect to foreign investment, Singapore's government is explicit. It strongly encourages export-oriented manufacturing industries that will contribute to rapid economic growth. It does not encourage foreign investment in shipping, shipping agencies, travel agencies, and the like, of which Singapore has more than enough. For retail ventures, including hotels, the government prefers to see a joint venture, with Singaporeans holding a 51 percent—i.e., controlling—interest.[38] It encourages multinational firms to establish regional and national offices in Singapore, with the hope that these offices will lead to the establishment of manufacturing facilities making higher-value-added products. In public pronouncements in the early 1980s, the government specifically pointed to the desirability of such high-value manufactures as integrated circuits, computers, industrial electronic equipment, aircraft components and machine tools, and medical instruments such as X-ray machines, blood counters, and specialty pharmaceutical products. The government sought to encourage increased employment in Singapore's skilled workers and for professionals such as engineers, accountants, lawyers, doctors, technicians, computer personnel, and managers as well.[39]

To bring about the establishment of new enterprises, the government promulgated tax-relief programs for "pioneer industries." Any industry so designated—i.e., one badly needed by Singapore—would get a zero tax on company profits for five to ten years, depending on the details of each proposed project, such as type of product, investment level, skills, technology, and so on.[40] Specialized projects involving the manufacture of new desirable products could be considered for pioneer status even if the investment was extremely small, say, below U.S. $1 million.

In addition to the pioneer industries program, Singapore also grants generous investment allowances to industry either in addition to or in lieu of other forms of tax relief. For an approved project, tax-exempt profits up to 50 percent of actual fixed investment on factory buildings and productive equipment can be permitted.[41] If there is insufficient chargeable income in a year, the investment allowance can be carried forward indefinitely until it is used up. Hence, such investment allowances are particularly suitable for long-gestation projects that may not generate profits for some time after the start of commercial production. Although qualifying fixed assets exclude land, separate office buildings, motor vehicles, and office equipment, and also the cost of interest during construction, the investment allowances are granted in addition to the normal capital allowances. Companies can also claim simultaneously accelerated depreciation on plant and machinery without loss of any portion of the investment allowance.

Yet another aid to a specific type of business activity is the "warehousing and servicing" tax reduction.[42] This entails over a period of five years a company tax reduction from the normal rate of 40 percent to 20 percent on profits derived from export sales of goods or services of desirable engineering products. Profits from domestic sales in the warehousing and/or repair of technical products continue to be taxed at the 40 percent rate. Where the incentive was granted for technical products already warehoused or serviced in Singapore, the tax benefits are limited to export revenue above predetermined base levels. The incentive applies to projects that involve primarily technical or engineering services.

Singapore also provides an international-consultancy-services incentive to encourage "brain" types of services in overseas projects that involve plant and civil construction and related activities. Eligible services include project management and supervision, computer and data-processing services, and others. The incentives are a five-year company tax reduction from the normal rate of 40 percent to 20 percent on export profits.

In addition, Singapore provides tax incentives whereby a manufacturing enterprise that increases its investment in productive equipment by approximately U.S. $5 million may be granted an exemption on the increase in income resulting from the expansion for a period of up to five years. Singapore also encourages the construction of industrial facilities via accelerated depreciation allowances. While the basic general depreciation allowances are 20 percent the first year and annual allowances of from 5 percent to 20 percent on capital expenditures on machinery or plant, as an incentive industrial enterprises may claim 33.3 percent per annum for three years. Accelerated depreciation allowances for industrial buildings are prorated over twenty five years after a first-year allowance of 25 percent.

The list of other aids to industry is a long one.[43] There are tax exemptions on interest on approved foreign loans, concessionary tax rates on income from approved royalties, duty-free imports of equipment, preferential government purchase of local products, tax incentives for relevant training programs; capital-assistance programs for specialized projects of unique economic and technical benefit to Singapore, loan programs for the development and technical upgrading of the generation of small industries, and product-development assistance programs to foster local applied research and product-development capability and to build up indigenous technology.

In addition to encouraging manufacturing and other industrial growth, Singapore's government strongly encourages exports. An export incentive is the 4 percent tax on export profits instead of the normal 40 percent on company profits. It is used to encourage exports, or in cases where it would be unjustified to award pioneer status because of existing local manufacture. The export incentive period ranges from five to fifteen years, with the latter applying to projects with a fixed capital expenditure exceeding approximately U.S. $75 million, provided 50 percent of the company's paid-up capital is held by permanent Singapore residents. There are other international trade incentives meant for trading companies that export Singapore-manufactured products or that trade in non-traditional commodities. The incentive for these exports is a five-year concessionary company tax of 20 percent on export profits instead of the normal company rate of 40 percent. To get the lower rate, companies must export either a minimum of about U.S. $5 million per annum of qualifying manufactured products or Singapore domestic produce or a minimum of about U.S. $10 million of nontraditional commodities.

There are still other incentives for export as well as those for industrial development, but those cited above underscore one of the central facts about Singapore's economic development: although Singapore taxes heavily, it is eager to reduce taxes sharply for enterprises that operate in a way that contributes to attainment of its objectives. The government taxes heavily and regulates in detail, but it also encourages selected economic activities in an extremely generous albeit forceful style. In contrast, as noted above, the government of Hong Kong taxes and regulates lightly, and does less to plan for and achieve specific economic objectives. Its approach is distinctly that of laissez-faire.

Which of the two approaches is the superior one? An answer to that question requires consideration of numerous noneconomic as well as economic factors that are simply too complex and too subjective to consider briefly. Suffice it to note that proponents of both libertarianism and central planning can find much to support their position in a review of the recent economic development and current levels of achievement of Hong Kong and Singapore.

Causes and Effects

The economic success of Hong Kong and Singapore in recent decades raises many interesting questions. What factors accounted for their rapid development? Was it economic assistance from more developed countries? No. Neither city-state was the beneficiary of U.S., British, Soviet, or other AID-type assistance. The monetary and physical as well as human capital all originated in Hong Kong and Singapore, in contrast to Japan, South Korea, and Taiwan, which benefited from U.S. economic assistance in the post-World War II years. Was the absence of strong labor unions and therefore the presence of low wage rates a major contributing factor? Possibly. However, if that is the main factor, how does one explain the retarded state of economic development of nations in Central and South America, Africa, the Middle East, and elsewhere in Asia? In those areas, labor unionism and wage rates were and are as underdeveloped as in Hong Kong and Singapore. Is the absence of heavy military expenditures the main reason that Hong Kong and Singapore have recorded such high growth rates? If that is so, then nations with heavy military expenditures would be expected to have low rates of growth. How, then, does one explain South Korea, Taiwan, and other nations that have experienced very high growth rates in spite of extremely large military burdens? Is it that states as small as cities are inherently more manageable and efficient than large national states? If that is so, how does one explain the deterioration of the quality of life in Mexico City, Cairo, and other cities comparable in size and to some degree in government to Hong Kong and Singapore? Is it a matter of culture? Possibly. However, Malaysia has a large Chinese population but is not nearly as productive and economically impressive as its smaller, less populous neighbor Singapore, which also has a large Chinese population. On the other hand, there appear to be great cultural differences between the populations of France and Germany that are reflected in their attitudes toward work and that may also be reflected in their respective productivities and national outputs. The question calls for intense statistical analysis, which lies beyond the scope of this paper.

What is clear at this time is that no one model of economic development is suitable for all nations. What is suitable for India or Algeria may not be suitable for China or Nigeria. Decision making can be either centralized or decentralized, depending on individual circumstances, and still work. Allocation of resources between the public and private sectors can vary widely from nation to nation and still be effective. The only factors that appear to be common to all national economic success stories are that the populations involved placed extremely high values on education and hard work. What Hong Kong and Singapore have most in common with Japan, South Korea, and Taiwan is not their Asian geographic and ethnic-group backgrounds but, rather, their willingness to study and to work to the maximum, and to stress investment in the future rather than current consumption. To illustrate the principle, let us briefly consider Israel, a Middle Eastern nation with a large number of European and other non-Asian Jews who also stress education and hard work. As with Hong Kong and Singapore, the paucity of natural resources and the small size of the population have not prevented Israel from experiencing rapid economic development since 1948. Were it not for Israel's heavy military expenditures, loss of manpower in five wars, powerful unions, high wage rates, and considerable economic assistance received from abroad, it would have made an excellent third small nation to be evaluated in this paper along with Hong Kong and Singapore. Perhaps it will be considered at a later date. What is clear at this time is that education and hard work have been important factors in its development.

What can also be stated with certainty at this time is that if Hong Kong and Singapore are not perfect models of economic development for other nations then they are certainly close to it. Which of the two is the better model is probably a matter of national economic taste and philosophy. What will happen to them as models if and when labor unions become more powerful in those areas and wage rates rise? I do not know. The possibilities include a British-type of economic stagnation, e.g., an average annual growth rate of real GNP from 1974 to 1981 of .9 percent; a West German-type of moderate economic growth, e.g., an average annual growth rate of real GNP from 1974 to 1981 of 2.2 percent; and continuation of their currently high rates of growth. Forced to make a choice, at this time I would bet on the latter. Let us wait and see.

Yet another interesting aspect of the question of what factors accounted for the rapid economic development of Hong Kong and Singapore is that which deals with the importance of the *dissimilarities* to Japan, South Korea, Taiwan, and other Pacific rim success stories. Specifically, if there were factors that were important in the economic development of Japan, for example, that were not important in the cases of Hong Kong and Singapore, then how important in the general area of economic development are they? In Japan, the state "built," "opened," "established," "initiated," "patronized," and "took risks" in a wide variety of light and heavy industries and in transportation and communication facilities to a degree far beyond anything that occurred in the two ministates to the south. Many students of Japanese economic development describe the entrepreneurial role of the state as being among the most important in its economic development. If it was so very important in Japan, why was it not necessary or important in Hong Kong and Singapore?

A second major difference is one that involves Japan and Singapore. In the post-World War II period, Japan has typically spent about 1 percent of its GNP on national defense and thereby avoided what might have been a large drag on its economic development. In contrast, Singapore has frequently spent 4 percent to 5.5 percent of its GNP/GDP on military programs and yet has suffered no perceivable loss of economic momentum. Are expenditures on national defense a dilution of the resources available to nations with which to develop themselves? If so, why? If not, why not?

In the same vein, there is the third question of the stimulus of war. In the 1950s and 1960s, Japan benefited from U.S. participation in the Korean and Vietnam wars. It was used as a major supply base by the United States as well as a rest and recreation (R & R) area. The United States rented or leased numerous supply and recreation facilities and U.S. service men and women spent huge sums of their personal funds on souvenirs and services. It is difficult to place a specific monetary value on all of these things, but it is clear that the economy of Japan experienced a prolonged boom in the postwar period as a result.

Because of British concern over sensitivity regarding People's Republic of China, the United States was able to use Hong Kong and Singapore for similar supply and R&R functions to a far lesser degree than Japan. Indeed, to minimize friction, members of the U.S. military were even required to wear civilian clothing on many occasions in these two areas. It is clear that the economies of Hong Kong and Singapore did not benefit from U.S. military expenditures to anywhere near the same extent as Japan; however, that did not prevent both from experiencing rapid economic growth in the same period. The question, then, is just how important in the general economic development process are expenditures of these kinds?

A fourth set of dissimilarities between Japan on one hand and Hong Kong and Singapore on the other is the character of business organization in those countries. Managers in Japan, like the workers, have job tenure. They receive regular annual pay plus increments based on seniority. It is only through annual bonuses that a manager is affected by the company's profitability. In contrast, in both Hong Kong and Singapore, job tenure for both managers and workers is conspicuously a function of productivity and profits. To what extent, if any, is either system superior to the other? Is job security unimportant as a factor in the economic development process?

The Future

In 1997 the British government's ninety-nine-year lease of the New Territories will expire. At that time, the People's Republic of China will resume sovereign jurisdiction over it and the huge manufacturing, trading, and service facilities therein. In 1980 there began large movements of capital and capitalists out of Hong Kong,[44] which accelerated in 1982, 1983, and much of 1984. As in 1949, when they fled the Chinese civil war to seek refuge in Hong Kong, entrepreneurs and others left Hong Kong to establish new lives in Singapore, other places in Southeast Asia, Canada, Australia, Western Europe, the United States, and elsewhere. They left while there was still time to liquidate their assets without sustaining severe losses. The exodus had a chilling effect on Hong Kong's economic development: the value of the Hong Kong dollar fell sharply, and Hong Kong real estate, finance, banking, and other economic activities plummeted. In September and October 1984 the situation changed dramatically when China and Britain signed an agreement that states that for fifty years after China regains sovereignty, Hong Kong will be a "special administrative region" of China and will "maintain the capitalist economic and trade systems" that have made it so prosperous. From 1997 to 2047 Hong Kong is to maintain its status as a free port and remain a separate customs territory. It will have an independent financial system, including freely convertible currency. Hong Kong will not be subject to Chinese taxes. Commercial shipping systems will be unchanged, and Hong Kong will regulate civil aviation flights that do not fly over China.[45]

In late October 1984 the economy of the People's Republic of China moved closer to that of Hong Kong and contributed to the revival of Hong Kong's economy, which began only weeks earlier after the signing of the Sino-British agreement on Hong Kong. China relaxed controls over much of its commerce and trade, emphasized the importance of competition, announced more toleration of differences in income, and outlined plans to eliminate controls over the prices of many products.[46] By early November 1984 low-priced and medium-priced apartments in Hong Kong were selling briskly, and real estate, which had been in a slump since 1981, appeared to be reviving rapidly. It now appears that the economic development of Hong Kong will continue.

The economic development of Singapore also seems likely to at least continue if not accelerate. A beneficiary of the exodus from Hong Kong, Singapore's more diversified economy—in particular its heavier higher-value-added industries—seem likely to experience continued rapid growth of its GDP and GDP per capita. Its imaginative approach since 1960 to its problems has already resulted in its becoming a model of economic development. Perhaps the chief dangers Singapore faces are excess population and depressed world markets. It has initiated population-control programs to deal with the former and export-diversification programs to deal with the latter.[47] As a first approximation, it seems reasonable to believe that these programs will succeed; and hence, that Singapore's currently impressive rate of development will continue.

Notes

1. See Sidney Klein, "Lessons for Less Developed Countries: The Japan and USA Cases," *Proceedings of the Tenth International Conference on the Unity of the Sciences*, Vol. I, 1982, pp. 233-261.
2. For economic histories of Hong Kong, see T.N. Chiu, *The Port of Hong Kong: A Survey of Its Development* (Hong Kong: Hong Kong University

Press, 1973); Alvin Rabushka, *Hong Kong: A Study in Economic Freedom* (Chicago: University of Chicago, Graduate School of Business, 1979); A.J. Youngson, *Hong Kong, Economic Growth and Policy* (New York: Oxford University Press, 1982). For economic histories of Singapore, see Iain Buchanan, *Singapore in Southeast Asia: An Economic and Political Appraisal* (London: Bell, 1982); Frederick C. Deyo, *Dependent Development and Industrial Order: An Asian Case Study* (New York: Praeger, 1981); You Poh Seng and Lim Chong Yah, eds., *The Singapore Economy* (Eastern Universities Press, 1971).

3. For earlier comparative studies, see Theodore Geiger, *Tales of Two City-States: The Development of Hong Kong and Singapore* (Washington, D.C.: National Planning Association, 1973); Mee-Kau Nyaw and Chan-leong Chan, "Structure and Development—Strategies of the Manufacturing Industries in Singapore and Hong Kong: A Comparative Study," *Asian Survey* 22, no. 5: 449-69.

4. Hong Kong Government, *Two Decades of Economic Achievement*, p. 9.

5. Ibid.

6. Hong Kong Government, *Hong Kong: The Facts—Industry* (n.d.), p. 1.

7. Ibid.

8. Hong Kong Government, *Hong Kong Into the 80s—Industrial Investment* (n.d.), pp. 10-15.

9. Hong Kong Government, *Hong Kong: The Facts—General Summary* (n.d.), p. 2.

10. Ibid.

11. Hong Kong Government, *Hong Kong: The Facts — Education* (n.d.), p. 1.

12. Ibid., p. 2.

13. Hong Kong Government, *Hong Kong: The Facts—Social Welfare* (n.d.), pp. 1-2.

14. Ibid., p. 1.

15. Republic of Singapore, *Economic Survey of Singapore, 1980* (n.d.)

16. Hong Kong Government, *Hong Kong Into the 80s*, table 6.

17. Republic of Singapore, *Economic Survey of Singapore, 1980*, table 2.3, p. 83.

18. Hong Kong Government, *Hong Kong for the Business Visitor* (n.d.), p. 21.

19. Federal Reserve Bank of San Francisco, *Pacific Basin Economic Indicators* 7 (December 1982): 2.

20. Republic of Singapore, *Economic Survey of Singapore, 1980*, p. ix.

21. Ibid., p. 30.

22. Hong Kong Census and Statistics Department, *Hong Kong in Figures, 1983*, p. 1.

23. Republic of Singapore, *Economic Survey of Singapore, 1980*, table 29, p. 51.

24. Republic of Singapore, *The Investment Environment in Singapore* (n.d.), p. 7.

25. Ibid., p. 2.

26. Price Waterhouse, *Information Guide: Doing Business in Hong Kong* (September 1979), p. 35.

27. Ibid., pp. 35-37.

28. Hong Kong Government, *Hong Kong Into the 80s*, pp. 29-32.

29. Price Waterhouse, *Information Guide*, p. 35.

30. Hong Kong Government, *Hong Kong Into the 80s*, p. 32.

31. Price Waterhouse, *Information Guide*, p. 75.

32. Hong Kong Government, *Hong Kong for the Business Visitor*, p. 14.

33. Price Waterhouse, *Information Guide*, pp. 7, 48, 52-53.

34. Hong Kong Government, *Hong Kong Into the 80s*, tables 12, 13.

35. Republic of Singapore, Ministry of Culture, Information Division, *Singapore, Facts and Pictures, 1982*, (n.d.), p. 85.

36. Republic of Singapore, *Economic Survey of Singapore, 1980*, p. 39.

37. Ibid.

38. Republic of Singapore, *Economic Policies and Economic Growth* (n.d.), p. 10.

39. Ibid., p. 11.

40. Republic of Singapore, *Industrial and Investment Incentives* (n.d.), p. 21.

41. Ibid.

42. Ibid., p. 22.

43. Ibid., pp. 24-27.

44. Michael Parks, "Hong Kong Is Suffering from Exodus of Cash," *Los Angeles Times*, 22 February 1983, pt. IV, pp. 1, 2, 3.

45. B.R. Schlender, J.P. Mangino, and J. Leung, "Detailed Sino-British Agreement on Future of Hong Kong Appears to Allay the Capitalist Enclave's Apprehensions," *Wall Street Journal*, 27 September 1984, p. 28.

46. Amanda Bennett, "China Embraces Free-Market Principles in an Attempt to Modernize Its Economy," *Wall Street Journal*, 22 October 1984, p. 1; J.P. Sterba and A. Bennett, "Peking Turns Sharply Down Capitalist Road in New Economic Plan," *Wall Street Journal*, 25 October 1984, p. 1.

47. Republic of Singapore, *Industrial and Investment Incentives*, p. 1.

Comments on Economic Development in Hong Kong and Singapore

Toshio Aoki

Professor Sidney Klein's View

In his conference paper "Economic Development in Hong Kong and Singapore," Professor Klein analyzes very clearly and concretely both the causes and the process of the post-World War II economic development of the two ministates. His analysis gives meaningful suggestions to these who have either an academic or a practical interest in the socioeconomic development of the developing countries (DCs) in general.

Klein points out that the two countries have, on the one hand, many similarities:

- small size of territory and population, paucity of natural resources

- strategic location commanding important sea lanes in Asia

- colonial history and commercial development before World War II

- industrial development and rapid GDP growth after the war, due mainly to hard-working and educated population

- prevalance of a free-market economy, dominance of the private sector, and government encouragement of investment and exports

But, on the other hand, the two countries are very different in the following ways:

- The composition of the industrial sector: Hong Kong industry is still concentrated in the labor-intensive textile and clothing industries. Singapore has already established capital-intensive heavy and chemical industries, including the second-largest oil refinery in the world.

- The role of government in economic development: Hong Kong, using a classic laissez-faire approach, taxes and regulates lightly; gives less assistance to business and does not seek to control it; but provides the population with many social services. Singapore, in somewhat authoritarian, paternalistic style, taxes and regulates heavily; gives much more assistance to business, yet at the same time implements centrally planned and socially oriented control of business; and provides fewer social services for the population.

Klein, cautiously refraining from judging which of the two approaches is superior, states that no one model of economic development is suitable for all nations. However, he also clearly attributes the success of the two countries to shared virtues: "The only factors that appear to be common to all national economic success stories are that the populations involved placed extremely high value on education and hard work."

Role of Clean Government and Hard Work

While entirely agreeing with the above-mentioned conclusion, I rather doubt whether the virtues of hard work and an emphasis on education can be transplanted to all DCs, and wonder why, where people in a DC already work hard and are very conscious of the importance of education, their efforts do not give their countries economic development like that enjoyed by Hong Kong and Singapore. On the basis of my own observation and experience, I believe that the ordinary people of the DCs, e.g., the paddy farmers of Java, the *becak* drivers in Jakarta, the fishermen on the Thai coast, or the forest workers in East Malaysia, invariably work very hard to earn their living. Even in modern factories, the efficiency of local labor is said to be not so low when compared with that of industrialized countries as far as normal day-to-day operation is concerned.

It seems to me, then, that it depends very much on the character of the upper structure of society whether the ordinary people's efforts lead to national economic development or not. In other words, the existence or nonexistence of clean and honest administration is one of the decisive factors determining the success or failure of national development efforts. Nobody doubts that government in Singapore is honest and clean, its officials' efficiency and orientation toward achievement are well known. Under such administration one can expect that harder work will naturally produce better results. Contrariwise, under corrupt and dishonest government consisting of status-oriented and lazy officials, there is no guarantee for the ordinary people that their efforts will enjoy a fair reward. In many cases, honest behavior leads to personal disadvantage while the dishonest and cunning prosper. There can be no doubt that such a situation is a disincentive to hard work and constitutes a prime obstacle to development.

In most cases, as described by Professor Syed Hussein Alatas in his famous study *The Sociology of Corruption* (1975), corruption usually originates in the upper echelons of government and big business, eventually pervades all strata of the administration, and finally spreads throughout the whole society. It is, therefore, only logical that the cure must also start with purification of the upper echelons themselves, not with moral preaching to the common people. The following diagnosis by Wang An Shih (1021-1086), quoted by Alatas, is still applicable today: "The two absolute prerequisites against corruption are power-holders of high calibre and rational and efficient laws. Neither can function without the other. The one conditions the other. Both have to be present for any effort to be successful."

Role of Value System and Education

Why do people in Singapore and Hong Kong work so hard? In addition to a favorable environment for hard work, the result mainly of the existence of clean government, mentioned above, traditional cultural attitudes appear to play a very important role as motive power for hard work. The role of traditional cultural attitudes, in other words, the value system of a society, must not be overlooked in the study of a society's development.

The eminent cultural anthropologist, Professor Koencaraningrat of the University of Indonesia, describes in *Kebudayaan, Mentalitet dan Pembangunan* (Culture, mentality and development)(1974) the features of the value system of the Javanese *priyai* (upper-middle-class administrative officials originally employed by the Javanese feudal dynasties) that still influence Javanese cultural attitudes and retard the society's economic development, as follows:

- The Javanese *priyai* attach prime importance to their status, authority, and social power and the consequent material comfort, not on achievement in their profession. (Status-oriented, not achievement-oriented.)

- Even when faced with a situation that clearly calls for urgent and drastic measures, they avoid realistic discussion or criticism, particularly with or of their superiors, as rude and impolite, and regard meetings as social rather than business gatherings. (Unwillingness to face reality, prevalence of wishful thinking, confusing of *sollen, wollen,* and *sein.*)

- Being extremely vertical-oriented, they always seek their superiors' blessing before doing anything; without supervision from above, they have no self-discipline. (Lack of built-in controls and personal initiative.)

- They want to obtain good results quickly and easily, neglecting the necessary, unavoidable process of cumulative efforts, which alone could give the desired results, and also forgetting the importance of the quality of the work done. (Easy-going society, to use Koencaraningrat's term.)

If we merely reverse the above, perhaps oversimplified description of the cultural attitudes of the Javanese *priyais*, we have a model of the modern official with the opposite virtues, those conducive to the development of a society. I believe that this type of official already exists in Singapore and Hong Kong, constituting an essential factor in its success. It appears to be obvious that education and training in the DCs, particularly of administrators, should emphasize the production of such achievement-oriented, well-disciplined people, able to face bitter reality with courage and clear minds, free from wishful thinking and the confusing of *sollen, wollen,* and *sein.* It may well be that education and training are even more important than technology or know-how transfer from industrialized countries.

5.

Lessons for Developing Countries: The Japan and United States Cases

Sidney Klein

Introduction

For nearly three decades one of my favorite examination questions, for undergraduates and graduate students alike, has been the following: "The year is 1840 just prior to the Opium War. You are comparing the potential of China and Japan for economic development over the next one hundred years. Which of the two countries would you choose as more likely to make the greatest progress. Why?" Most if not all of my students quite rationally, given the time constraint of 1840 vision, choose China. After all, in 1840 China had land area and resources many times those of Japan, a much larger population and labor force, and by far the richer, more varied, more promising economic history. Japan, comprising only four small, heavily mountainous islands in toto about the size of California, with limited inanimate and human resources and a relatively unimpressive economic history, hardly merited mention in the same breath as China. Of course, as we all know, the next century was marked by extraordinarily rapid development on the part of Japan rather than China. By 1914 Japan was the leading industrial power in Asia and by the 1930s, after acquiring Formosa (now called Taiwan), Korea, and Manchuria, felt able to challenge the United States economically and politically in the Pacific and brought on World War II.

We all know the results of that war. However, writing in September 1981 with some thirty six years of postwar experience behind us, it now seems appropriate to update my old dependable question as follows: "It is the fall of 1945. You are comparing the potential of the United States and Japan for economic development over the next one hundred years. Which of the two countries would you choose as more likely to make greater economic progress? Why?" Again, rational students of economics, given a constraint of 1945 knowledge and vision, would choose the larger, far better endowed, technologically far more advanced, militarily unscathed, financially powerful economy of the United States. After all, by the fall of 1945 Japan had lost all of its colonies and a significant portion of its labor force, industry, and economic infrastructure. Japan's economy was epitomized by the war-caused rubble in which so many of its cities and towns were still enveloped. And once again, rational students of economics, those using 1945 vision and knowledge, would have been wrong. Now, over a third of the way into the century defined, Japan's is the third-most-powerful economy on the planet, the second most powerful in the free world. Japan appears to be inexorably over-taking both the United States and the USSR economically and by the middle of the next century may well have done so.[1]

Given these two dramatic contrasts based on economic races roughly a century apart, the following questions arise: What can developing countries (DCs) learn from Japan? What has Japan done since 1840 and particularly since 1945 that DCs might well emulate? Further, even allowing for near closure of the gap between the United States and Japan, what lessons can DCs learn from the United States, both positive and negative?

Favorable Factors in Japan's Economic Development

There are at least nine factors that explain Japan's economic success and from which DCs can benefit. The first and perhaps the most important of these is the role of the state.[2] In 1868, a conscious decision was made by the government to modernize the economy as quickly as possible. Students were sent to Europe and the United States to learn the most advanced technology; the principle of compulsory public schooling was adopted; the postal and telegraph systems were introduced; and railroads were built. The government took the initiative not only in these areas but in shipping, textiles, and other types of production and transportation enterprises as well. Many commercial and special-purpose banks were organized, for example, the Hokkaido Colonization Bank. After many of these diverse business ventures proved successful they were sold to private interests; however, before and after sale, there was close coordination and cooperation between the government and major business interests. It was long before the post-World War II period that use of the term "Japan Incorporated" became warranted.[3]

The rapid industrialization process was facilitated by rapid growth of the population, labor force, tax base, tax rates, and productivity, concurrently with relatively low growth of real income for the overwhelming majority of workers.[4] As that suggests, the willingness of the population of Japan to work hard for, pay heavy taxes to, save with, and invest through the government was a major factor in the growth of the pre-World War II economy. Between 1902 and 1918, Japanese government expenditures tripled and the national debt increased over five times. Domestic economic needs for raw materials, markets, and an outlet for its population led to the acquisition by force of colonies in East and Southeast Asia. Preferential tariffs and other types of legislation that favored Japanese interests were enacted in the home islands and in all of the areas controlled by Japan. In the colonies, as earlier in the home islands, the state pioneered and financed new ventures in a wide variety of economic sectors. The operative words are that it "built," "opened," "established," "initiated," and "patronized" in many light and heavy industries. And, as necessary, it imported from the West and elsewhere.

All of that was accomplished without coercion on the part of the state; rather, it was the result of a national consensus and national cooperation. In the post-World War II period, the major positive role of the state is best exemplified by the Ministry of International Trade and Industry (MITI). MITI works closely with private industry in the construction and modernization of plants and equipment. It helps "guide" resources into industries where they can compete more effectively both domestically and in foreign trade, but particularly the latter. It organizes multiyear plans to help provide a flexible framework for foreign trade and technology transfer. Although it does not "command" businesses, it does issue analyses that identify long-term trends and indicate what is necessary to attain specified targets for balanced national growth. Essentially a catalyst, it coordinates the diverse estimates of future growth made by various government agencies and the business community. It draws attention to present and future needs and provides input into the estimates of other government agencies and private firms. Just as they react to MITI information releases, MITI reacts to their announcements and actions.[5]

Indicative of the coordinative approach is that since the 1960s MITI has encouraged firms to channel resources from labor-intensive to capital-intensive industries, where rising wages in Japan would have less of a negative impact on Japan's ability to compete internationally. After the oil crises of 1973-74, MITI guided Japanese firms out of energy-intensive industries into service industries not dependent on oil imports and attempted to ease the problems of those oil-dependent firms that could not do so. It has helped declining firms to move elsewhere geographically or functionally or both. Where entire industries have had severe problems, it has worked out agreements like those of the 1930s National Recovery Administration in the United States—agreements to limit output and other aspects of competition.

A second major factor in Japan's unusually rapid economic development has been superior education and training. As noted earlier, a compulsory free public school system was adopted immediately after the decision to modernize was made in 1868, and it has been enlarged in scope consistently since then. By the early 1970s Japan had a literacy rate of 99.3 percent and in 1978 some 39 percent of all high school students were going on to a higher education.[6] That educational system in the late nineteenth century and in the twentieth century produced a continuing flow of well-trained, highly motivated managers and a middle class with values and ideals most conducive to development, such as the importance of hard work, self-discipline, and personal, institutional, and national savings and investment. Difficult but fair examinations characterized the system and made possible the recruitment from all segments of society fresh supplies of the capable leaders needed for the rapid modernization of the country. Over the decades since the Meiji Restoration, a diploma from a major national university has been literally the only ticket needed for an ambitious young man to reach the top of the socioeconomic hierarchy, and it was attainable to all with the ability and fortitude to withstand the stress of competition.[7] It should be noted that while degrees from leading non-Japanese universities were helpful, they were no substitute for those from Japanese universities, and that factor contributed further to the unity and cohesiveness of Japanese society and the establishment of a consensus on national goals.[8]

Closely related to the factor of education is the third factor, the character of the population. It has been and is advancement oriented, achievement oriented, work oriented, and imbued with a psychology of mutual dependence. Historically, the population and labor force have not only been willing but eager to defer gratification in the present in the interest of future production. The labor force is loyal to employers, to the public at large, and to the concept of "Japan Incorporated" and has a classically intense work ethic. In 1971, for example, the Ministry of Labor surveyed worker attitudes and found that 37 percent of all Japanese workers found their greatest satisfaction in life when absorbed in their work, compared to 21 percent when at home with their families and another 21 percent when taking part in leisure activities.[9] That Japanese workers identify strongly with their work is reflected in how they introduce themselves to others. Instead of stating their occupation, they state the name of the organization that employs them.

The employing organization represents more than just a source of income to the worker. Because of the practice of, in effect, lifetime job tenure in Japan, the organization is the mechanism by which individuals can attain higher social and economic status, and the means by which they can maximize psychic as well as monetary income over their lifetimes.[10] The company's fortune is their fortune. Consequently employees tend to work harder for the firm, knowing that they will still be with the firm when their efforts bear fruit, and that the results will reflect favorably on them. The custom of lifetime job tenure makes for high employee morale and a heavy commitment by employees to economic progress by the company and hence the nation as well. Thus, employees willingly—indeed even enthusiastically—work overtime and on holidays and weekends to complete assignments. They are not imbued with the "9-to-5" or "it's-not-my-problem" psychologies so evident in the United States and elsewhere. After jobs have been completed, Japanese employees habitually stay after regular hours to conduct critiques of the efforts of all so that the firm may profit from their experience.

A fourth factor in Japan's economic development has been its consistently steady emphasis on research and development and the establishment and expansion of high-technology industries. Although historically Japan has benefited from the importation of foreign technology and indeed even as recently as in 1977 was benefiting from foreign patents at the rate of about 25,000 per year, it was concurrently developing domestic alternatives to foreign technology. In the late 1960s, the general index of Japan's technological level, with that of the United States equal to 100, was about 22, just slightly less than France and the United Kingdom (24 and 25, respectively). For the late 1970s, with the U.S. index at 200, Japan's was 50, nearly twice that of the United Kingdom (26), and well above that of France (38). Whereas in the late 1960s it had been about half that of Germany (40), it was now nearly equal to Germany's (56). By the late 1970s Japan alone had 272,000 personnel in research and development work, compared to a total of 234,000 for West Germany, France, and the United Kingdom combined.[11]

That progress came primarily from the efforts of the private sector of the economy. In 1977 the governmental contribution to total national research expenditures was only 27.4 percent, compared with 50.5 percent in the United States and 48.5 percent in West Germany.[12] The proportion reflects national policy that technological innovation should be the job of the businesses themselves. The main contribution of the government was in other ways, which include the formulation of industrial policy and measures in support of that policy, such as favorable tax and depreciation schedules and industry nationalization measures. They also included direct control over technological imports up to the early 1970s.

The efforts clearly paid off. In 1966, of 68,406 patents issued by the U.S. Patent Office, some 1,122 or 1.6 percent were issued to Japanese firms or nationals. In 1976, of some 70,236 patents issued by the Patent Office, 6,542 or 9.3 percent were issued to Japanese.[13] These data do not include improvements in patents held by others made by Japanese businesses that were incorporated into the product or process by the non-Japanese patent owners. It should also be noted that the Japanese approach to research and development has been extremely cost effective. Between 1950 and 1978 the Japanese entered into 32,000 contracts for the transfer of foreign technology to Japan. The cumulative cost to the Japanese of all of the technology represented was only $9 billion. In 1980, U.S. research expenditures alone were estimated at about $50 billion. As two students of the subject put it, "For a fraction of the U.S. annual expenditure, Japan closed the technology gap."[14] One can only speculate what the rate of research and development would have been like if, as in the United States, there had been large military and space budgets to provide a subsidy base. In any case, there is no deprecating the effectiveness with which tax concessions and very fast depreciation schedules have been and will continue to be used.

A fifth factor in Japan's economic development was expert export management through collective yet competitive market-oriented capitalism. In the post-World War II period, the Japanese government created JETRO (Japan External Trade Organization) to promote Japanese trade and to disseminate information about Japanese goods and services. In addition, the government offered firms effective incentives to promote exports. These included tax reductions for export earnings, subsidized interest rates for export financing, long-term export credit on a deferred payment basis, and subsidies for export and export-oriented production that would increase the rates and levels of export profits.[15] Even more imaginatively, reparations payments for World War II and the provision of tied aid to DCs also made exporting activity more profitable. Foreign exchange bills that conformed to standard settlement rules were made eligible to be discounted by, or qualified as collateral acceptable to, the Bank of Japan. Thus, they could be discounted or borrowed against at interest rates lower than those prevailing in Japan.[16] In international trade, where capital is frequently limited, the early availability of sales revenue via discount at low interest rates is a major factor in business continuance and expansion. These export incentives coupled with others made it profitable for Japanese firms to export goods at prices significantly lower than those prevailing domestically, and led to charges of "dumping" from foreign businesses adversely affected.

As the foregoing suggests, JETRO helped Japan change from a nation that imported manufactured products to one that exported them; it provided assistance to "infant trade" rather than the "infant industries" described in classical economics writing. Without in any way interfering with the competitive process, JETRO helped many hundreds of Japanese firms identify the absolute and comparative costs involving Japan and other countries, and to make direct investments in Japan and abroad that would maximize the likelihood of their success. It is for that reason, among many, that the term "Japan Incorporated" developed. By 1980 Japanese firms had invested about $33 billion overseas; and it is possible, given current developments, that the figure could quadruple by 1990.[17]

Perhaps even more significant, by 1980 it was clear that the level of Japanese investment in the industrial West was rising sharply at the expense of investment, in raw-materials-rich Asia. Thanks to JETRO, and their own ability, as one government official put it, Japanese "enterprises are gradually getting more confidence in investing abroad. . .they feel they are at a technological level where they can compete with advanced countries."[18] Thus, they are investing in capital-intensive, state-of-the-art manufacturing plants instead of more conventional and traditional labor-intensive industries. These include, among many other products, automobile plants in the United States, jet engines in the United Kingdom, liquefied coal in Australia, a petrochemical complex in Saudi Arabia, and refrigerator compressors in China. Moreover, because Japanese firms take more minority positions and joint ventures than U.S. firms, "the real overseas assets controlled by Japanese companies are far larger than the raw numbers suggest."[19] To encourage still more overseas investments in areas considered critical to Japan's economy, in late 1979 the government passed a liberalized foreign exchange law. For projects considered of "national significance," Japan's Export-Import Bank would provide low-interest loans for up to 30 percent of a project's cost while other government agencies would insure against political and exchange rate risks. And, as diplomats of other governments do, Japanese diplomats were to aid the firm when projects involved foreign local governments.

Yet other aids to export management include Japan's exemption from personal income taxes earnings abroad of company employees and its "benign neglect" of laws inhibiting "commissions" to foreign officials. Also, Japan does not require companies to resist boycott clauses in contracts nor does it require them to take account of human rights violations.[20] Indeed, the only real pressure felt by Japanese firms is to invest abroad in areas of concern to MITI and JETRO before the foreign nations concerned impose restraints on such investment.

Such economic nationalism has clearly paid off. By 1980, eight of Japan's largest overseas investments were held by large trading companies that have evolved from export-import houses into multinational companies with large stakes in overseas manufacturing and raw materials extraction and exploitation. JETRO's strategy was that the gigantic trading firms must have production functions and not merely serve as commission agents so that they could completely control the product from manufacture to sale at retail. The presence of trading firms abroad with production functions also served to encourage smaller Japanese firms to follow. Thus, JETRO was able to orchestrate a "bandwagon effect"; a few large companies lead and many smaller ones follow. Indicative of the "guidance" roles of JETRO and MITI is that while Japan's multinationals are still focusing on direct investment abroad and the trade that accompanies it, Japan's planning organizations are looking far into the future when the direction of the investments will be changed. Over time the government expects to serve as a catalyst so that investment in the home islands will concentrate on "knowledge-intensive" and automated industries, while heavier, more labor-intensive production will lead a migration of multinationals to the labor-intensive, lower-cost Third World.[21]

A sixth factor in Japan's economic development is that it has spent very little on national defense in the post-World War II period, thus avoiding what was a large drag on its economic development in the late nineteenth century and the first half of the twentieth century. Typically, military expenditures have been in the range of 5.4 percent to 8.2 percent of its national budget and about 1 percent of its GNP. In 1978 the military expenditures of the USSR, the United States, China, and West Germany were 11-13 percent, 6 percent, 8.5 percent, and 3.4 percent of GNP, respectively.[22] Japan, with 0.9 percent in 1978, spent far less than any of the other major economies, a situation that resulted in much greater investment and consumption in Japan than would otherwise have been the case. International comparisons of per capita national income and taxes are, of course, suspect for a wide variety of reasons. A first approximation to data for the fiscal years 1977 and 1978 suggests that per capita taxes in relation to per capita income in Japan were 70 percent and 67 percent, respectively, of those in the United States and West Germany.[23] If the general tenor of these data is correct, and I believe it is, corporations and individuals had proportionately more disposable income left after payment of taxes in Japan than in other comparable nations.

These data explain in part why in fiscal year 1976 Japan's government expenditures accounted for only 10 percent of GNP, while private consumption and gross domestic capital formation accounted for 58 percent and 31 percent respectively. In contrast, government expenditures in the United States and West Germany in 1977 were 18 percent and 20 percent, respectively, while gross domestic capital formation in the two nations was 17 percent and 21 percent, respectively. These data suggest why, except for the "oil-shock" years of 1974 and 1975, when it was minus 0.5 percent and plus 1.4 percent respectively, real economic growth in Japan from 1965 to 1978 ranged from 5.1 percent to 14.0 percent, and for the fourteen-year period averaged 7.8 percent.[24] It should be noted that in contrast real economic growth in the United States, West Germany, and the United Kingdom was much lower. For the United States, for the periods 1960-1970 and 1970-1977, it was 4.3 percent and 2.8 percent, respectively; for West Germany, 4.4 percent and 2.4 percent; and for the United Kingdom, 2.9 percent and 1.8 percent.[25]

A seventh reason for Japan's rapid economic development is that it spends very little on welfare, again freeing resources for more productive activities. In 1972, for example, Japan spent 6.9 percent of its GDP on three major areas of welfare: health and medicine, social security and welfare, and government transfer payments to persons. In that same year, the United States spent 9.7 percent and the United Kingdom spent 15.2 percent.[26] The basic reason the Japanese can spend so little on welfare is that aside from health care and old-age pensions, the population does not feel a sense of entitlement to welfare. There is a stigma attached to welfare and it is sought and given sparingly. The extended family and the firm are expected to bear the responsibility for family welfare and to set aside funds to provide for family security. And that they have done. In 1977 total savings deposits in Japan were $1,085 billion; much more than the $944 billion in the United States, the $235 billion in West Germany, and the amounts recorded for any other nation. On a per capita basis savings in Japan were $9,531, second only to Switzerland's $11,285. In 1977 some 49.2 percent of the Japanese were saving 15 percent or more of their annual income. In terms of the ratio of accumulated savings to annual income, the lowest ratio was 63.7 percent for the cohort under the age of twenty-five. For the age group sixty and over, the ratio was over 200 percent.[27]

The high levels of savings make possible smaller-scale and more limited types of welfare aid programs than those found in the

United States and the United Kingdom. Although Japan has far fewer broken homes than the West, the primary factor keeping welfare costs low, in addition to the high level of national savings, is that the payments made are not enough to live on comfortably. Thus, there is an incentive for welfare recipients to get back on the work rolls as soon as possible. Unemployment insurance compensation, for example, is not only low in general but is lower yet for workers under thirty and those with one year of unemployment.[28]

An eighth reason for Japan's rapid economic development has been the stimulus of war, particularly in the post-World War II period when Japan was a supplier of goods and services rather than a participant in the war. During World War I Japanese industry benefited tremendously from British and German preoccupation with the war in Europe. The conflict brought unprecedented prosperity to the Japanese economy via the elimination of foreign competition in Asia. In particular, the machinery, parts, and intermediate industrial goods industries benefited as a shortage of such goods caused a sharp increase in their prices and created a more favorable environment for their production in Japan.

World War II, of course, resulted in the destruction of much of Japan's industrial potential. However, during the Korean War from 1950 to 1953 and throughout U.S. major participation in the Vietnam war, Japan was used as a major supply base as well as a rest-and-recreation area. The United States rented or leased numerous supply and recreation facilities, and U.S. servicemen and servicewomen spent huge sums of their personal funds on souvenirs and services. While it is difficult to place a specific monetary value on all of these things, it is undeniable that the economy of Japan experienced a prolonged boom in the post-World War II period as a result of U.S. involvement in the wars. The boom allowed numerous companies to earn large profits, which to a large degree were retained and subsequently used to pay for plant modernization and expansion and for the importation of the latest technology from abroad.

A ninth reason for Japan's rapid economic development is the character of business organization in Japan. Managers in Japan, like the workers, have job tenure. They receive regular annual pay increments plus increments based on seniority. It is only through annual bonuses that a manager is affected by the company's profitability. Thus, Japanese managers are more interested in the size and growth of the firm than profits, and as a result are more willing to take risks. In a typical Japanese firm in the 1970s, the equity ratio was about 14 percent, whereas for a typical U.S. or U.K. firm it was about 50 percent.[29] In the typical Japanese firm interest costs were about 5 percent of revenue, roughly equal to depreciation costs or net profits. In the United States, interest costs were generally about 1 percent of gross sales and much smaller than depreciation charges and net profit. Ordinarily, such a risk-taking posture would make a firm severely vulnerable in business recessions and therefore be considered dangerous. However, in Japan, many large firms are affiliated with banks, with which they have established close personal and financial ties, and under such circumstances the bank will not let the firm fail. In return for such support, the bank usually requires that a bank officer or officers be placed in the company's management. It should be noted that without such guaranteed financial support by a bank, the firm is indeed vulnerable to the sudden calling in of loans by a bank, which could cause other lenders to do the same and thus cause bankruptcy. That can and has happened. However, the system as a whole has worked to the advantage of the Japanese economy.

In addition to having privately owned commercial banks to fall back on when pressed, large firms can call on the resources of the government's Japan Development Bank (JDB) and the Export-Import Bank of Japan. The JDB was established in 1951 to provide long-term loans for reconstruction and industrial development; it supplements rather than competes with private banks. In the past three decades, the JDB has made loans to many heavy industrial firms as well as for urban and regional development and for the development of new technology. Established in 1950, the Export-Import Bank supplies medium- and long-term loans to finance the export of heavy industrial equipment but particularly to finance activities associated with the shipbuilding industry. It has also made loans to finance the importation of key commodities and the making of overseas investments, and direct loans to foreign governments to finance their purchase of goods and services from Japan.[30]

The collective yet nonsocialistic nature of the Japanese management system and the Japanese economy is reflected in the attitudes of the owners and of the managers of large firms.[31] The managers frequently insistently state that their firms' activities serve the larger public purpose of economic growth rather than the selfish one of profit maximization. The owners support these public utterances. Such idealistic posturing adds to the prestige of the firm. Profit making for its own sake has long been a cultural no-no. Further, a higher degree of worker identification with the firm is achieved when the firm's goal is more altruistic and therefore more respectable. A "public-spirited" firm is the beneficiary of worker loyalty and commitment in a way that is not possible when the profit motive is paramount. Thus, when required, the firm can persuade the workers to make sacrifices for the company in the name of greater economic growth and social welfare, which would be rejected if made in the name of greater company profits.

The owners too, as noted above, also make sacrifices on the altar of economic growth. They do not insist that profits be maximized; only that they be adequate. As long as the profit rate is reasonably respectable, given the firms's position in the industry, the owners as well as management continue to maintain face. Reduced profits would also probably lead to reduced dividends, which would be another loss of face. By maintaining a large and ever-increasing volume of sales concurrently with adequate profits, managers also frequently capture for their firm a greater share of the market, and thus more prestige for all associated with the firm. That same kind of volume of sales means quicker and better promotions for the managers, higher wages and larger bonuses for all employees, more generous executive expense accounts, and more welfare and recreational programs for the employees. It also means fewer employee layoffs and dismissals, and contributes to the firm's ability to make the interest payments on its typically dangerously sizable debts to banks and other creditors. If a firm is unable to make the interest payments, the banks would probably take a direct role in the management of the firm and, among other things, thereby cause a loss of face to both owners and management.

In summary then, the nine factors that explain Japan's unusually rapid economic growth are (1) the role of the state; (2) superior education and training; (3) the character of the population; (4) consistently steady emphasis on research and development; (5) expert export management; (6) minimal expenditures on national defense; (7) minimal expenditures on welfare; (8) the stimulus of Asian wars in which Japan was a nonparticipant; and (9) the character of business organization in Japan. DCs can profit by emulating at least many if not all of these ways. Now, what of the United States? What can DCs learn from that country?

What Can Developing Countries Learn from the Experience of the United States?

In examining the period 1929 to 1957, Denison found five factors that in toto accounted for over 90 percent of U.S. economic growth: increased employment, increased education, increased capital input, the advance of knowledge, and economies of scale associated with the enlargement of the national market.[32] The reduction of working hours in that time period was the largest negative influence on economic growth. For the years 1909 to 1929 increases in capital and in employment were more important than after 1929, while improvements in the labor force were less important. None of these factors is unusual or different enough to warrant extended discussion and indeed in many respects they are obvious, particularly after our discussion of Japan. What does require discussion, however, are the strategies based on the U.S. experience available to DCs that would permit full use of the information; strategies that would result in increased real income over many years.

The first strategy is that of the agricultural surplus.[33] Agricultural sectors perform many functions in developing societies. First, they supply food for the population and raw materials for industry. Second, they create an investable surplus of savings that can be used to finance industrial or other development. Third, the incomes generated are used by agriculturalists to buy the output of other expanding sectors. Fourth, the agricultural products exported generate foreign exchange and contribute to a healthy balance of payments situation. Fifth, even if not exported, agricultural products contribute to a better balance of payments situation via import substitution.

Clearly the U.S. experience substantiates these generalizations. In 1800, 60 percent of the GNP was agricultural. By 1850 agriculture had fallen to between one-third and two-fifths of GNP, and employment in agriculture had fallen from 80 percent of the labor force to about 60 percent. However, gross farm product had increased four to five times in that same period. By the period 1897-1901, some 40 percent of the labor force was in agriculture but farm product had increased more than six times.[34] By 1920, only about one-fourth of the labor force was in agriculture and agricultural output had grown by 15 percent between 1897-1901 and 1917-21. The same general trends have continued since then. It is significant that as agricultural incomes rose, the food needs of the farm population were met by successively smaller proportions of farm output and that therefore successively larger proportions of agricultural output were surplus. As suggested above, the surpluses were the engine of growth in the industries processing agricultural products, industries that were the source of capital for investment in light and heavy industries, the source of capital for investment in labor-saving agricultural machinery, and the origin of the foreign-trade and balance-of-payments surpluses.

That the agricultural sector of the typical DC can perform so well so rapidly is of course doubtful. Many DCs have very unfavorable person-land ratios. There are already too many mouths to be fed in the nation as a whole and in the rural areas particularly to duplicate the U.S. experience. Measures to control population growth are required concurrently with such specific aids to agricultural output as rationalization of farm size; elimination of fragmentation of the fields; increasing the number and quality of labor animals and farm implements; elimination of the nonagricultural use of agricultural land; increasing the availability of chemical fertilizers and newer, better strains of seeds; increasing the availability and lowering the cost of loans to farmers; reforming the conditions of tenancy, including the elimination of oral land leases and implicit rents and the lowering of explicit rents; easing the tax burdens of farmers; improving water storage and drainage facilities; expanding and improving agricultural educational facilities; organizing better national disaster prevention and remedial facilities; improving transportation and communication facilities in rural areas; and minimizing if not eliminating political instability in agricultural areas. It is easy for economists to recite litanies of such improvements; in DCs they require decades of steady effort.

It should be noted that there was one important element in the agricultural history of the United States that should not be reproduced in the DCs, namely, slavery. Between 1802 and 1860, the slave population in the pre-Civil War South grew from 569,000 to 2,407,000. Although the question of how profitable or unprofitable slavery was to the slaveholder is still controversial in some respects, the latest judgments are that it was profitable. The internal rate of return on investment in male field hands—slaves—averaged 4.5 percent to 8 percent, and on the better soils was as high as 10 percent to 13 percent. In contrast, 6 percent could have been earned in comparable alternative investments.[35] In the late twentieth century, one hopes and expects that, whatever its economies, the institution of slavery will not obtain in DCs or anywhere else.

A second strategy that DCs can borrow from the United States is the industrialization model.[36] Factories provide employment for surplus agricultural labor, stimulate the urbanization process as ancillary urban services develop around new firms and industries; create investment and consumer goods for the population at large; contribute to the growth of such service occupations as banking, finance, insurance, transportation, and real estate; and stimulate technological progress. Light and heavy industrial exports, as do those of agriculture, create foreign-exchange earnings and contribute to balance-of-payments stability. They also lessen or eliminate dependence on foreign imports via the import-substitution process. DCs can learn from the experience of the United States and begin with light industries rather than rushing into heavy industry too soon with dire consequences, as happened in the USSR and the People's Republic of China.[37] Light industries are not only technologically simpler and less capital intensive than heavy industries but permit the employment of the large numbers of women and children typically found in DCs. If and when a DC reaches the heavy industrial phase, adult male labor can take over the more dangerous and physically demanding work—which also happens to pay better, as pro-Equal Rights Amendment persons are quick to point out.

In the United States, one of the first industries to develop was the textile industry. Of course, everyone is familiar with the story of the industrial revolution, Samuel Slater, and the rapid rise to preeminence in the pre-Civil War economy of textiles. What may not be well known is that the same phenomenon occurred in the industrialization of Germany, France, Japan, South Korea, Hong Kong, Singapore, Taiwan, and a long list of other nations that were DCs at the time and that are now or are about to become advanced industrialized nations. The development of a textile industry has been and still is a major milestone on the road to industrialization and economic growth.

Even more important is the development of steel and automobile industries.[38] These heavy industries do more than create important investment and consumer goods, high-paying jobs for skilled workers, diverse service-type jobs in those two and related industries, and a basis for the promotion of exports. They are, in addition, important symbols of higher levels of economic attainment; in some respects "economic cathedrals" that symbolize the new economic structures that DCs and others are seeking to create. Prior to the Civil War agriculture and the textile industry dominated the U.S. economy; after the Civil War, the steel industry dominated. During World War I the automobile went into mass production, and since that time psychologically and economically has exerted a major influence on the U.S. economy and on the perceptions of economists and the general public on the state of health of that economy. Confidence and pride in the economy have risen and fallen with the fortunes of the automobile industry. As this is written in September 1981, the w rldwide great demand for Japanese automobiles and the worldwide respect accorded Japanese economic performance are paralleled by red ink in Detroit and doubts about the long-term viability and stability of the U.S. economy. In the 1950s, a U.S. secretary of defense said that what was good for General Motors was good for the United States. The statement created a political furor, but as economic reasoning it contained a large element of truth.

A third strategy for economic development that DCs might copy from the United States is based on foreign trade.[39] The areas of consideration in this strategy include: (1) the monetary volume of trade conducted; (2) the physical composition of the goods exported and imported; (3) the geographic distribution of the exports and imports; (4) the balance of payments, with particular emphasis on the capital account; and (5) tariff and quota policies. Between 1790 and 1920 U.S., real imports per capita more than tripled while real exports per capita increased by about five times.[40] Although the foreign trade sector grew slightly less rapidly than the economy as a whole and far less rapidly than domestic trade, it contributed substantially to the economic growth and rapid industrialization of the nation. Along with changes in the volume, trade composition changed. Prior to the Civil War the United States exported raw materials of agricultural

147

origin and imported manufactured and semimanufactured products. After the Civil War, when the United States had industrialized, it imported more raw materials and foodstuffs and exported more manufactured and semimanufactured goods. The numbers are that typically, before the Civil War, manufactured goods accounted for one-sixth of all goods and by 1920 accounted for slightly more than half of all exports.[41] DCs with high-value raw materials to export, such as petroleum, undoubtedly would find this particular strategy appealing.

The geographic distribution of the foreign trade of the United States changed over time and was the registry of greater economic growth. Until the twentieth century the United States continued to import manufactured and semimanufactured goods from Great Britain, then the most industrially advanced nation in the world. However, as the United States itself industrialized, inevitably it traded more with nations that were suppliers of raw materials, such as Canada and the nations of Asia, which in addition were markets for an increasingly larger production of finished goods and of services. Improvements in transportation made possible the expansion of U.S. trade in the nineteenth and twentieth centuries. It is not unreasonable to expect continued improvements in the next century, which would benefit DCs seeking to capitalize on an advantage in the raw materials that they possess.

Another benefit to DCs of the foreign trade strategy accrues through the balance of payments mechanism. While it is true that raw materials have lower values than manufactured goods and that nations that are exporters of raw materials and importers of manufactured goods typically have deficits in their balance of payments, it is not true that this is a permanent condition. As the character of foreign trade changes, as exports of raw materials are replaced by exports of manufactured goods, surpluses replace deficits. This is particularly true where a DC has encouraged foreign investment. The inflow of foreign capital not only serves to offset deficits in the balance of trade but creates direct employment in the geographic area of investment and indirect employment and economic opportunities in related supporting economic activities, including service occupations. DCs can profit from the U.S. experience and aid their balance of payments situation by using their own carriers rather than those of foreigners; discouraging any immigrants or others in their country from sending funds back home or otherwise sending funds out of the country; encouraging foreign tourists to visit and spend; discouraging any of the population from nonbusiness travel abroad; and carefully regulating the flow of interest payments abroad on loans made by foreigners. These measures coupled with encouragment of foreign investment in a DC should soften considerably the initial impact on the balance of payments of a foreign trade strategy based on the export of raw materials.

The last element of a foreign trade strategy involves tariffs and quotas, and in some respects it is the most dangerous. Such restrictions can be costly internally, for, as the U.S. experience shows, they usually benefit special-interest groups rather than the general public. In the nineteenth century in the United States high tariffs in textiles benefited the New England textile producers at the expense of the public, which paid higher prices for foreign and domestic textiles. More recently, in 1981, the "voluntary" quota of 1.6 million automobiles in exports to the United States accepted by the Japanese—down from 1.8 million in nonquota exports from the previous year—benefited inefficient U.S. automobile manufacturers and ironically the efficient Japanese automobile producers as well, as a result of higher prices for automobiles paid by the U.S. public.[42]

If the purpose of tariffs and quotas is to encourage the growth or permit the survival of a specific industry, then in the short run perhaps such policies may be constructive. However there are dangers. One is that one or more other nations may retaliate by imposing tariffs and quotas on the products of the nation that first initiated such moves. The retaliation may harm the DC more than the DC may benefit from its own tariff and/or quotas. A second danger is that tariffs passed "temporarily" to aid "infant industries" tend to be semipermanent. The "infant industries" do not grow—or do not seem to grow—enough to cause the tariff to be removed. There are many reasons that U.S. domestic trade grew more rapidly than its foreign trade from 1790 to the present, but certainly one of the more important is the persistent existence of artificial obstacles to trade. Nevertheless, DCs should consider the selective limited use of tariffs and quotas. In addition to aiding selected industries, such policies contribute to diversification of the economy. DCs that depend on single products for export are vulnerable to changes in the marketplace, such as newer technologies, changing consumer tastes, and political and/or economic problems in or with the nations that purchase the export products. Further, supplies of the one product a DC can export may dry up. Witness the very different fears and therefore different policies of the OPEC nations with relatively little oil left on one hand and Saudi Arabia, which has the largest reserves in the world, on the other.[43]

The last positive element of economic growth in the United States to be offered as a lesson for DCs is technological change. It matters not whether a nation selects the strategies of agricultural surplus, industrialization, or foreign trade, or any combination thereof; technological progress is an important element. Technological progress occurs when major new products are developed, when product alterations and quality changes occur, and when productivity is increased. Technological progress occurs in extraordinarily diverse human activities, as for example the electrification of industrial plants and homes, the mass production and use of effective birth control devices, the development of ballpoint pens and 78-rpm phonograph records.[44] Whether such progress is innovation or adaptation of existing technology is irrelevant; the fact is that a product or process is created that has sufficient value to be demanded in the marketplace and that acts as a catalyst with respect to economic activity.

The U.S. economy benefited tremendously from technological progress. In the nineteenth century much of the technology came from Great Britain, for example, the substitution of machinery for hand work, the application of new sources of power to transportation and industry, and the widespread use of iron and steel. However, the United States independently developed the system of interchangeable parts in the nineteenth century, and in the twentieth century developed the assembly line and made innumerable advances in the chemical, electrical, electronic, biological, and nuclear engineering fields.[45] The progress was so diverse and so great that it is extremely unlikely the typical DC could duplicate it. But it is possible for DCs to copy the U.S. and other advanced technologies and to develop technological improvements appropriate to their resource base, current development strategy, and current level of achievement. The developments can and should come in a wide variety of activities: production, transportation, and modification of the basic product itself. It should be noted that in the case of consumer goods, more skill in the marketing of the product, although not a technological improvement, would have the same effect.

It may come as a surprise to DCs to learn of their economic potential in the area of economic growth. As Japan has demonstrated, small size, a paucity of resources, and a slow start on the road to modernization are no bar to great economic progress. As the United States has demonstrated, huge size, abundant resources, and an early start on the road to modernization are no guarantee of continued great economic progress. The latter suggests, rather unfortunately, the United States offers some negative lessons in development to DCs as well as positive. The negative lessons center on productivity. During the 1960s and 1970s U.S. manufacturing productivity steadily declined. During the period 1960-66 the annual rate of increase averaged 4.0 percent; during the period 1966-76, 2.2 percent, slightly more than half the previous rate. Over the entire period 1960-76, the average of 2.9 percent was less than that of eleven major industrialized nations, including Japan's, which at 8.9 percent was three times the U.S. rate.[46]

The major causes of declining U.S. productivity were (1) a slower growth in the amount of capital per laborer; (2) a decline in research and development; (3) an increase in government regulations; and (4) changes in the composition of the work force.[47] The capital-labor ratio, which exceeded 2 percent each year in the 1950s and 1960s, dropped to an average of less than 1.4 percent from 1970 to 1975. The possible causes of the decline in capital growth include an increase in taxes, which may have made capital investment less attractive. In an inflationary period, accounting methods that understate the cost of replacement of capital goods tend to overstate profits and thus overstate taxes. When machines wear out and inventory is sold and thus need to be replaced, the proportional increase in the drain on corporate finances tends to discourage capital investment. The capital gains taxes on the increases in the value of capital goods sold, which are attributable solely to inflation, also lessen incentives for investment. Under these circumstances, the gain is usually illusory and, after the capital gains taxes, may in fact be negative. DCs can benefit from the negative experience of the United States by attempting to restrain the inflationary processes that frequently accompany growth. Should they be unsuccessful in restraining the inflation, the lowering of corporate taxes and capital gains taxes, *ceteris paribus*, would seem to be desirable.

The decline in research and development expenditures in the United States amounted to about 30 percent between the mid-1960s and 1978.[48] Although primarily in the area of military and space-related research, it affected other areas as well. Having discussed the significance of research and development in connection with Japan's rapid industrial development, I will not repeat it here. Suffice it to note that DCs can learn from the U.S. experience that nations must maintain a continuously high level of research and development; intermittent reductions in it will be reflected in their rates of growth.

The third contributing negative factor in recent U.S. economic experience has been sharply increased government regulation of business. Although clearly such regulation has saved many lives and made life much more enjoyable for most Americans through improved industrial safety, safer consumer products, less air and water pollution, and so on, it has also been expensive in both monetary and real terms.

In late 1972, a National Archives team trying to cut down on federal paperwork had counted over 700,000 federal forms, and predicted that the total would go over a million. All 700,000 forms were being used actively according to the agencies polled. Government sources in the early 1970s estimated that it cost the government $18 billion a year to print, distribute, and store all its forms, and another $18 billion was spent by businesses to fill out those forms. The figures may seem high, but they are probably not. In 1972 a representative of the Associated General Contractors of America testified that estimated paperwork costs in the construction industry alone in the early 1970s amounted to $4.5 billion. In the same year the General Services Administration estimated that 4.5 million cubic feet of federal records are filed annually; they include not only the authorized forms (14,000 by the IRS alone) but numerous "bootleg" forms used widely internally.

As these data suggest, DCs can profit from the U.S. experience by carefully controlling the growth of regulation. I yield to no one in my appreciation of the value of human life and of the quality of life; in recommending extreme caution in the growth of government regulation, I am merely saying that embryonic firms and industries need all the encouragement they can get. Unnecessary regulation and paperwork, particularly to the degree suggested above, not only would have a distinctly negative impact on productivity but would probably encourage bribery and corruption. Unfortunately, bribery and corruption are so far from being unknown in many DCs that even the growth of the most extremely desirable government units would probably spawn them; hence, the extreme caution required when dealing with still other types.[49]

Yet another contributing factor in the decline of productivity in the United States in the 1960s and 1970s was the entry into the work force of many young people and women. Both groups consist largely of unskilled workers whose efforts tend to bring down the average rate of output generated by older, more skilled workers. In DCs young people and women tend to predominate in the work force because mortality rates are high, particularly among adult males. Undoubtedly, their lack of skills have the same effect on productivity as does that of their U.S. counterparts. What is required of DCs is an intensive effort to upgrade the skills of young people, women, and other unskilled groups concurrent with their employment. Private as well as public funds must be used toward that end; again, the Japanese model is one that DCs can profitably copy.

DCs can learn from the U.S. experience of the 1960s and 1970s in still other respects. During the years 1966-73 some 40 percent of the increase in national output was the result of an increase in labor input, compared with only about 10 percent for the years 1948-66.[50] Quantity of labor to a degree can compensate for quality. The quantity of labor in DCs can be increased by changes in the numbers of hours worked per employed person per year, sharp increases in health and sanitation facilities, the encouragement of in-migration, stabilization of current domestic labor force participation rates, and stabilization of the length of current workdays and workweeks. In DCs there are many underemployed individuals of all ages who can be given full-time work. With improvements in health and sanitation facilities, they and other members of the labor force could not only live longer but work longer. Encouraging immigrants to work permanently or temporarily in DCs with low person-land ratios would also add to labor input and hence to increased national output.

Yet other contributions to a larger labor force include avoiding haste in the passage of both child labor and early retirement laws. Keeping young people and the elderly working may be questionable from the point of view of humane treatment and social welfare, but the costs and benefits of doing so are something that each nation must determine for itself. For better or for worse, much of the economic progress of the United States in the nineteenth century and early twentieth century was created by what in the late twentieth century we call "sweatshop labor." Today sweatshop labor is characteristic of many DCs. Maintenance or at best slow modification of the status quo would contribute to a high level of labor input.

In summary then, DCs can benefit from the experiences of the United States. They can adopt the strategy of agricultural surplus, industrialization, or foreign trade, or any combination thereof. They can and should emphasize technological progress, whatever the strategy selected. They ought to maintain an optimum capital-labor ratio, avoid excessive and certainly unnecessary government regulation, and make appropriate investments in human capital as the character of their work forces changes. Thus, *ceteris paribus*, they ought to be able to duplicate some of the success of the United States without duplicating some of its errors.

Concluding Remarks

How good our economic vision is depends on whether we are looking forward or backward. Our hindsite is 20/20—amazingly good. Unfortunately, as our two examination questions demonstrate, our foresight is extremely myopic. Even so, it seems reasonable to say that both Japan and the United States have had experiences from which DCs may profit. Both Japan and the United States offer lessons that are in some respects unique to each of them. Japan offers the incredible saga of an economic David who at least in relation to economic growth can seem to do no wrong. The United States offers DCs the soap opera of an economic Goliath spoiled by power and success who must now use resources and declining power far more effectively than in the recent past or lose planetary economic supremacy. Thus, the United States offers negative as well as positive lessons. DCs are a varied lot, and they have many social, political, religious, philosophic, and military problems with which to contend as well as the purely economic. Undoubtedly, the lessons described above will have to be modified greatly to suit individual circumstances.

However, even after allowing for these individual circumstances and major modifications, I believe the Japanese and U.S. experiences will retain much of their value for DCs.

Notes

1. In September 1981 a private forecasting group in Japan predicted that by 1990 at the latest Japan's per capita gross national product would exceed that of the United States. See Urban C. Lehner, "Aid to Japan's Growth: Pleading Poverty," *Wall Street Journal*, 14 September 1981, p. 1.

2. For excellent analyses of this role, see William W. Lockwood, *The State and Economic Enterprise in Japan* (Princeton: Princeton University Press, 1965); G. C. Allen, *A Short Economic History of Modern Japan* (London: Allen & Unwin, 1946).

3. For a brief extremely lucid description of the concept of "Japan Inc.," see Eugene J. Kaplan, "The Concept of 'Japan Incorporated,'" in *Japan: The Government-Business Relationship* (Washington, D.C.: U.S. Department of Commerce, Government Printing Office, February 1972), pp. 14-17.

4. For a brief description of Japanese worker real incomes, see J. Hirschmeier and T. Yui, *The Development of Japanese Business, 1600-1973* (Cambridge: Harvard University Press, 1975), pp. 154-57, 197-99.

5. For a much more detailed account of the functions of MITI, see Ezra F. Vogel, *Japan as Number One: Lessons for America* (Cambridge: Harvard University Press, 1979), pp. 70-78.

6. *Facts and Figures of Japan* (Tokyo: Foreign Press Center, 1980), p. 93.

7. For a detailed discussion of the competition, see Kanji Haitani, *The Japanese Economic System* (Lexington, Mass.: D.C. Heath, 1980), pp. 29-37.

8. Wilbur F. Monroe and Eisuke Sakakibara, *The Japanese Industrial Society* (Austin: University of Texas at Austin, Bureau of Business Research, 1977), pp. 24-26.

9. Katsumi Yakabe, *Labor Relations in Japan* (Tokyo: Ministry of Foreign Affairs, 1977), p. 75.

10. For an excellent discussion of life within the company for laborers and managers, see *Japan: A Businessmen's Guide* (New York: American Heritage Press, 1970), pp. 35-60; Yakabe, *Labor Relations in Japan*, pp. 1-18.

11. James Abegglen and Akio Etori, "Japanese Technology Today," in *Dynamics of Asian Business* (Honolulu: University of Hawaii, Pacific Asian Management Institute, 1981), pp. 214-16.

12. Ibid., government sources cited, p. 217.

13. Ibid., p. 229.

14. Ibid., p. 228.

15. Kiyoshi Kojima, "Industrialization and Trade Growth in Japan," *Hitotsubashi Journal of Economics* (February 1973), in *Dynamics of Asian Business* (Honolulu: University of Hawaii, Pacific Asian Management Institute, 1981), p. 100.

16. Ibid.

17. "Japanese Multinationals Covering the World with Investments," *Business Week*, 16 June 1980, p. 92.

18. Yoshitomo Tanaka, Japanese Finance Ministry, quoted, ibid.

19. Lawrence G. Franko, International Management Institute in Geneva, quoted, ibid., p. 93.

20. Ibid., p. 94.

21. Ibid., p. 102.

22. *Facts and Figures of Japan*, p. 31.

23. Ibid., p. 37.

24. Ibid., p. 36.

25. *Statistical Yearbook, 1978* (United Nations), cited in *Taiwan Statistical Data Book, 1980* (Taipei: Executive Yuan), pp. 296-97.

26. *Nihon Keizai Shinbun*, 1 September 1975, cited in Haitani, *The Japanese Economic System*, p. 173.

27. *Facts and Figures of Japan*, p. 105.

28. For an excellent extended discussion, see Vogel, *Japan as Number One*, pp. 186-203.

29. Haitani, *The Japanese Economic System*, p. 147.

30. Ibid., p. 158.

31. For an extremely well-written, extended discussion, see ibid., pp. 92-95.

32. Edward F. Denison, "United States Economic Growth," *Economic Growth: An American Problem* (Englewood Cliffs, N.J.: Prentice-Hall, 1964), pp. 84-100.

33. For excellent discussions, see Everett E. Hagen, *The Economics of Development* (Homewood, Ill.: Richard D. Irwin, 1980), pp. 356-82; Gerald M. Meier, *Leading Issues in Economic Development* (New York: Oxford University Press, 1976), pp. 561-80.

34. Richard K. Vedder, *The American Economy in Historical Perspective* (Belmont, Calif.: Wadsworth Publishing Co., 1976), pp. 227-28.

35. Alfred H. Conrad and John R. Meyer, "The Economics of Slavery in the Antebellum South," *Journal of Political Economy* (April 1958): p. 103.

36. For arguments and critiques of arguments on industrialization by various individual economists and UN organizations, see Meier, *Leading Issues in Economic Development*, pp. 629-84.

37. See Jerzy F. Karcz, "An Organizational Model of Command Farming," and Frederick W. Crook, "The Commune System in the People's Republic of China," in *Comparative Economic Systems*, ed. Morris

Bornstein (Homewood, Ill.: Richard D. Irwin, 1979), pp. 238-60, 342-76, respectively.

38. For a brief discussion of the role of the automobile and steel industries in the United States, see Vedder, *The American Economy in Historical Perspective*, pp. 283-85.

39. For extended discussion of the foreign trade strategy by various economists, see Meier, *Leading Issues in Economic Development*, pp. 685-779.

40. U.S., Department of Commerce, *Historical Statistics, Colonial Times to 1957*, cited in Vedder, *The American Economy in Historical Perspective*, p. 208.

41. Ibid., p. 211.

42. See "Reagan Downshifts on Auto Import Policy," *Business Week*, 20 April 1981, pp. 29-30.

43. See William D. Marback, "Economics 101 for OPEC," *Newsweek*, 8 June 1981, p. 79; James Nelson Goodsell, "Perils of a Petropower," *Christian Science Monitor*, 11 September 1981, pp. 1, 6.

44. For an insightful and comprehensive analysis of the subject, see L. E. Davis, R. A. Easterlin, W. N. Parker, et al., "Technological Change," in *American Economic Growth: An Economists' History of the United States* (New York: Harper & Row, 1972), pp. 233-79.

45. Ibid., pp. 251-61.

46. "Sources of Productivity Growth and of the Recent Slowdown," *Reaching a Higher Standard of Living* (New York: New York Stock Exchange, 1979). pp. 14-20, cited in Timothy Hannan, "The Productivity Perplex: A Concern for the Supply Side," in *Economics 81/82*, ed. Glen Beeson and Reuben E. Slesinger (Guilford, Conn.: Dushkin Publishing Group, 1981), p. 219.

47. Hannan, "The Productivity Perplex," pp. 218-22.

48. Ibid., p. 221.

49. Among the many excellent articles on the subject of bribery and corruption that have appeared in recent years is Edwin McDowell, "In Brazil 'Mordomia' Is Rampant," *Wall Street Journal*, 9 November 1976, p. 22.

50. Hannan, "The Productivity Perplex," p. 218.

6.

Development Strategies in Chile, 1964-1983: The Lessons of Failure

Paul E. Sigmund

One of the fascinating aspects of the study of Chilean development policy over the past twenty years is that it offers a series of case studies in the direct application of contrasting theories of development. The Christian Democratic administration of President Eduardo Frei (1964-70) attempted to apply the ideas of the Alliance for Progress and the Economic Commission for Latin America (ECLA) to promote a mixed economy that could combine social reform and economic development within a free democratic political system—the "Revolution in Liberty." Salvador Allende's Marxist-dominated Popular Unity government (1970-73) promised a "transition to socialism" that would be based on the abolition of capitalism, carried out by a government based on "the power of the people" (*poder popular*), especially workers, peasants, and shantytown dwellers (*pobladores*). "The Chicago boys," the economists and technocrats who dominated economic policy under the military junta led by Augusto Pinochet that overthrew Allende, were committed to the promotion of free markets, an open economy, a sharp reduction in the role of the state, and the maximization of individual choice—in economics, if not in politics.

Each of these policies may be said to have ended in failure. Yet each can also teach us important lessons about the problems and prospects of development—not only in Chile but in the developing world in general—and some of those lessons have even wider implications for all contemporary political and economic systems.

Frei's Revolution in Liberty

It is difficult to recapture the enthusiasm that greeted the election of Eduardo Frei in 1964. In retrospect, it should not have been surprising that he won such a large share of the vote—56 percent, compared to 39 percent for the candidate of the Socialist-Communist coalition, Salvador Allende—because the rightist parties threw most of their support to Frei in a stop-Allende movement, offering only a token third candidate for those members of the anticlerical Radical party who could not bring themselves to vote for Frei because of his church connections. Frei's program contained three central elements, each of them a response to the challenge offered by the Left. To the Left's proposals to nationalize Chile's American-owned copper mines, Frei responded with the idea of "Chileanization," that is, purchasing part ownership—if possible 51 percent—of the mines, with the compensation to be used to develop refining and smelting facilities in Chile. To leftist efforts to mobilize the poor, Frei offered the Popular Promotion program, which would organize neighborhood committees, centers for mothers, and peasant unions to give effective expression to the needs of the lower classes. To the Left's criticisms of Chile's oligarchical landholding patterns, Frei offered a program of agrarian reform that set upper limits on amount of arable landholdings, and endorsed peasant cooperatives and independent family farms as a preferable alternative to collectivism, echoing the ideas advanced by the Alliance for Progress in the early 1960s. All of these programs were to be carried out by democratic processes through congressional legislation and, where necessary, constitutional reforms.

How did Frei's "revolution" work out in practice? Initially there were political obstacles because, although he won an absolute majority in the 1964 presidential election and control of the lower house of Congress in the legislative elections six months later, holdovers in the Chilean Senate, only half of which was elected every four years, were sufficient to require support from other parties. Frei's strategy was to get the support of the Left for his agrarian reform law, and of at least part of the Right for the copper Chileanization. He was successful in this effort, and both pieces of legislation were adopted by the Congress, but it took until halfway through his term to get legislative approval, and the agrarian reform debates deepened the hostility of the Right, already incensed by the tax increases required to finance the Christian Democratic welfare programs. The Left sabotaged a good part of the Popular Promotion program, which it correctly saw as an effort to win over for the Christian Democrats what the Left considered to be its own clientele among the lower classes. The Chileanization proposals also ran into opposition from the Anaconda Copper Company, which opposed any sharing of ownership of the lucrative Chuquicamata mine, the largest open-pit copper mine in the world, which was able to produce copper at a very low cost. Frei ultimately secured U.S. government support for a negotiated deal with Anaconda that involved a phased-in transfer of ownership ("nationalization by agreement"), with retention of management and a sliding scale of compensation based on earnings.

If Frei was able to get the key elements of his program through the Congress, what went wrong? To answer this question we must look at events in 1967, halfway through his six-year term. In that year the Radical party, which had been aligned primarily with the Right, switched alliances and began to negotiate with the Communists and Socialists to form what eventually became Allende's Popular Unity coalition. Within Frei's own party the delays and compromises required for the adoption of the implementing legislation led to internal splits that ultimately resulted in the departure in 1969 of the party's left wing to form the Movement of United Popular Action (MAPU) that also later supported Allende. Within the Congress the Left and Right opposition began working together to frustrate presidential initiatives, particularly those of a financial nature, with the result that the Chilean inflation rate, which had been dropping since Frei's election, began to rise once more. Most important in terms of its impact on the 1970 election, the Right began to promote the candidacy of former President Jorge Alessandri at the same time that Christian Democratic heir-apparent Radomiro Tomic (Chilean presidents may not succeed themselves, so Frei was ineligible) was talking of an alliance with the Left.

The result was that in 1970 instead of a two-way fight there were three major candidates for the presidency—Allende, Tomic, and Alessandri—and Allende won with 36.1 percent of the vote (less than the 39 percent he had received in 1964, but still more than the 34.9 percent of Alessandri or the 27 percent of Tomic). The Chileanization program, which was just getting going in terms of increased production and refining, was junked in favor of outright nationalization. The agrarian reform that had so alienated the Right had resettled only about 35,000 peasants, rather than the 100,000 promised in 1964. The Popular Promotion program meant increased Christian Democratic votes in certain lower-class areas, but the rising inflation was more important in persuading Chile's perennially dissatisfied electorate to vote against the Christian Democrats in 1970.

In retrospect, what should Frei have done to avoid the debacle of the election of a Marxist president in 1970? One obvious strategy would have been to broaden his government to include the Radicals, who, like the Christian Democrats, were a centrist-reformist party—but this was difficult when both parties were competing for the same voters. Another might have been to de-emphasize the agrarian reform issue, or at the very least to make the compensation provisions somewhat less confiscatory. (Payment was in bonds, which were only partially readjustable for inflation.) In addition, further efforts to control inflation would have lessened the criticisms of the Frei government—and with Radical support this might have been possible. Most important, however, we now realize was an attempt to work out a candidacy more acceptable to the Right than the leftist-sounding Tomic, but here Alessandri's personal prestige and popularity made things difficult. The U.S. supported strategy of persuading the Christian Democrats to vote for Alessandri in the October 1970 congressional runoff between the top two candidates was another possibility, but the Christian Democratic commitment to Chile's democratic tradition, and Allende's rapid acceptance of Christian Democratic demands for the addition of the Statute of Democratic Guarantees to the Constitution undercut that maneuver as well.

Perhaps, as some Chileans insist, the situation had all the elements of inevitability of Greek tragedy. Certainly, however, there were enough special circumstances to prevent the conclusion being drawn—as it was by part of the Left—that democratic reform is impossible. Frei, more than his party, had broad support in the country, and there was a sense that his reforms were long overdue. Personalities, parties, and constitutional peculiarities (the prohibition on recandidacy of Frei, the lack of a second-round electoral runoff that Alessandri would have surely won) were more important than systemic inhibitions on reform. Combined with the perennial problem of inflation, they made Frei's administration look much less successful than in fact it was. He did, after all, achieve all of the reforms that he promised, although at the considerable political cost of increasing inflation and polarizing the opposition in ways that contributed to the triumph of the Marxist-dominated Popular Unity coalition in 1970.

Allende and the Transition to Socialism

In his inaugural address in the National Stadium on 5 November 1970, Salvador Allende promised a *via chilena* to socialism, anticipated in the classics of Marxism (he quoted a speech of Engels), that would be characterized by "democracy, pluralism, and liberty" and that would destroy the large landholdings, take over banking and credit, and nationalize foreign-owned mines and industries. His subsequent efforts to do so succeeded only in destroying the economy, polarizing the society, and provoking a bloody and repressive military coup.

At first, Allende made good on his promises to respect democracy and liberty. He nationalized the copper mines through the regular constitutional processes, achieving a nearly unanimous vote in the Congress, and he respected Chilean institutions, such as the courts, the military, and the controller general. Yet there were other aspects of his policy that led ultimately to his downfall.

In his zeal to redistribute land and industry, Allende tolerated seizures of land and factories that undermined his effort to portray his program as one carried out within Chile's legal framework. It is true that his goverment used what it called "legal loopholes" *(resquicios legales)* to provide a legal justification for the seizures. The seized land was officially described as "abandoned by its owners," a category that permitted expropriation under the 1967 agrarian reform law. The factories were "intervened," supposedly on a temporary basis, under provisions for the settlement of labor disputes, or by the use of a 1932 law concerning the maintenance of supply of articles of basic necessity. When the courts would not accept many of these justifications, court orders were simply ignored. The controller general's legal objections were overridden, as provided in the Constitution, by a cabinet "decree of insistence." When the Congress attempted to limit the nationalizations by law, Allende vetoed the legislation and the executive and legislative got bogged down in dispute as to whether the veto could be overridden by a simple or two-thirds majority. The basic point, of course, was that over time the reliance on legalism, which had permitted Allende to reach power in the first place, was increasingly eroded as an atmosphere of lawlessness and arbitrary actions by the executive overrode the objections of the other two branches in ways that made Chilean constitutionalism appear to be inoperative.

A related and more serious problem was the increasing use of violence on the part of extremist groups of the Left and the Right. Allende himself had assembled a personal bodyguard that he called his Group of Personal Friends (*Grupo de Amigos Personales, GAP*) to defend himself against reported assassination attempts. In early 1971 he attempted to cover up Cuban arms shipments to the extreme Left when they were discovered in Chilean customs. By 1973 he and several of the parties in his coalition were carrying out programs of arms training, which were duly reported by the intelligence branches of the armed services. On the Right a quasi-fascist group, Fatherland and Freedom (*Patria y Libertad*), was organized to oppose Allende's election, and by 1973 was resorting to armed terrorism. In addition, some factories and shantytown areas organized their own internal police organizations and would not permit the national police (*carabineros*) to enter. Thus the threat to military control of the instruments of violence, the classic precipitant to coups d'etat in many countries, became increasingly evident during Allende's three years in office.

A third element that undermined the Allende program was his mismanagement of the economy. Chile's already existing price control system was extended to three thousand items—requests for price increases were denied—partly as a way to subsidize consumption and in some cases as an effort to bankrupt private companies and replace them with state companies. In addition, the printing presses kept printing money to subsidize an large and inefficient state sector, while tax collection efforts were stymied both by rising inflation and political opposition (the opposition-controlled Congress would not impose new taxes). Thus, after Allende had some initial success with the economy as a result of postelection stimulation of unused capacity by Keynesian-type spending, the inflation rate began to take off and by the time of the coup had reached an annual rate of 323 percent in official figures, and in excess of 600 percent as a real rate. Investment ceased, agricultural production ground to a virtual halt, savings were nonexistent, and foreign exchange reserves were run down by the end of Allende's first year. Some credits from European and Latin American sources kept food imports coming, but the credits were not likely to be renewed after Chile declared a moratorium on nearly all foreign debts. After three years of the transition to socialism the economy was in ruins, giving the military yet another reason to intervene.

On the positive side, the Allende experiment had forced the Chilean upper classes to recognize the magnitude of the distribution problem in their society—the enormous differences in income and social class that had been concealed by the veneer of social consensus that had been created by an almost-uninterrupted history of 140 years of constitutionalism with at least the trappings of democratic participation. The continuing problem of foreign control of Chile's most important natural resource, its copper mines, had been solved by a constitutional amendment that was a reflection of a genuine national consensus. And various experiments in worker control of industry in the Allende period had shown that economic democracy was not simply a wild theory but a real alternative to capitalist managerial relations. The Allende years had also shown that the Soviet Union was determined not to give the same kind of unrestricted support to a second Cuba that it had given to the original model.

What the Allende experiment had not shown is that a polarizing politics based on Marxist doctrines of the class struggle is an effective method of democratic reform. Indeed, it seemed increasingly clear during the Allende years that Marxist slogans were more effective in mobilizing the middle and upper classes in opposition to the regime than in expanding its support among the lower classes. If reform was to take place under democratic auspices, it could not pit one group against another but needed to be based on the expansion rather than the contraction of national support. To come to power with only slightly over one-third of the vote and then expect to carry out fundamental social and economic changes required at the very least negotiation with the additional political and social groups besides the original electoral base if democratic legitimacy was to be maintained.

The Allende experiment then did not prove that democratic reforms to promote the welfare of the lower classes were impossible, only that they must be carried out more incrementally and consensually than the Marxist formulations of the Popular Unity leadership would argue. A *via chilena* only became a kind of self-fulfilling prophecy from which the very groups that the Marxists were attempting to assist would suffer the most—the peasants, the workers, and the poor.

Finally, another lesson of the Allende years was the importance of the economy in providing the wherewithal to carry out programs of social reform. Chile may not have been as dependent on the capitalist world-system as some of the Chilean Left believed, but cutting itself off from the sources of investment, technology, and markets of the United States could be viable only if it was assured of alternative outlets in the Communist world—or as occurred for a time, in Europe and Latin America. The alternative was to engage in the kind of bargaining and manipulation that the Christian Democrats had practiced with considerable success during the 1960s. To propose, for instance, that compensation for the copper nationalizations would be dependent on company performance in marketing and technology contracts, as the Venezuelans later did when they nationalized their petroleum companies in 1976, rather than using, as Allende did, a fallacious theory of excess profits to avoid paying compensation to the companies.

One additional lesson that other Latin American Marxists, notably the Sandinistas in Nicaragua, drew from the Chilean experience was the importance of control of the armed forces. Allende did better on this score than many expected at the time of his election, carefully cultivating the top military leadership, never opposing their views on important issues of national security, and, unlike Frei, maintaining the living standards of the military at a level at least equal to that of other sectors of Chilean society. His most successful accomplishment in this area was the conversion to his support of General Carlos Prats, the army commander in chief, not only moving him from opposition to defense of Allende's programs but even encouraging him to believe that he might well be elected as Allende's successor in the 1976 presidential elections.

Pinochet and "the Chicago Boys"

After the September 1973 coup led by General Augusto Pinochet, Chile set out on another and radically different experiment in development. Before the coup many political observers believed that the Chilean armed forces would embark on a corporatist nationalist program not unlike that being undertaken by General Juan Velasco in neighboring Peru. In fact, however, the armed forces' rejection of the statism of the Allende government, and their belief that the Christian Democrats had paved the way for that government by their populist measures in the 1960s led them to embrace a third alternative approach to development, the free market policies recommended by "the Chicago boys," the professors of the Catholic University School of Economics who since the mid-1950s had been imbued by Milton Friedman and Arnold Harberger at the University of Chicago with the virtues of private enterprise and competitive markets. With the support of the military, the professors dismantled the huge statist bureaucracy developed by the Left, removed most of the three thousand price controls and freed the exchange rate, returned the confiscated agricultural lands and industries (but not those, like the copper mines, that had been taken over by legal means), and lowered tariff protection from an average of 94 percent to 52 percent in 1975, 22 percent by 1977, and 10 percent by 1979. At the same time, the military dismantled Chile's Left-dominated trade unions, took over its universities, and dissolved or declared in recess its political parties and the Congress. Defenders of the Chicago economists argued that their attempt to create a libertarian economic system would provide the preconditions for a decentralized and depoliticized democracy, which would maximize the possibilities for economic and political choice for all Chileans. But the economic and political changes were enforced by a repressive security apparatus; from 1974 to 1977 the dreaded DINA was responsible for the torture and death of thousands of Chileans. Thereafter the National Information Center engaged in somewhat less repressive methods but still ensured that Pinochet would maintain control.

More strictly economic arguments used by the Chicago reformers attacked the irrationality of the Allende economic system with its six different exchange rates, subsidized food but controls on prices paid to farmers, negative interest rates, and statist protection of industry. The attack went beyond the Allende policies, and argued that they were only the logical extension of earlier statist and politically skewed policies that had crippled the Chilean economy for decades. Removing the state from the economy and letting market forces make most decisions would leave government free to concentrate on a supportive social role that included targeted social programs such as nutritional aid to preschool children, free lunch programs, subsidies to employment and public works, and educational reforms that emphasized primary and secondary education and put university education on a pay-as-you-go or low-interest loan basis.

The Chilean Economic Miracle

What were the results of the Chicago program? It started slowly, partly because the economists did not have total control of economic policy in the first two years after the coup. Sergio de Castro, the former dean of the Catholic University Social Science Faculty and head of its School of Economics, became minister of economics only in mid-1974 and minister of finance in 1976. By the latter date, however, the Chicago control over economics was complete, and de Castro remained as finance minister until April 1982, making all major economic decisions over a period of six years.

During the period of Chicago dominance, over four hundred companies were returned to their former owners or sold to private interests. Only two of the nineteen banks in state hands at the time of the coup did not become privatized. Thirty percent of agricultural holdings that had been taken over were returned to their owners, and another 35 percent were distributed to small holders. In 1975-76 public employment was cut by 20 percent and the economy contracted violently, with a drop in GNP of 11 percent and an increse in unemployment to 16 percent. Inflation began to drop rapidly; in 1976 and each year thereafter with the exception of 1979 (the year of the second OPEC price hike) it dropped in half, bottoming out at 9.8 percent in 1981. Economic growth took off, beginning in 1976 with a 4.1 percent increase, followed by 8.6 percent in 1977, and 7.3 percent in 1978, and similar rates for the following two years. As the Chilean "economic miracle" brought Japanese cars, Hong Kong television sets, Adidas shoes, and Scotch whiskey at lower prices than in London and New York, it seemed that the Chicago policy was an astounding success. Never mind that critics complained of "the social cost" of the great experiment: unemployment rates in the 13 percent to 15 percent range; malnutrition among the lower classes that could not pay "realistic" prices for basic goods; low wages for the workers, for until 1979 trade unions were not permitted to function; and a 20 percent to 25 percent drop in savings and investment as Chile's new affluence financed consumer imports and financial speculation rather than productive enterprise.

Collapse of the Model

Yet as sudden as was the takeoff in the mid-1970s came the crash of the early 1980s. In mid-1981 the first bankruptcy (a large sugar-refining company) made the government violate its non-interventionist principles and bail the company out. Then several banks and financial holding companies were taken over in late 1981. By early 1982 a wave of bankruptcies and a soaring unemployment rate (23 percent by June) revealed that something was radically wrong with the economy. Pinochet reluctantly fired de Castro but replaced him with another Chicago economist. Then just after Pinochet announced that Chile would never devalue its currency, the first of a series of devaluations took place, followed by interventions and takeovers of more banks, and a dizzying succession of finance ministers, a rise in inflation to 30 percent, and an increase in unemployment including government make-work programs to nearly a third of the population. The Chicago policy was in ruins. What had gone wrong?

At first the government blamed external factors: the drop in the price of copper, Chile's principal export, to its lowest price since the depression, combined with very high international interest rates, especially for short-term loans. What the Chicago economists admitted only reluctantly, however, was that part of the problem was the direct result of their policies. In the first place, to bring inflation down, de Castro had first revalued the Chilean peso, then had fixed it in mid-1979 at a permanent rate of thirty nine to the dollar and kept it there regardless of the fact that in 1979 and 1980 Chilean inflation rose faster than the world rate, thus pricing Chilean exports out of the international market and making imports very cheap. Second, controls on dollar loans had been lifted in 1978 and 1979 and Chilean banks and even private individuals began to run up huge debts because the world interest rate was so much lower than the internal rate in Chile. Third, Chilean wages under the 1979 Labor Plan were indexed and rose even faster than the cost of living. The result was that once confidence was shaken by the first bankruptcies, the whole house of cards collapsed. Yet the government refused to devalue for at least a year after the first signs of trouble, and ran up a $4 billion balance of payments deficit in 1981, increasing Chile's international indebtedness by mid-1982 to $17 billion—on a per capita basis one of the highest in the world. Now it is saddled with IMF austerity programs, bank renegotiation, and an economy in the depths of a depression from which there does not seem to be a way out.

What are the lessons to be learned from the failure of the Chicago experiment in Chile? Does it prove that the free market and export-oriented policies were wrong? Not really, because the only problem that was directly related to free market ideology was the refusal to regulate private foreign borrowing, on the theory that such borrowing was being done at the risk of borrower and lender and did not involve the government in any way. In fact, of course, once the private debtors got into trouble, the government was forced to step in both because of the domestic economic consequences and the adverse impact default would have on the Chilean government's ability to borrow on international financial markets.

The other policies that got the Chileans in trouble, however, the indexing of salaries and, above all, the dogged insistence on a fixed exchange rate, did not follow directly from the Chicago approach—and indeed might be regarded as violations of its free market principles. Moreover, as Milton Friedman himself observed in 1981, a free economy is usually associated with free politics—and the lack of political freedom is what enabled the Chicago economists to override or ignore all criticism. It is also true that even the Chicago school accepts some protection for infant industries, and Chile opted for an undifferentiated 10 percent rate, which did not distinguish among desirable and undesirable, productive or unproductive imports, on the grounds that such distinctions would provide the opening wedge for a return to the politicization of the economy.

In the wake of the financial collapse, the Pinochet government allowed tariffs to double and inflation to rise to 30 percent, and took over 85 percent of banking credit. Within the limits of IMF austerity programs it increased public expenditures on labor-intensive projects and subsidized bankrupt "smokestack industries." Yet it still maintained that Chile was basically a "social market economy," despite the criticism of the "Chicago way to socialism" by the financial groups that have been adversely affected by the takeovers.

Further changes are likely in the direction of a greater state role in the economy, especially if the anti-Pinochet feeling that was fueled by the failure of the economic policy with which he identified himself results in a change of government. Yet some elements of the Chicago model will remain, for there is no one who wants to return to the completely centralized statism of the Allende period, and, despite the recent reverses, there is still a widespread belief in the superiority of the market in making economic choices in many areas. Whether this belief has in fact taken permanent root in Chilean society or will fall victim to the political pendulum that has plagued the country for two decades will be revealed in the coming years.

Conclusion

What are the lessons of the three contrasting policies that we have examined? We have described them all as failures, but in so doing we have employed different criteria for each. A more useful way to evaluate them might be to make these criteria explicit and apply them in a more differentiated fashion.

Contemporary governments all seek stability and legitimacy. Since Keynes, they have also attempted to promote economic growth. Democratic governments also boast of their support for freedom and popular participation. Since the rise of the welfare state, there has been a concern for social justice and equity. How do the three governments just examined measure up on these standards?

The Frei government (1964-70) was elected with a 56 percent majority but faced increasing threats to democratic stability—

especially from the Left, which rejected "bourgeois democracy" and, in the case of the Movement of the Revolutionary Left (MIR), engaged in violence and terrorism in 1969-70. The growth record of the Frei government was very positive in the first two years of his *sexennio* but later slowed down, although it kept ahead of population increases. Similarly, there was a sharp drop in the inflation rate for the first three years, followed by an increase in the last half of his administration. Frei was successful in maintaining civil liberties, and he increased popular participation substantially with the organization of peasants and slum dwellers. This resulted in some increase in income distribution favoring the lower classes, but at the end much of that increase was eroded by inflation. The general lesson to be drawn from his administration is that it is difficult to carry out reforms that alienate both Left and Right in a multiparty system that permits a "negative majority" to block action through the combined action of both extremes. Yet it is also possible, at least at the outset, to use democratic majorities to take action on fundamental social reforms, although the delays necessitated by the democratic system will inevitably limit the degree of social change that is possible.

The Allende government began with the legitimacy derived from Allende's election in a congressional runoff after having received 36 percent of the vote in the popular elections. He had also agreed to the Statute of Democratic Guarantees, a series of constitutional amendments to reassure the opposition that he intended to observe democratic freedoms in carrying out his program. Yet his government gradually undermined constitutional processes by bypassing the opposition-dominated Congress, and there were members of his coalition who were convinced that violence at some point would be required to carry out the revolutionary changes proposed by the Left. This became a self-fulfilling prophecy. The economy grew during Allende's first year, as government expenditures produced an artificial boom that exploited Chile's considerable unused capacity, but it turned sharply negative in the second and third years as private investment in industry and agriculture ceased, and the accelerating inflation approached Weimar terms. Income was redistributed to the lower classes as a result of wage increases, price controls, and government employment programs, but again this was only a temporary phenomenon as inflation wiped out the workers' gains and shortages led to a flourishing black market patronized principally by the upper and middle classes. Democracy and participation increased to the point that government-encouraged *assembleismo* interfered with normal production, but genuine freedom diminished as the government put economic pressure on the opposition and rioting and violence replaced democratic procedures. The bloody demise of the regime in a military coup replaced the flourishing democracy with repressive military rule.

The Pinochet government imposed the stability of the sword but lacked democratic legitimacy, except such as could be derived from the claim that it had saved Chile from communism. In 1980 Pinochet won a hastily called plebiscite on a constitution that was designed to ensure him eight and possibly sixteen more years in power, but the circumstances of the vote were such as to lead it to be challenged by the church and by the political opposition. After sharp declines in economic growth in 1973 and 1975, the Chicago free market policy brought impressive economic gains until late 1981. The intrinsic weakness of the policy and the mistakes regarding the fixed exchange rate led to a collapse the following year and unemployment that affected a third of the working population. Although the government attempted to target its social expenditures to the areas of extreme poverty, the general result of its economic program was a sharp reduction in the living standards of the lower classes and, in 1982 and 1983, of the middle classes as well. Democracy and freedom were destroyed in 1973, but in response to the protests that followed the economic collapse there has been some liberalization and increasing talk of legislative elections in the middle-term future.

What the Frei government understood and its successors did not was that extremist policies of the Left and Right will lead to disaster. The Left's lack of concern for investment and growth and its desire to produce immediate structural changes in industry and agriculture led to economic paralysis, runaway inflation, and societal breakdown. The Right's insistence on the maintenance of economic freedom produced a sharp drop in investment, a redistribution of income upward, the destruction of domestic industry and agriculture, and wholesale bankruptcy. The lesson from those concerned with democracy, development, and social justice is that a balanced approach that does not sacrifice any of those goals to any of the others will in the long run turn out to be the most successful. Whether Chile will be able to achieve such a balance will be tested when it returns once again to its historical tradition of constitutionalism, freedom, and democracy.

Selected Bibliography

There is a large but highly partisan literature on the Allende period, but very little on Frei, and even less on Pinochet. All three are analyzed with an emphasis on the interaction of politics and economics in my *The Overthrow of Allende and the Politics of Chile* (Pittsburgh: University of Pittsburgh Press, 1977). Related material also appears in chapter 5 of my *Multinationals in Latin America: The Politics of Nationalization* (Madison: University of Wisconsin Press, 1980). A contrasting point of view is presented in Barbara Stallings, *Class Conflict and Economic Development in Chile* (Stanford: Stanford University Press, 1978). Stefan de Vylder, *The Political Economy of the Rise and Fall of the Unidad Popular* (New York: Cambridge University Press, 1976), analyzes Allende's economic policy. On the economic policy of the Pinochet government, see Alejandro Foxley, *Latin American Experiments in Neoconservative Economics* (Berkeley: University of California Press, 1983), and the papers by Ricardo French-Davis and Rolf Luders in *Chile Under Military Rule*, edited by Arturo Valenzuela (University of North Carolina Press, forthcoming) as well as my article, "The Rise and Fall of the Chicago Boys," *SAIS Review* (Summer-Fall 1983). Some libraries will also have Juan Carlos Mendez, *A Socio-Economic Overview of Chile* (Santiago: Matte and Mendez, 1980). The best single discussion of the collapse of the Chicago model is the debate among Ricardo French-Davis, Juan Andrés Fontaine, Alvaro Garcia, and Thomas Wisecarver, "Que Pasó con la Economic Chilea?" *Estudios Publicos* (Santiago), no. 11 (Winter 1983): 5-134. The best source for pre-1979 statistics is the 1979 World Bank study, *Chile: An Economy in Transition* (3 vols.).

Comments on "Development Strategies in Chile, 1964-1983: The Lessons of Failure"

Takao Fukuchi

In 1982 Latin American countries experienced the worst stagnation since the decade of the 1930s, as cited by Enrique Iglesias in ECLA's report "Balance of the Year." The rate of growth of per capita income was, on the average, minus 3 percent, and negative for all nineteen countries. The rate of growth of inflation was 80 percent, and net foreign capital inflow decreased drastically from $42 billion in 1981 to $19.2 billion in 1982. Accumulated international debt reached $300 billion by the end of 1982, $23.5 billion beyond ECLA's estimate.

The lack of economic achievement and accumulated international debts are causing further shrinkage of international trade, threatening private banks in developed countries with a possible moratorium crisis. How can this crisis be averted in the short run by bridging loans from developed countries? How can the debt amortization program be adequately rescheduled in the future? How can Latin American governments persuade their people to accept this austere policy to meet the stringent requirements set by the IMF? How will the results of these new policies affect the new tendency to call for civil government in the southern zone? These are disturbing questions of great concern for all the peoples of the world.

Chile is not an exception in the Latin American economic situation. As of now it faces an accumulated international debt of

$18 billion or a very high per capita debt level of $1,500. Naturally, there are some common factors in Latin America and some original ones in Chile for these bad results after many decades of futile efforts for economic development.

As Sigmund clearly analyzes in his paper, Chile has tried very different development strategies in the two past decades: (1) gradual industrialization under a capitalistic regime and a protective tariff up to the Frei government; (2) socialistic planning with nationalization of important sectors, including the big copper companies by the Allende government; (3) economic development through the formation of the five-nation Andean Common Market, with preferential tariffs and assignment of industrial factories up to the government of Pinochet (this arrangement is not intensively discussed in Sigmund's paper); (4) a liberalization policy, with the abolition of subsidies, protective tariffs, wage control, and the return of nationalized firms to private sector by the government of Pinochet; and we might add another, (5) industrialization through export promotion, which differs from the past industrialization in that it leaned towards import-substitution.

The five strategies seem to me to be the development strategies open to every developing country. Chile tried (1), (2), and (4) without success, according to Sigmund's discussion. Chile voluntarily withdrew from the Andean Common Market, as it sought to increase foreign capital inflow by relaxing regulation of amortization of profits. However, the current stagnation even after the liberalization policy seems to reveal the weak competitive power of Chilean agriculture and industry. If Chile is really interested in the promotion of industry, at least some selective protection of its infant industries will be necessary. The "Revolution in Liberty" of the Frei government could not succeed mostly due to low productivity in agriculture and long industrial protectionism because of political power struggle in Chile. To quote Sigmund, "In the Chilean case, ideology divided the country into three groupings, and when any one came to power, the other two would combine to prevent it from governing."

The strengthening of two basic sectors, agriculture and industry, remains the key issue for economic development. Agriculture is suffering because of the hasty redistribution policy of the Allende government; hence, it is not sufficiently productive to feed the Chilean people. The industrial sector needs a market

176

large enough for its products, but after Chile's withdrawal from the Andean Common Market and trade liberalization, the industrial sector cannot compete well against products from developed and Association of Southeast Asian Nations (ASEAN) countries. Low growth rates in agriculture and industry drove large numbers of people into Greater Santiago, creating an informal sector and the need for massive public expenditure. As one knows well, the existence of a sizable informal sector is an unstable factor in politics.

To overcome its short-term debt management crisis, Chile must meet the following requirements:

- Follow the conditions set by the IMF to lower inflation and improve the balance of payments.

- Obtain financial cooperation from developed countries to set up a suitable rescheduling program.

- Cut off imports and increase export-earning capacity.

Such an austere program will, of course, increase the frustration of workers in the informal sector, which suffers from a high unemployment rate and very low standard of living.

What is necessary in the long term is to establish a long-running strategy to overcome common Latin American problems (incomplete agrarian reform, unequal distribution of income, monocultural sectoral structure, high dependence on foreign capital inflow, and so on) and the Chilean problems (small domestic market, big informal sector in Santiago, a city of consumption). Such a strategy may be and must be a careful combination of development strategies (3), (4), and (5) and satisfy the following conditions: advance gradually the income redistribution policy that is necessary to enlarge the domestic market and mitigate the social frustrations of the informal sector in the urban area; strengthen cooperation with developed countries and increase the inflow of foreign capital; and promote investment in the most productive industries and cultivate selective export, which is necessary to change the monocultural structure and stabilize the increased export earnings. The implementation of these policies may require at least some political independence of the group of technocrats in charge of the implementation of policies.

I still firmly believe that the basic problem of Latin American countries, including Chile, is to "develop a political regime that can overcome the obstacles to economic development and social justice without sacrificing freedom." From the viewpoint of an economist, it is noteworthy that simultaneous achievement of these targets implies a compromise among various social groups, and that stable economic development requires a somewhat middle-of-the-road political position. The prospect of a long-run development strategy is a prerequisite condition to effecting a harmonious political regime and vice versa.

7.

Economic Crisis in the Philippines

Charles W. Lindsey

The murder of Benigno Aquino, Jr., last August 21 marks the nadir into which the Marcos regime has sank. It may never rise again from that muck. There are just too many questions which Filipinos—and they aren't cowed anymore—want answered, questions which the regime has, so far, either ignored or dealt with deviously.
—*Solidarity*, no. 96 (1983)

The assassination of former Senator Benigno S. Aquino, Jr., on 21 August 1983 triggered the severest political and economic crisis in the history of the Philippine republic. In the late 1960s and early 1970s Aquino was a powerful political opponent of President Ferdinand E. Marcos, and was considered by many as the man most likely to succeed Marcos to the presidency in 1975. At the time the country's democratic system—limited largely to competition among elite factions—was coming under severe strain, with debate raging over the proper direction for the nation. The declaration of martial law by Marcos in September 1972 put an end to the debate and to existing democratic processes, deficient as they were. Marcos instituted an authoritarian regime —which he proclaimed "The New Society"—that has continued beyond the formal ending of martial law in January 1981.[1]

©1984 by the Regents of the University of California. Reprinted from *Asian Survey*, Vol. 24, No. 12, December 1984, pp. 1185-1208, by permission of the Regents. Some of the text has been slightly revised to update it.

Aquino was among the first of an estimated thirty thousand Filipinos arrested and detained during the first few weeks of martial law.[2] For the seven years he remained in prison, and afterward in exile in the United States, he was considered the one individual who could rally the nonrevolutionary opposition to Marcos. Thus his decision to return to the Philippines in the summer of 1982 and lead the opposition in the parliamentary elections to be held in May 1983 created consternation among regime supporters. The president's ill health exacerbated the situation. Imelda Marcos, the president's wife, and Minister of Defense Juan Ponce Enrile, among others, warned Aquino that his life was in danger if he returned. They were correct.

The immediate reaction to Aquino's assassination was a demand for the resignation of Marcos. Rallies were held, marches undertaken, speeches made. The immense size of the protests, particularly in Metro Manila, gave witness to the widespread disenchantment with the regime. Perhaps most surprising was the participation by the business community in Makati, the financial and corporate center of the country. Although certain business people had begun to speak out, at times vociferously, against the economic policies of the regime, most of the economically powerful had gone along with Marcos. For the first few years of the martial law regime, business had benefited; there was little reason to complain. Later when the economy turned down and the bailouts of Marcos's close business associates—dubbed "cronies" —became excessive, business people generally kept their complaints to themselves or expressed them in subdued terms.

Beyond the obvious revulsion of what was almost universally believed to be an assassination initiated by the Marcos administration, there are at least two reasons that members of the Makati business community perceived the need to become actively involved in the anti-Marcos movement. First, it was important that they be able to dominate the aboveground, political opposition to the regime. Their involvement in the May 1983 parliamentary elections, despite Marcos's refusal to meet their demands for electoral reforms to ensure fairness, demonstrates this point. Second, it became increasingly obvious that the economy was in disarray. At the time of Aquino's assassination, business activity was purportedly showing favorable signs after having weathered a prolonged recession. The prices of coconuts, copper, and gold were beginning to turn up, and the government was speaking of a recovery phase. Subsequent events, however, showed the economy to be in fragile shape, with most elements of the crisis already being problem areas prior to the events of mid-August 1982.

It is quite likely that the Philippines would have undergone an economic crisis even if the assassination of Aquino and the Filipinos' response to it had not occurred, for the situation was becoming difficult to sustain. But in the world of business where appearances are as crucial as reality, the murder was precipitous. Survival demanded that the capitalists begin to assert themselves.[3] This paper examines the origins of the economic crisis, the impact of the assassination, and the response by the Philippine government, domestic capitalists, the IMF and World Bank, transnational banks, and foreign governments, particularly the United States.

The State of the Economy before 21 August 1983

In the first few years after independence in 1946, Philippine economic growth was sustained by war-reconstruction assistance from the United States. By 1949, however, inflows had decreased to the point that the country found itself in a balance of payments crisis, and it entered into a *de facto* import-substitution phase of development. Initially the policy was successful, with real gross national product (GNP) in the first half of the 1950s growing at an average of 7.7 percent.[4] The buoyant period was rather short-lived; growth rates in the latter half of the decade were less than 5.0 percent. At the beginning of the 1960s there was some liberalization of the economy, but government policy remained essentially protectionist, with tariffs replacing the earlier import and exchange controls. Between 1960 and the onset of martial law in 1972, the GNP growth averaged slightly over 5 percent.

In 1965 Marcos was first elected president. He gathered around him a group of economists and policymakers—widely referred to as technocrats—who advocated a shift toward a more open economy and an export-oriented economic policy. Their ideas were partially put into practice, but in the face of considerable resistance. To some extent the opposition was from elements of the business community who stood to lose their protected status, but it also came from other quarters. Economic nationalists argued that Philippine economic problems were a result of the country's continued reliance and dependence upon the United States, not protectionist policies. What was needed were even more stringent policies, particularly in the area of controlling foreign investment.

In declaring martial law, Marcos made it clear that he intended to create a "New Society." The economic policies he pursued, however, were to be largely those already advocated by the technocrats, the difference being that under the new regime—constitutional authoritarianism—there was to be no opposition, no debate. According to the regime's chief economic planner, policies could now be implemented with speed and flexibility.[5]

From 1973 to 1979, GNP growth annually averaged 6.9 percent. Initially this was taken to be a vindication of the open-economy model. In reality the dismantling of tariff walls began relatively late in the decade. The impressive growth rates were largely based on a few years of good export prices and massive international borrowing. In the 1980s the economy turned down, with real GNP increasing by 4.7 percent in 1980, 3.6 percent in 1981, 2.8 percent in 1982. The estimated increase for 1983 was 1.4 percent, a rate less than that of population growth.[6] Much of the blame for the slowdown was placed on the depressed world market, particularly for primary products. Exports had been diversified somewhat to include more manufactured goods, but sugar, coconut products, copper and other mineral products, wood products, and pineapples and bananas still dominated. Their prices fell dramatically after 1979, often by more than half, and the economy felt the impact. Terms of trade in early 1983 stood at only 57.3 (using 1972 as a base of 100).[7]

Another major factor affecting the economy was the financial scandal that occurred in January 1981, when businessman Dewey Dee disappeared owing an estimated P700 million. More than eighty firms became virtually insolvent and several investment houses closed their doors. In an attempt to avoid widespread bankruptcies, the Central Bank and other government-owned financial institutions made large emergency loans to distressed companies. However, given the combination of Dee's debts, mismanagement, and the depressed state of the Philippine economy, the situation for many of the firms did not improve appreciably, and for some it got worse. The government continued to pour in money and began converting existing loans to equity.

Recently it was reported that the Development Bank of the Philippines has an approximately P2 billion exposure in 122 companies; in addition, repayments are not being made on 65 percent (P17 billion) of its loans. The National Development Corporation has an equity interest in over 50 distressed firms, including full ownership of 12, with an investment of some P2 billion. And the Philippine National Bank, the National Investment Development Corporation, and the Government Services Insurance Corporation have over P3 billion in equity investments in domestic firms.[8]

As time passed charges began to arise that close associates of Marcos were being favored in the bailouts, the most notorious being the Construction and Development Corporation of the Philippines (CDCP). Between 1981 and 1983 the government injected P6.2 billion into CDCP, an amount roughly equivalent to 25 percent of the country's money supply and 30 percent of tax collections by the Bureau of Internal Revenue in 1981. Some P4 billion of the loans were recently converted from debt to equity, an act described by one businessman, Jaime Ongpin, as "'the most obscene, brazen and disgraceful misallocation of taxpayers' money in the history of the Philippines.'" The result is that funds needed by other firms are not readily available.[9]

Finally, the country experienced its worse drought since 1972. Virtually no rain fell in the Visayas and Mindanao between September 1982 and April 1983, resulting in substantial shortfalls in the production of the staple crops rice and corn (16 percent and 25 percent, respectively, for the first six months of 1983), as well as in coconuts, sugar, and other export crops.

All this occurred at the same time the government was instituting a restructuring of Philippine industry instigated and funded by the World Bank, dismantling tariffs to encourage efficiency and an orientation toward exporting. The loans were to tide the Philippines over what was hoped to be a transitional period until some import-substituting industries became more competitive, new industries replaced inefficient ones, and exports caught up with the increase in imports that was expected to occur as the level of protection fell. During the adjustment period, a World Bank report estimated, unemployment would increase by at least 100,000 workers, about 5 percent of the work force in manufacturing.[10]

Whatever the merits of the reconstruction, the timing was miserable. Imports did increase but exports fell, so that by 1982 the current account deficit was equivalent to 8.5 percent of GNP.[11] The country could not sustain such a deficit and meet its debt-servicing commitments. During the 1970s the Philippines had become increasingly indebted to multilateral lending institutions (it is the sixth-largest recipient of World Bank funds) and transnational banks. Its foreign-currency debt grew from about $2.1 billion in 1970 to $3.8 billion in 1975 to $12.7 billion in 1980 to what would turn out to be officially pegged at more than $25 billion in 1983. (Informed observers place the actual debt figure as high as $40 billion.) Debt-service payments in 1982, $2.24 billion, were greater than the total debt in 1970 and approximately the level of foreign borrowing that year.[12]Traditional reliance on loans to cover trade deficits was no longer a viable policy.

Indications of a Crisis

The Philippine economy was in a very precarious situation by late 1982; one headline put it, "Emergency Aid From IMF, World Bank Helped the Philippines Avert Default." To keep the country from going under, the IMF agreed in February 1983 to a $543 million emergency loan to the government, which was followed by a $300 million loan from the World Bank. Another loan of $300 million from major New York banks with significant interests in the Philippines was made, it was said, to proclaim "Manila's return to grace" as well as to keep the Philippines from being cast as "Asia's only Latin American debtor."

Achieving this state of grace required the Philippines to agree to comply with stringent conditions imposed by the IMF; resistance delayed the IMF loan for several months, but on 31 December 1982 Central Bank Governor Jaime Laya indicated the government would follow the IMF dictates: to reduce the balance of payments deficit, to limit the growth of the money supply, to reduce government spending, and not to resort to tariff increases or import controls. As subsequent events showed, compliance would be difficult and costly in terms of economic growth. When the loan conditions became known in Manila, even many of Marcos's political supporters turned against the technocrats, accusing them of selling out. Prime Minister (and Finance Minister) Cesar Virata indicated his willingness to resign over the issue, but after letting him "take the heat," Marcos refused the offer.[13]

A major condition of the IMF loan was that the Philippines limit its balance of payments deficit for 1983 to $598 million, about half the 1982 figure of $1.14 billion.[14] By midyear the deficit had already reached $562 million. In an effort to stem the tide, the government took four steps, each of which was connected to commitments to the IMF or World Bank.

First, the government devalued the peso by 7.3 percent, to P11 to the U.S. dollar—this on top of a 10.3 percent drop that had occurred during 1983. Although no evidence was produced to link the devaluation with IMF dictates, observers could not fail to note that the devaluation occurred just when an IMF team finished a review of the country's economic situation. Second, the IMF team recommended a further reduction in the government budget, to which Budget Minister Manuel Alba did not accede; two weeks later Prime Minister Virata, who was attending an IMF/World Bank consultative meeting, cabled Alba to order that the projected budget of P9.4 billion be trimmed by P1 billion.[15]

Third, import-restricting measures were increased. In early 1983 an across-the-board 3 percent ad valorem tariff had been imposed. Then beginning in July capital goods imports in excess of $50,000 were allowed only if the importer could secure suppliers' credits or was covered by Asian Development Bank or World Bank credit lines.

Finally, in August 1983 Central Bank approval became necessary for the importation of over five hundred relatively high tariff items. The latter actions may have been in violation of commitments the government had made. The agreement for the World Bank structural adjustment loan, as well as for loans from the IMF, requires the government to refrain from imposing import or foreign exchange controls. Apparently the initial ad valorem tariff did not violate any covenants the government had entered into but subsequent measures did. It is unclear if action was contemplated by either the IMF or the World Bank; however, by mid-October the issue became moot.[16]

Measures were also taken to control the allocation of foreign exchange. The Central Bank had expressed concern that commercial banks were placing too large a portion of their allowable holdings of foreign currency abroad, thereby limiting the amount available for local importers. In March 1983 the first of a series of steps were taken to reduce the level of the foreign exchange holdings of commercial banks, steps that became increasingly severe as the crisis worsened.

The government also ended a subsidy on petroleum products. Before a meeting of the ruling political party (*Kilusanq Baqonq Lipunan*, or KBL) In April 1983 the prime minister had argued that the government could no longer afford the P55 million-a-month subsidy, but objections were raised and the matter was sent to committee. In June agreement was reached within the KBL to eliminate the subsidy, and oil prices were increased across the board by about 32 centavos a liter. The delay and discussion turned out to be only for political show, for the government had committed itself in March to the World Bank to end the subsidy as part of its request for a second structural adjustment loan.[17]

Last, the government cancelled five highly controversial major industrial projects. Initiation of the projects, which had an estimated cost of $3 billion, was already problematic, given the budget reductions and loan limitations that the government had agreed to in its negotiations with the IMF. [18]

Impact of the Assassination

In the midst of the belt-tightening adjustments, Senator Aquino returned from a three-year, self-imposed exile in the United States. Within seconds of stepping off the airplane, he was murdered. The reaction in both the Philippines and overseas was shock and disbelief. The stability of the Philippines became an issue, with discussions in the Manila media about a possible freeze on new international loans to the Philippines and the country's ability to meet its commitments; capital flight, runs on local banks, and a selling spree on stock markets in the Philippines were mentioned. The actual size of the foreign debt was being questioned, with estimates ranging from the IMF's $17.5 billion to private bankers' $20.8 billion; even the latter figure, it was said, might be low. Would major banks be willing to roll over Philippine short-term debt to keep the country from defaulting?[19]

None of the talk regarding economic stability was new. Two-thirds of the business people surveyed by the prestigious Makati Business Club in mid-1983 believed that capital flight was a "serious problem" for the economy; the rest acknowledged it as a problem but considered it manageable.[20] Although the run on the commercial banks was distressing, the selling spree on the stock market, given its already depressed state, did not appear to be of significance. Concern over the size of the debt was in part a consequence of the government's having recently disclosed that the country's actual short-term indebtedness was double the $4 billion shown in official reports.[21]

By the end of September 1983 it was obvious that the measures taken by the Marcos administration in June after announcement of balance of payments figures for the first semester had not stopped the hemorrhaging. The seriousness of the situation was plain: the balance of payments deficit for the third quarter alone was $780 million, bringing the total for the year to $1,342 million. Virata pointed to capital flows rather than the trade account to explain the situation. Net inflows of medium-term and long-term capital at the end of September 1983 were down to $913 million, a 22.8 percent drop from the same period a year earlier. More distressing was that for the first time in ten years, short-term capital registered a net outflow ($607 million). This being the case, the government had to draw on its stock of foreign exchange to cover the deficit. The gross international reserves of the Philippines were then $1,431 billion, a fall of $851 million in three months.

In an attempt to stem the tide, the government devalued the peso by 21.4 percent (from P11 to P14 to U.S. $1) on October 5, bringing the total change for the year to almost 35 percent, and increased the ad valorem tariff on certain imports from 3 percent to 10 percent. But the descent continued. By the middle of October 1983 the balance of payments deficit had swelled to over $2 billion, and the international reserves of the country had fallen by another $1 billion to $430 million, less than the value of one month's imports. Later it was reported that during October reserves hit a low of $290 million.[22] The country was on the verge of defaulting on its international commitments. Prime Minister Virata and Central Bank Governor Laya rushed to New York on October 12 to confer with ten of the country's leading bank creditors. On October 17 it was announced that the Philippines could no longer meet its debt obligations and was asking for a ninety day moratorium on principal payments; interest payments were to continue.[23]

Complications

The reasons for the crisis, it has been widely claimed, were political in nature. Certainly, reaction to the assassination of

Aquino created difficulties for the regime. Normal ninety-day, short-term credits were being reduced to two-week, one-week, or twenty-four-hour loans, or creditors were not rolling over the loans that they had extended. In addition, capital flight estimated as high as $5 million per day were occurring.[24] But soon additional factors that pointed to more fundamental problems began to come to light. First, the size of the debt was revised upward by some $7-$8 billion to a total of about $25 billion; it was noted that certain nonmonetary capital liabilities and short-term liabilities of the Central Bank had not been included previously.

Second, the structure of the country's debt had been changing; at the time of the moratorium, short-term debt constituted about 40 percent of the total. The reason for the change, according to Virata, was to keep from defaulting earlier. He gave the following explanation in a cabinet meeting:

> There was a general erosion of confidence in the entire system, such that towards the end of 1982 or beginning of 1983, about $710 million of existing [credit] lines were already withdrawn from the Central Bank of the Philippines. . . .What happened during the rest of 1983, was a continuous cutting of the various lines and at the same time a shortening of maturities.[25]

The problem was a combination of an increasing current account deficit and a tightening of international credit. The government had begun covering external-payments shortfalls with overnight borrowings as early as October 1982. At the same time the country's international reserves, particularly its gold holdings, were being used. By March 1983 the Central Bank's overnight liabilities had reached $150 million.[26]

One consequence of the increased reliance on short-term debt was that the cost of servicing the debt, and hence the debt-service ratio, began to rise (annual interest payments, for example, rose by 27 percent between 1981 and 1982). By Philippine law, the ratio of debt-service payments to total foreign exchange receipts of the previous year is limited to 20 percent. However, using current account receipts (the more normal procedure), the ratio was reported to be about 28 percent. Debt servicing in 1983 was eating up more than half of export earnings.[27]

Third, it became clear that the Central Bank had been drastically overstating the size of its foreign exchange reserves so as to maintain the confidence of the international banking community. The Central Bank was engaged in a practice known as "back-to-back" credit; the operation involved the Philippine National Bank (PNB) and perhaps some other government-owned financial institutions as well as some private banks. The procedure was outlined in a resolution passed by the board of directors of the PNB:

(1) Central Bank deposits with a PNB overseas office/s for lending to PNB congenerics. (2) The FX (foreign exchange) is sold by the PNB congenerics to PNB head office, which in turn sells to the Central Bank. (3) The peso proceeds of the PNB congenerics are deposited/lent to the PNB head office. In turn, PNB head office deposits such proceeds with the Central Bank. (4) The procedure and entries are reversed upon advice of the Central Bank.[28]

The president of the PNB, Placido Mapa, pointed out that the procedure served both to increase the Central Bank's reserves and to reduce the country's money supply. Of the $2.43 billion in reserves at the end of the first quarter 1983, $960 million reportedly represented back-to-back transactions with the PNB. Some officials question whether these funds were in fact actually liquid. In addition, the Central Bank increased its foreign exchange reserves by using credit lines of government institutions, in particular the Philippine National Oil Company.

The practice of resorting to back-to-back transactions is not unique to the Philippines; some Latin American countries have also engaged in it. What is different in Manila's case is that when some of the funds were repaid, the Central Bank kept the amounts on its records. Virata admitted that some of the withdrawals occurred as early as March 1983. In addition, the extent of the "window dressing" was much greater in the Philippine case, constituting nearly 40 percent of the declared reserves at the end of March 1983, and 43 percent at the end of September. There is a dispute in at least one instance about whether the transaction took place at all. Central Bank records show an increase in reserves of $215 million resulting from the deposit of a loan from the London branch of PNB to a PNB subsidiary in the Philippines; PNB President Mapa denies the transaction occurred.

Corrections in the foreign exchange reserves statement were made in mid-October 1983, and accounted for $600 million of the reported $1 billion fall in reserves during the previous two-week period. The entire fall was initially attributed to capital flight after the Aquino assassination, but in December foreign bankers who were inspecting Central Bank accounts discovered the true situation.[29]

Announcement of the overstatement was met with shock and criticism by the IMF and foreign banking community, although one banker claimed that the foreign banks knew about the window dressing of the reserves from the beginning.[30] Questions were raised about the suitability of Central Bank Governor Jaime Laya. Laya offered his resignation in late December 1983, but it was declined by Marcos. KAAKBAY, the movement for Philippine sovereignty and democracy led by Jose Diokno, a former senator and a Marcos critic, has alleged that the highest officials were aware of overstatement of reserves and that their actions involved violations of several sections of the Central Bank Act. They have called for dismissal and prosecution of those involved.[31]

In January 1984 a new irregularity surfaced. Under an agreement with the IMF, the Central Bank was to limit money supply growth to 3 percent between September 1983 and January 1984, but in October and November alone it grew at a rate of 20 percent. According to one account, the reaction was strong:

> The discovery of such blatant disregard of IMF dictates, whether a politically inspired resort to the currency-printing presses or simply financial mismanagement by the government, destroyed much if not all the trust built up over the years with the Marcos government—as much as did the controversy over the inflated reserve figures.[32]

Several possible explanations were put forward beyond simple mismanagement. One was that government officials may have used new notes to buy U.S. dollars on the black market. Prime Minister Virata, on the other hand, expressed hope that the figures might simply reflect the adjustment in foreign exchange reserves. If that was the case, he suggested, the IMF might be less severe with the country. The IMF, however, extracted a price.

> On 9 January. . .the IMF team leader [in Manila] Hubert Niess indicated to Marcos that if the IMF was to continue with the Philippine programme, [Central Bank Governor] Laya would have to go. The monetary data, so out of kilter, would have to be audited to find out what happened. All the new money injected into the system would have to be reabsorbed by the central bank, and in all likeli-

hood the effects of the money surge would demand a new peso dollar parity shift—the third since last June—or possibly multi-tiered exchange rate.[33]

Laya left the Central Bank the following week. He was replaced by Jose B. Fernandez, Jr., the president and chairman of the Board of Far East Bank and Trust Company, one of the largest commercial banks in the Philippines. Negotiations between the Philippines and the IMF to salvage the Philippine economic mess had to begin anew.

"Corrective" Actions

At the time the moratorium was declared, the Philippines needed a complete overhaul of its international commitments. Negotiations began almost immediately between Philippine monetary officials, on the one hand, and the IMF and the twelve-member (up from ten members) bank advisory group on the other. The government wanted three things: standby credits of $650 million from the IMF; a restructuring of existing loans that amounted to $9 billion; and $3.3 billion in new loans, half of which would come from commercial banks, and the other half from the World Bank, Asian Development Bank, and the U.S. and Japanese governments, among others.[34]

Agreement with the IMF is most important, for the banks, multilateral lending institutions, and the U.S. and Japanese governments are demanding an IMF stamp of approval before they are willing to reach agreement with the Philippines. Initially events appeared to be going smoothly. In November 1983 Prime Minister Virata had been ready to sign a letter of intent with the IMF outlining the austerity measures that the government would take as part of a recovery program, and the managing director of the IMF, Jacques de Larosiere, had approved in principle IMF's assistance. However, as the understatement of debt, the over-statement of reserves, and the ballooning money supply came to light, everything began to unravel. Larosiere refused to telex his support for the financing package for the Philippines to the banks, multilateral lending institutions, and governments of Philippine trading partners. Negotiations dragged on, with a fourth, ninety-day moratorium beginning July 16, 1984. The IMF was insisting on verifying Philippine economic-performance data before negotiating what will surely be a harsh austerity program. This being the case, politics as much as economics will dictate when agreement is reached. In mid-March 1984 it was reported that the Philippine government informed the IMF that it would not be prepared to agree to the IMF's conditions for the standby credit until late May, after the parliamentary elections. Central Bank Governor Fernandez said that the rescheduling of the foreign debt and extension of new loans with the country's creditor banks was expected to be reached by late August.[35]

To cope with the crisis, the government undertook actions in several areas: restrictions on imports, control of foreign exchange, reduction in government expenditures, limitations on expansion of domestic credit, and a loosening of regulations on foreign investment. Commercial banks were required to turn over all foreign exchange holdings to the Central Bank. Foreign exchange would then be distributed depending upon its need and availability. Priority uses were as follows: (1) payment for oil imports; (2) servicing of official development assistance loans; (3) financing of imports for use in export industries and vital domestic industries and of food grains; (4) servicing of bank loans; and (5) servicing of interbank loans and trade credits. In addition, items for which banks could open letters of credit were limited to some four hundred critical commodities.[36]

Most of the restraint on letters of credit, however, was external. A week after the onset of the moratorium of October 1983 the local media reported that the opening of letters of credit had virtually stopped. A number of foreign banks that normally handled letters of credit issued in the Philippines were refusing to honor them because they were afraid that the issuing bank would be unable to remit the foreign exchange. Later Marcos claimed that difficulties in securing letters of credit were having an adverse impact upon production, adding, "'We spend sleepless nights thinking of ways to solve the problem.'" Although difficulties continue, in March 1984 it was reported that the Philippines had been able to attract some short-term credit from small U.S. banks through the assistance of the U.S. Export-Import Bank and its loan guarantee program.[37]

The effect of the import-priority system and limitation on letters of credit was that from the fall of 1983 until mid-1984, private business was allocated on $225 million for imports. The Central Bank estimated that for all of 1984 only $1.6 billion would be allocated for imports other than oil, including $700 million to agriculture and $870 million to manufacturing industries. Some businesses have been able to secure credit from their suppliers or additional inflows of capital from foreign joint-venture partners, but this has not made up the difference. Moreover, the situation has the nature of a vicious circle because many export products, particularly the newer, nontraditional ones, have large import contents; limiting imports thus has an adverse impact on foreign exchange earnings.[38]

As part of the loan agreement in early 1983 with the IMF, the Philippine government agreed to limit both the growth of domestic credit and the size of the government budget deficit. Funds spent in bailing out distressed companies, plus countercyclical spending, caused the budget deficit to mushroom to some P14 billion in 1982. It was to be reduced to 2 percent of GNP in 1983 (about P7.6 billion) and 1.5 percent (P6.5 billion) in 1984. One impact of such reductions would be to lower economic growth and, consequently, reduce the demand for imports.

Having an effect similar to that of reductions the budget deficit, as well as supposedly helping to control inflation, was the agreement to limit the growth of domestic credit to 16 percent for the year. Although the government undertook measures to restrict credit by increasing commercial bank reserve requirements, actual money supply growth was much larger than scheduled. Partly because of the need to assist banks that found themselves in a precarious position, the Central Bank allowed currency to expand 54 percent in the last quarter of 1983 alone.[39]

Liquidity remains far above levels agreed to with the IMF, no doubt because of spending prior to the May 1984 election. How much the government actually spent is subject to speculation; estimates range from P2 billion upward. At a campaign rally in Cebu City, the wife of President Marcos told the crowd she was offering "prizes" of P50,000 to each *barangay* and P100,000 to each town in the province that delivered a straight KBL vote. Unlike poorly financed opposition candidates, those on the KBL ticket relied extensively on television advertising. It was reported that the government borrowed P4.7 billion from the Central Bank in the three weeks before the election.[40]

After the election, Marcos apparently decided to move toward agreement with the IMF. On 5 and 6 June 1984 he announced a series of austerity measures. First, the peso was devalued by 22 percent to P18 to the U.S. dollar, bringing the total devaluation since the end of 1982 to just under 100 percent. In addition, a 10 percent excise tax was placed on the peso value of foreign exchange purchased for non-commodity-import purposes. A 30 percent export stabilization tax was placed on profits of exporters stemming from changes in exchange rates. The government budget was trimmed by 5 percent (on top of an earlier cut of 10 percent) to bring it in line with the IMF requirement of no more than 1.5 percent of GNP. And, attempts are being made to reduce the money supply. Nonetheless, with a minimum foreign exchange requirement for the year of $8.8 billion and estimated earnings of $4.33 billion, the country will still experience a shortfall of at least $4 billion.[41] Projections of real economic growth for 1984 range from zero to a negative 6 percent.

Impact on the Domestic Economy

Philippine industry has traditionally been import dependent. During the 1970s the policy of the government was to create an even more open economy. In addition, its development program was dependent to a large extent upon funding from abroad. When, after the Aquino assassination, the country found that it could no longer borrow, the effect was devastating. The inability of producers to obtain raw materials and intermediate products from abroad could only for a short time be compensated for by depleting inventories. The main alternative has been to cut back on or cease operations, increasing unemployment in an already depressed economy. The National Economic and Development Authority's employment index for manufacturing stood at 87.9 in January 1983 (January 1981 being the base of 100), with reported layoffs of 54,000 during the year. In December 1983 the Employers Confederation of the Philippines estimated that its members would lay off 68,000 by mid-1984, and in January 1984 it was reported that some 1,400 firms had applied to the Ministry of Labor and Employment for permission to reduce their work forces. Projections of layoffs during 1984 run as high as 300,000, although government figures are not anywhere near that level. From the first of January until early March 1984 the Ministry of Labor and Employment has recorded 28,000 layoffs. These figures are most probably only from larger establishments because ministry officials say that normally layoffs of fewer than 100 workers are not reported.[42] Undoubtedly unemployment will continue to worsen in 1984.

The real wage has also been affected. During 1982 it declined by 5.7 percent and the fall continued in 1983 and 1984. The minimum wage (including cost-of-living adjustments) was increased in July 1983 and again in November by a total of P10.00 for industrial workers in Metro Manila to a level of P42.00 per day. In percentage terms it is only slightly below the preliminary estimates of inflation of 32 percent for the year.[43] Published minimum wage data, however, are only minimally useful because it is widely recognized, even by the labor ministry, that compliance is low. Also, there are exemptions for distressed industries. According to the NEDA compensation index, at the end of 1983 the growth of total compensation since 1982 lagged behind inflation 16 percent.

Further, reports in the media suggest the cost of living has risen by more than official statistics indicate. A sample of price increases in the eight weeks after the 1983 Aquino murder is enlightening: white sugar, 25 percent to 40 percent; salt, tomatoes, garlic, 100 percent; cooking oil, 100 percent; chicken, 75 percent; pork, 66 percent; onions 66 percent.[44] Also, during November there were reports of shortages of rice and cooking oil.[45] Panic buying occurred again in June 1984 when the peso was devalued to P18 to the U.S. dollar. On 6 June petroleum prices increased an average of 26 percent. Then in the next few days, prices of controlled items increased by an average of 12 percent; uncontrolled items, 20 percent to 30 percent. Even prior to the surge, unofficial estimates of the inflation rate were as high as 50 percent.[46]

In the hope of increasing inflows of foreign currency, as well as presenting a more favorable image abroad, the government has taken several measures to encourage more foreign investment. Throughout the crisis, it has appealed to subsidiaries of multinational firms and domestic capitalists in joint ventures with foreigners, to use their influence to get the multinationals to provide credits and to invest more in their Philippine operations. To make this action more attractive, Marcos signed Presidential Decree 1892, effective for one year beginning 4 December 1983, which allowed foreign investors to own up to 100 percent of local companies engaged in nonpioneer industries; the previous limit was 40 percent. Foreign firms can exchange raw materials with their local affiliates for shares of stock. The decree does not change constitutional provisions limiting foreign investment in the area of natural resources, public utilities, and real estate, but almost everything else is open, and domestic business people fear the move is a threat to local ownership.

Foreign investment in the Philippines declined in the early 1980s, with net foreign investment in 1982 amounting to only $259 million. It is difficult to imagine an increase in inflow of sufficient size to make a dent in the Philippines problems, and this is apparently the case. At the end of March 1984 it was reported that most foreign investment coming into the country was either in the form of raw materials and machinery or the conversion of unremitted profits and royalties into equity, a total of approximately $40 million. However, with the current crisis on top of an economy that has not performed well in the past two years, foreign firms should be able to acquire equity at bargain prices. In addition, those without foreign partners are incurring more difficulties in getting foreign exchange for imports. No doubt many would welcome the opportunity to find a joint-venture partner.[47]

Business versus Marcos

One of the more unexpected developments after the assassination of Aquino, at least to this observer, was the reaction of the business community, particularly in the financial center of Makati. For virtually all of the martial law period, the members of the community were quiet. In the beginning they fared rather well economically, and if they had criticisms, they kept them to themselves.

Recently there has been some speaking out against various economic policies of the government; the bailing out of bankrupt firms owned by friends of the president, for example, has come in for considerable criticism. Such complaints, however, pale in comparison with the forcefulness of the attacks on the Marcos regime after 21 August 1983: participation in rallies and demonstrations, public speeches, articles in the media, and, in general, demands that Marcos change his policies and/or step down. Marcos has responded by alternatively cajoling and berating representatives from the business sector.

One of the best examples of this interaction occurred at the close of the ninth annual Philippine Business Conference, November 1983. Those attending met with Marcos and presented him with a statement signed by the presidents of the Philippine, Filipino-Chinese, American, Australian, European and Japanese Chambers of Commerce. The business community wanted the following: (1) the clear designation of a presidential successor, (2) freedom of the press, (3) an independent and honest judiciary, (4) restoration of constitutional rights, and (5) an end to pervasive militarization.

Marcos, on his side, said business was partly responsible for escalating the country's problems. For one thing, he wanted but did not receive substantial proposals from business people that would help raise foreign exchange. For another, he complained that Filipino companies, compared with the multinationals, were not "faithful" in paying their taxes; he estimated the nonpayment to be from two to four times the amount paid. Further, he pointed among other things to what he called flagrant violations of customs laws, bribery, dollar "salting" (not remitting foreign exchange earnings to the Philippines), smuggling, misdeclaration of imports, undervaluing of exports, and hoarding prime commodities.[48]

Business people were described as feeling "helpless" after the president's comments. The items on the list presented to Marcos were characterized as being "supernational," and in need of solution first if capital flight was to be arrested, foreign investment attracted, and private enterprise stimulated. One columnist asked if the president's cronies were among those at whom he directed his comments. Although courageous and on the mark, the question was almost too easy; it let the business people off the hook. They had gone along with the conditions they now asked to be changed for more than a decade. In terms of bailing out the economy, the president's list is more compelling, but not by much. The practices Marcos mentioned are surely problems but, by the same token, he has gone along with them ever since he became a politician. Neither side dealt with the fundamental issues of Philippine development: the nature of economic policy that has been pursued under the Marcos regime, on the one hand, and the structure of control and utilization of the nation's resources and wealth, on the other. But, of course, that is not the point. Both sides are concerned with power, and the lists reflect what each wants from the other to maintain or achieve power.

The crisis has limited Marcos's ability to dominate the situation. It is apparent that he can no longer stifle all critical comment. The church hierarchy, particularly its leader Cardinal Sin, has distanced itself from the regime, and investigatory reporting has returned to segments of the press. The latest round in what has now become an open struggle was the May 1984 parliamentary election in which the opposition won approximately one-third of the seats. Marcos, on the other hand, does retain his dictatorial powers and control over the military. Unable and unwilling to resort to force, that part of the opposition that participated in the parliamentary election is heavily dependent on external support: the IMF and international bankers, whose financing the regime needs, and the United States government, whose political support has been traditionally a requirement for successful ascension to power in the Philippines.

It is clear that the opposition believed that pressure from Washington was vital to their efforts during the May 1984 election. Two comments—one by Cardinal Sin in an interview; the other by Jaime Ongpin, president of Benguet Corporation, in a speech to the Makati Business Club—illustrate the point.

> In a recent interview Sin made it clear that he believed the US, as the country's main creditor and friend in its hour of need, was applying effective pressure on Marcos to ensure that the coming National Assembly elections in May will be fair and honest. "The democratic system here was introduced by Uncle Sam," said the cardinal. "There must be conditions [attached to the Americans' economic aid]. I think the president is conceding."[49]

> The involvement of the US government and the foreign banks is of special significance [Ongpin said], because for the first time in his 18-year reign, Mr. Marcos is confronted with a political crisis in which he cannot ignore, much less manipulate or coerce, the most crucial participants. The US government and foreign bankers have become the most crucial element in the political equation because they alone control the purse strings that hold the one thing Mr. Marcos cannot do without—US dollars.

> . . .Despite all their public denials to the contrary, neither the US nor the foreign banks are about to throw more dollars down the drain by letting Mr. Marcos have as much money as he wants without substantive political reforms.[50]

The United States, for its part, appears to be pursuing a middle course. On the one hand, the Reagan administration reportedly believes that Marcos is the only person currently capable of stabilizing the situation. Thus, during the protracted negotiations with the IMF, the United States, along with the World Bank and Asian Development Bank, has continued to supply the Philippines with loans and aid. The United States accelerated disbursal of $50 million in economic support funds; $225 million in Commodity Credit Corporation Funds was made available (of which, only $106 million is reported to have been drawn down); and $700 million of Export-Import Bank loan guarantees were created. In addition, the U.S. Treasury was reportedly willing to provide an emergency bridge loan to the Philippines between the time agreement is reached with the IMF and negotiations with the country's creditors are completed. The World Bank granted loans of $100 million in December 1983 and $125 million in March 1984; a $150 million agricultural loan was approved in September.[51]

Elections are seen as necessary, according to one U.S. official, to ensure "'that the government enjoys authority, legitimacy and remains congenial to the US.'" The then-ambassador to the Philippines, Michael Armacost, stated the Reagan position in a speech to the Makati Rotary Club last November. He pointed to American investment in the Philippines (book value, approximately $2 billion) and to Filipino-Americans as reason for the deep U.S. interest in Philippine affairs. "'It is not for us to prescribe political reforms for the Philippines,' Armacost added, 'but we do have an interest in the fundamental stability of political and economic life in this country.'" He went on to refer to the U.S. preference for free elections.[52]

The U.S. position has not been to assist toward Marcos's ouster but to seek stability and pave the way for an orderly succession by elements supportive of U.S. interests. This has angered some of those opposed to Marcos. They point out that following the assassination of Aquino, the entire opposition had one objective: the resignation of Marcos. Actions of U.S. officials that focused on clean elections helped defuse the opposition.[53] Debate now centers on the ins and outs of parliamentary politics rather than on more fundamental issues. This may change, but because the major actors among the oppositionists participating in the elections are mostly long-time politicians, it is doubtful.

Prospects for the Economy

Why did the Philippines get into the economic mess in which it now finds itself, and what are the proper corrective measures?

The most common answer to the first part of the question points to Marcos and his cronies. Cardinal Sin, in a commencement address at Brandeis University, referred to the current government as a "'plague of locusts'" on the country. A prominent business critic, Jaime Ongpin, estimated that between $6 and $7 billion of the Philippine's $26 billion debt can be linked directly or indirectly to crony-related handouts. But, he went on, "'The heaviest cost of crony capitalism was not out-of-pocket dollars but the devastation of confidence of the private sector. . . . Without confidence, there's no investment; without investment, there's no growth.'"[54]

From this perspective, the issue is to replace Marcos without disturbing the underlying pattern of economic relations. The response of Salvador Laurel, president of the opposition organization UNIDO, is illustrative.

> A Filipino reporter asked Mr. Laurel what he had to offer the Filipino people. "Democracy," he replied. No, the reporter pressed, Mr. Laurel didn't understand. For example, the reporter had an aunt in southeast Luzon. Her biggest problem was that her nearest source of clean water was about half a mile from her house. What did the opposition have to offer her? "Democracy," replied Mr. Laurel.[55]

A variant of the "Marcos-is-the-cause" theme is to place the blame for the crisis and, particularly, obstacles to its solution on politicians while looking to the technocrats as nonpolitical managers. As a foreign banker in Manila put it, the technocrats "'want to get on with the job of restoring economic health'"; and the problem is that the Filipino people are unwilling to subject themselves to the discipline of an austerity program and that politicians are anxious about their popularity.[56]

The difficulty with both explanations is that they ignore the role of the technocrats, the multilateral lending institutions, and the transnational banks in Philippine affairs throughout the past decade. Either that or the explanations assume that these individuals and organizations willingly lent their prestige to the Marcos government and provided billions of dollars to a regime that they knew was engaged in massive mismanagement. This makes little sense. Since Marcos first assumed the presidency in 1965, he has surrounded himself with technocrats. This fact is often used to differentiate his administration from previous ones.

It is difficult to believe that these individuals, purportedly non-political, would have associated themselves for almost twenty years with an administration that used them only to provide a gloss for its actions. Further, it is these same technocrats who negotiated the billions of dollars in loans that the Philippines cannot repay and who oversaw the actions that have delayed reaching agreement with the IMF. Finally, we now know that the IMF and World Bank have had significant and ongoing influence in Manila.[57]

Economic nationalists in the Philippines have long criticized the approach of the multilateral lending institutions, as have some groups of business people. (Those in favor of the move toward a more open economy often argue that the nationalists are being used by local capitalists to further the latter's monopolistic desire to avoid competition.) They argue that the power of multinational firms is such that they can destroy Filipino-run business, and that such business should be protected so as to develop the economy.

A long-time partisan of economic nationalism, Alejandro Lichauco, made a different point with respect to the consequences of an open economy. He noted that between 1970 and 1982, the importation of consumer goods and unclassified items (which he claimed to be mostly unessentials) totaled about $13.6 billion, about the same amount as the aggregate trade deficit for the period ($13.2 billion), and continued:

"The government responded to a fundamental disequilibrium by relying on inflows of short-term speculative capital with which to window-dress a balance-of-payments position that has been steadily deteriorating due to the trade deficits. . .This placed the entire international reserves completely at the mercy of foreign money speculators."[58]

The state of the world economy, as well as tendencies toward protctionism in any of the industrialized nations has not gone unnoticed by technocrats in the Philippines. Their export-oriented development strategy requires that foreign markets be open to Philippine goods. In June 1983 Prime Minister Virata, speaking to business people, even went so far as to suggest that the government take a second look at import substitution as an economic strategy.[59] No doubt the suggestion was made in exasperation, for the prime minister is fully aware that the import-substitution process, as it is normally practiced, had run its course in the Philippines by the end of the 1950s.

The pure types of export orientation and import substitution do not exhaust the possibilities, but whatever type or combination may be followed, it will be contingent upon those who control economic resources—the capitalists—doing their job of producing. It is not clear that this is the case in the Philippines, where the acquisition of wealth appears as much related to "cutting deals"—political and economic—as to producing. Both the economic nationalists and those in favor of an open economy assume that the current crop of capitalists will undertake their responsibility to produce only if conditions are appropriate: in the one case, if they are protected; in the other, if they are not protected. It may well be, however, that those with the will to develop the Philippines do not have control of the requisite resources.

Undoubtedly the Philippines will survive the current crisis, but how long it will take and in what condition the country will emerge remains to be seen. In July 1984 Marcos named a new cabinet led by the incumbent prime minister, Cesar Virata. Only five of its twenty seven members are new faces, and even some of them were previously deputy ministers.[60] There is little to suggest any significant change in economic policy. The primary concern of those oppositionists who participated in the May 1984 elections has been to wrest some power from Marcos and secure their position in the political structure when he leaves office. Critical comments have been directed at "crony capitalism," the understating of the debt, and the overstating of international reserves, but not at the underlying—IMF- and World Bank-supported—policy of an open economy.

Those more critical of the existing economic structure and development orientation—segments of the legal opposition and the National Democratic Front—have little current influence. To enact the policies of the economic nationalists, as has been done to some extent in the past, without changing the pattern of monopolized control of economic resources, will have questionable impact on Philippine economic development. The progressive groups will have to overcome the entrenched interests first, but because the latter are generally supportive of U.S. interests, and the former are not, attempts at significant alterations in economic policy will undoubtedly be opposed by Washington. Success will not come easily.

Yet, reaction to the assassination of Aquino has created a climate where a call for change cannot be easily suppressed. Hostility is being expressed toward not only the excesses of the regime but also its economic policies, and for the first time in over a decade alternative economic strategies are being openly discussed. The reality of poverty and the desire for development may yet prevail.

Notes

1. For a detailed discussion of the events leading up to, and the reasons for, the declaration of martial law, see David A. Rosenberg, ed., *Marcos and Martial Law in the Philippines* (Ithaca: Cornell University Press, 1979).

2. Claude A. Buss, *The United States and the Philippines* (Washington, D.C.: American Enterprise Institute, 1977), p. 67n.

3. See, for example, Ricardo Saludo, "Mixing Business with Politics," *Business Day*, 12 September 1983, p. 4.

4. All statistics are from the National Economic and Development Authority, *1981 Philippine Statistical Yearbook* (Manila, 1981).

5. Gerardo P. Sicat, *New Directions in the Philippines* ([Manila]: National Economic and Development Authority, 1974), p. 121. For a discussion of government policy toward foreign investment, see Charles W. Lindsey, "The Philippine State and Transnational Investment," in *States and Transnational Corporations in the Capitalist World Economy: Case Studies in Relationships*, ed. Robert B. Stauffer (forthcoming).

6. Statistics for 1981 and 1982 are from the National Economic and Development Authority; 1983 figures are reported in "The Turn of the Screw," *Far Eastern Economic Review*, 9 February 1983, p. 54.

7. "Overall Deficit Drops to $343 Million as Net Terms of Trade Pick Up," *Business Day*, 27 June 1983, p. 26.

8. Peter Truell, "Business Prospects in the Philippines Grow Gloomier," *Asian Wall Street Journal Weekly*, 26 March 1984, p. 1; Teodoro Y. Montelibano, "The New Politics: Government Priorities," *Business Day*, 2 December 1983, p. 8.

9. Montelibano, "Government Priorities;" "None for You, All for Me," *Veritas*, 12-18 February 1984, p. 9; Guy Sacerdoti, "A Bailed-Out Case," *Far Eastern Economic Review*, 24 March 1983, p. 80.

10. Rigoberto D. Tiglao, "The Structural Adjustment Program and the World Bank," *Business Day*, 14 June 1983, p. 9. An import-substituting industry is one whose initial development is based on restricting imports and producing for the market that is thereby created.

11. Guy Sacerdoti, "Biting the Peso Bullet," *Far Eastern Economic Review*, 7 July 1983, p. 43. The current account portion of the balance of payments is equal to the sum of exports of goods and services plus net transfer payments to the Philippines minus imports of goods and services.

12. "RP Growth Rate to Slow Down to Improve Creditworthiness," *Business Day*, 19 September 1983, p. 2; Guy Sacerdoti and Malcolm Subhan, "Keeping Faith in Manila," *Far Eastern Economic Review*, 21 July 1983, p. 50; Teodoro Y. Montelibano, "The New Politics: Where Does the Money Go?" *Business Day*, 1 December 1983, p. 8.

13. Eduardo Lachica, "Emergency Aid from IMF, World Bank Helped the Philippines Avert Default," *Asian Wall Street Journal Weekly*, 16 May 1983, p. 13; Richard Nations, "The Lengthening Shadow of Short-Term Debt," *Far Eastern Economic Review*, 9 June 1983, p. 66.

14. Roughly, the balance of payments is the sum of exports and non-official capital inflows minus the sum of imports and nonofficial capital outflows.

15. Rigoberto D. Tiglao, "Drastic Cuts Set on Gov't Budget Cash Deficit Goals for 1983, 1984," *Business Day*, 13 July 1983, p. 16.

16. "CB Moves Aimed to Delay Imports," *Business Day*, 7 September 1983, p. 16; "CB Tightens Import Rules Further," *Business Day*, 12 September 1983, p. 2; Guy Sacerdoti and Leo Gonzaga, "The Knives Are Out," *Far Eastern Economic Review*, 22 September 1983, p. 79; Conrado R. Banal III, "Business Slowdown to Result from Recent Gov't Measures," *Business Day*, 10 October 1983, p. 6.

17. Guy Sacerdoti, "The Economy May Be Marcos' Nemesis," *Far Eastern Economic Review*, 4 August 1983, p. 30.

18. Leo Gonzaga and Guy Sacerdoti, "Marcos Hits the MIPs," *Far Eastern Economic Review*, 7 July 1984, p. 44; Andy McCue, "Manila Puts Freeze on Five Major Projects," *Asian Wall Street Journal Weekly*, 27 June 1983, p. 11.

19. Guy Sacerdoti and Leo Gonzaga, "Capital Flies from Fear," *Far Eastern Economic Review*, 15 September 1983, p. 56; Eduardo Lachica, "Banks Fear Philippine Political Unrest May Spark Dollar Flight, Debt Problems," *Wall Street Journal*, 14 September 1983, p. 36.

20. "Businessmen Worried by Flight of Capital, MBC Survey Shows," *Business Day*, 21 July 1983, p. 1.

21. Nations, "The Lengthening Shadow," p. 66.

22. "BOP Gap Hits $2B; Reserves at $430M," *Business Day*, 31 October 1983, p. 3; Andy McCue and Matt Miller, "Manila's Foreign Exchange Shortage is Likely to Persist Until Early 1984," *Asian Wall Street Journal Weekly*, 26 December 1983, p. 4; Peter Truell, "Manila, IMF Are Unlikely to Reach Pact Before May," *Asian Wall Street Journal Weekly*, 12 March 1984, p. 8.

23. Guy Sacerdoti, "Buying Some Time," *Far Eastern Economic Review*, 27 October 1983, p. 58.

24. Ibid.

25. *ASIAWEEK*, 16 December 1983, p. 32.

26. Jose Galang, "The Financial 'Wizards,'" *Far Eastern Economic Review*, 29 March 1984, pp. 56-57.

27. *ASIAWEEK*, 4 November 1983, p. 54; Sacerdoti and Gonzaga, "Capital Flies from Fear," p. 56; Jose Galang, "Waiting on the IMF," *Far Eastern Economic Review*, 29 December 1983, p. 58.

28. Rigoberto D. Tiglao, "Non-Existent PNB Transactions Used in Reserve Overstatement," *Business Day*, 13 March 1984, p. 2.

29. Ibid.; Jose Galang, "Dressed Up or Padded?" *Far Eastern Economic Review*, 5 January 1984, p. 48; Galang, "The Financial 'Wizards'"; "The International Reserve Scandal," *Veritas*, 18-24 March 1984, p. 16

30. *ASIAWEEK*, 27 January 1983, p. 47.

31. "The International Reserve Scandal."

32. Guy Sacerdoti and Jose Galang, "Manila Money Games," *Far Eastern Economic Review*, 26 January 1984, pp. 42-43.

33. Ibid.

34. Galang, "Waiting on the IMF," *ASIAWEEK*, 3 February 1984, p. 38. "Financial Rescue," *Business Journal* (Philippines) 59 (December 1983): 3.

35. Guy Sacerdoti, "The Standby Standoff," *Far Eastern Economic Review*, 10 November 1983, p. 90; Galang, "Waiting on the IMF"; Truell, "Manila, IMF Are Unlikely to Reach Pact"; "RP Sought Delay in IMF Approval," *Business Day*, 13 March 1984, p. 2; Rigoberto D. Tiglao, "Debt Rescheduling, New Loan Agreement by August," *Business Day*, 16 March 1984, p. 2.

36. "Package of Import Controls Bared," *Business Day*, 28 October 1983, p. 3; "Philippines Stiffens Its Rules on Imports, Foreign Exchange," *Wall Street Journal*, 28 October 1983, p. 35; Rigoberto D. Tiglao, "CB Controls All Forex, Some Profit Remittances," *Business Day*, 7 November 1983, p. 2.

37. Rigoberto D. Tiglao, "Import Credits Slowdown Noted," *Business Day*, 20 October 1983, p. 2; "FM Anxious Re L/C Crisis," *Business Day*, 10 November 1983, p. 8; Truell, "Manila, IMF Are Unlikely to Reach Pact."

38. "CB Budget for Non-Oil Imports: $1.6B," *Business Day*, 29 March 1984, p. 3.

39. "Bank Loan Rates Up: 20%-30%," *Business Day*, 16 November 1983, p. 2; Galang, "Waiting on the IMF."

40. Guy Sacerdoti, "Preparing for the Poll," *Far Eastern Economic Review*, 17 May 1984, p. 20; Paul Quinn-Judge, "Filipinos Vote After Costly Campaign," *Christian Science Monitor*, 14 May 1984, p. 11; Paul Quinn-Judge, "Philippine Surprise: Elections So Far Clean, but Opposition Wary as Tallies Roll In," *Christian Science Monitor*, 18 May 1984, p. 1.

41. Rigoberto D. Tiglao, "RP Expected to Incur Forex Shortfall of $4B

This Year," *Business Day*, 27 March 1984, p. 2; Guy Sacerdoti, "Politics of Expediency," *Far Eastern Economic Review*, 21 June 1984, pp. 80-81.

42. "Manufacturing Employment Index Still Below '81 Level," *Business Day*, 3 June 1983, p. 2; Jose Galang, "Domestic Woes Widen the Government/Business Rift," *Far Eastern Economic Review*, 15 December 1983, pp. 70-72; Sacerdoti and Galang, "Manila Money Games"; Andy McCue, "Low-Income Filipinos Lose Jobs as Foreign-Debt Woes Hurt Firms," *Asian Wall Street Journal Weekly*, 20 February 1984, p. 3; "28,000 Workers Laid Off from January to March 6," *Business Day*, 28 March 1984, p. 3; "A Clearer Picture," *Veritas*, 4-10 March 1984, p. 15.

43. William Branigan, "Foreign Lenders Aim to Change Crony Capitalism in Philippines," *Washington Post*, 20 February 1984, p. A21.

44. Corito Llamas, "Spector of High Prices Hovers Over Supermarket and Palengke," *Veritas*, 20-26 November 1984, p. 19.

45. "Cooking Oil Disappears from Shelves of Supermarkets," *Business Day*, 1 November 1983, p. 7; "Rice Begins to Disappear from Manila Retail Stores," *Business Day*, 11 November 1983, p. 10.

46. Nick G. Benoza, "Panic Buying Empties Stores," *Philippine News*, 13 June 1984, p. 1; Sacerdoti, "Politics of Expediency," p. 80.

47. *ASIAWEEK*, 16 December 1983, p. 32; Cheah Cheng Hye, "Philippine Credit Punch Puts Foreign Investors in a Bind," *Asian Wall Street Journal Weekly*, 5 December 1983, p. 1; "Firms Without Partners Abroad Hit Hard by Dollar Shortage," *Business Day*, 15 March 1984, p. 2; "Multinationals Convert Imports into Equity," *Business Day*, 27 March 1984, p. 2; "Foreign Firms Convert Royalties, Raw Materials Imports into Equity," *Business Day*, 27 March 1984, p. 6; *Business Journal* (Philippines) 59 (March 1983): 6.

48. Daniel C. Yu, "Gov't; Business View Issues Differently," *Business Day*, 11 November 1983, p. 3; William Branigan, "Marcos Blames Businessmen for Economic Crisis," *Washington Post*, 11 November 1983, p. A20.

49. Rodney Tasker, "Our Rich Uncle Sam," *Far Eastern Economic Review*, 15 March 1984, p. 41.

50. "Marcos: Anyone Who Does Not Register or Reregister is Violating the Law," *Philippine News*, 4-10 April 1984, p. 7.

51. Robert Manning, "A Bridge Too Far," *Far Eastern Economic Review*, 12 January 1984, p. 51; Tasker, "Our Rich Uncle Sam"; Marjorie Niehaus, "Philippines in Turmoil: Implications for U.S. Policy," Issue Brief IB84113, Library of Congress, Congressional Research Service, July 1984, p. 7; Eduardo Lachica, "Manila Sets Accord with IMF, but Credits Hinge on Settlement With U.S. and Banks," *Wall Street Journal*, 27 September 1984, p. 34.

52. Guy Sacerdoti, "Vote Early, Vote Often," *Far Eastern Economic Review*, 5 April 1984; Tasker, "Our Rich Uncle Sam."

53. Belinda A. Aquino, "The U.S. Role in Philippine Politics," *Asian Wall Street Journal Weekly*, 18 June 1984, p. 14.

54. Steve Lohr, "Marcos Plays Down Opponents' Gains," *New York Times*, 21 May 1984, p. A3; Bob Spector, "Philippines: Regal Reign is Imperiled," *Los Angeles Times*, 19 June 1984, p. 1.

55. Andy McCue, "Waiting for Aquino: Philippines' 'Irrelevant Opposition' Seeks a Focus," *Asian Wall Street Journal Weekly*, 22 August 1984, p. 1.

56. Anthony Spath, "Technocrats Pitted Against Politicians As Philippines Seeks Cure for Economy," *Asian Wall Street Journal Weekly*, 9 June 1984, p. 10.

57. See Walden Bello et al., *Development Debacle* (San Francisco: Institute for Food and Development Policy, 1982).

58. *ASIAWEEK*, 3 February 1984, pp. 39-40.

59. "Virata Urges New Look at Import Substitution," *Business Day*, 3 June 1983, p. 1. An import-substitution strategy is one in which industrial growth occurs by limiting imports and replacing them with domestically produced goods.

60. "Marcos Retains Most Members of Philippine Cabinet," *Asian Wall Street Journal*, 9 July 1984, p. 10.

8.
The Value and Shortcomings of National Development Comparisons

Alexander King

T he present discussion has attempted to look at the process of development in the Third World by examining a series of case studies of a few countries in East Asia and Latin America. The purpose of this short paper is not to summarize the conclusions of the meeting but, rather, to use some of the points raised to illustrate a number of the contemporary issues of development.

The sample of countries examined was too small and too unrepresentative to enable important generalizations to be made, but the wealth of useful detail was such that many elements from each of the case studies have significance for many other countries striving to develop, not as suggestions for emulation, certainly, but for deep consideration.

The International Conferences on the Unity of Science naturally recognize the need for interdisciplinary and multidisciplinary approaches to development. Some of the present cases were written by economists, others by political scientists; this writer was able to comment from his concern with the role of technology in the development process. On many issues we could have profited from the insights of other social scientists, particularly demographers and anthropologists.

It was to some extent fortuitous, of course, in view of the smallness of the sample, that the studies were mainly the work of economists and political scientists, but, as Kuznets has pointed out, it does appear that in the East Asian countries selected economic policies have dominated the development process, and in Latin America political and social considerations have played a major role. Likewise, it was noted that the success stories were told by the economists and the failures reported by the political scientists. Many quite false or misleading generalizations might have been drawn from this small sample of countries, for example, that the recently decolonized countries (one of the group is indeed still a colony) have been economically successful, and those with more than a century of independence are lagging behind!

A fundamental weakness in international comparisons of this type is the extreme diversity of the countries currently classified as developing. Our present group consisted mainly of countries with considerable development success, or with the potential to achieve it; however, none of the really underdeveloped countries was included. Furthermore, the sample was biased by the inclusion of so many of the Newly Industrialized Countries of East Asia (which we shall refer to as the NICs for brevity), a group that has no analogues in Latin America and that is, indeed, significantly unique among the nations. The Philippines is an interesting case study in the Asian group, for the recent history of that country has many features that contrast with development in Chile.

The inevitable heterogeneity in the circumstances and levels of development of the 160-odd countries of the world casts doubt on the currently accepted classification into the three worlds of the industrialized market-economy countries, the Marxist group, and the Third World of the so-called developing countries. Each of these categories contains a whole spectrum of national conditions, and this is particularly so with the third group. There is little in common between Botswana, Brazil, and Bangladesh or Saudi Arabia, Surinam, and Singapore. Although there has been considerable political advantage in these designations, the massing together of all the disparate environments for the consideration of development issues leads to generalizations that have little or no relevance when applied to most of the individual countries. It is likewise this wild variety of conditions—climate, physical environment, population density, possession of mineral resources, water and fertile soil, educational levels, land-tenure systems, ideology, social history, ethnic homogeneity, religion, sheer size, and a host of other elements—that limits the value of international comparisons of the type we are discussing.

In his opening speech Chairman Kim stated that the main concept of development in the 1960s was increase in GNP; that of the 1970s stressed the fulfillment of basic needs; and that of the present decade remains ill defined. We may, indeed, be at a turning point in the approach to development, a broadening of the concept from economic development alone to human development in the larger sense comprising freedom from poverty, disease and exploitation, justice, and equity. Hitherto development has been considered in essentially economic terms with other benefits regarded as subsidiary and flowing spontaneously from economic growth. This is, for example, the assumption behind the reports of the Brandt Commission. A second implicit assumption is that the success of the industrialized countries in achieving an overall prosperity, unique in history, makes their type of development the model for all countries and all cultures. This means that the systematic pursuit of a technology-driven economic growth is taken to be the unique and inevitable path to development. Furthermore, it is assumed that the economic benefits of such growth will "trickle down" from the rich to the poor. These assumptions are increasingly challenged, especially by the developing countries themselves. There is a growing feeling that development strategies must take greater account of the traditions, values, and cultural objectives of the various nations rather than drift into situations where countries become ineffectual copies of the materially oriented countries of the North. This type of changing approach emerged clearly from our discussion of the papers on East Asia in which the strong influence of the inner values of those countries in selecting from development options became apparent.

The spectacular success of the NICs gave rise to much discussion as to its causes, especially because, in the cases of Hong Kong and Singapore, these territories are completely lacking resources other than human skills and intelligence. It was concluded that the reasons were diverse and complex. It seemed as if the essential precondition was a national will expressed politically but shared by the people. Backing this up was a strong feeling for education and efficient systems for education and training as well as the related appreciation of the need to build up an infrastructure for research and development, without which it is difficult to scan the world development of technology, to be aware of the significance of innovations and to select the technologies and industries basically appropriate to national conditions. But such attributes are by themselves insufficient. It seems that in all the countries concerned there existed a strong sense of entrepreneurship and a propensity for hard work inculcated by the Confucian work ethic. In addition, they have mainly had strong governments able to devise wise economic policies and to enforce them without a high degree of intervention in the day-to-day operations of enterprises.

Relative proximity to Japan has obviously influenced the development of the NICs. Whatever their national policies toward that country have been, they have watched its economic miracle closely, have appreciated the value to their economies of importing and exploiting advanced technologies, and have understood the concurrent need to develop education, training in skills, and research.

The question arises as to whether the success of these countries could be emulated by others. The general conclusion seemed to be that this would be difficult if not impossible unless the prerequisites mentioned above could be provided, and it is not easy to identify many countries where these exist or could be created. However, there are many elements of these success stories that could be studied with profit by many other countries when considering the relative merits of import substitution and export orientation.

The economy of the NICs surged during the period of general world prosperity of the 1960s. With their heavy reliance on export earnings, they are exceedingly vulnerable to external forces and, as does Japan, depend greatly on access to imported raw materials and energy that could easily be imperiled by distant political events completely outside their control. With the advent of the advanced technologies, such as microelectronics, which are revolutionizing the industries of the North through making complete or partial automation economically and technically possible for the first time, the NICs are facing a new challenge. In such labor-intensive manufactures as textiles, apparel, and shoes, and in the assembly of electrical and electronic equipment—in all of which the NICs excel—automation is already reducing and, in some cases, almost eliminating the labor component. Thus, the advantage of low-wage countries, such as the NICs, is being eroded and the industries are being reborn in the North. This situation is well understood in countries like Singapore, where the scientific structures have been soundly built up and are articulated with the planning and production efforts to the extent that it should be possible to go a long way toward the automation of the production lines. Because of its limited population, Singapore has found it necessary to import workers to sustain its present volume of production, so loss of jobs through automation should not be too serious. Some of the other NICs may have greater difficulty in adjusting to the new conditions, especially if populations are large and growing and the provision of jobs is a first priority. In some cases, also, the research and development structures may not be sufficiently strong to accomplish this task quickly. Here again, however, the proximity of Japan may be determinative. That country is at present leading in the *application* of the microprocessor to industrial processes and is already marketing some of its new production facilities actively in the other countries of East and South East Asia.

The descent of neighboring Chile into sociopolitical darkness is clearly due to several causes. Chile has a deeply democratic history and, under the Frei regime, seemed to be securely on the way to becoming a modern democratic state with clear economic objectives and a concern for equity and welfare. It has always had difficulties resulting from its geographic configuration, being excessively long and narrow, which makes for communications difficulties. Its natural resources have concentrated the economy excessively—saltpeter in the last century, copper in this—making it extremely vulnerable to fluctuations on the world market and technological replacements in connection with demand.

The failure of the three last waves of policy in Chile has important lessons for all developing countries. Indeed, of all the national studies presented at our meeting that of Chile has the greatest general relevance. The downfall of the Frei policies was to an extent a political accident and indicates some of the dangers of an essentially three-party system that depends on alliances of a central party with either the Right or the Left, according to the reforms it is determined to carry out. Frei played the game of manipulating coalitions rather skillfully in attempting to strengthen the economy and at the same time to achieve agrarian reform and other social improvements. However, his apparent concession to the Left infuriated the Right, and in the elections of 1970, with three strong candidates for the presidency, Allende obtained 39 percent of the popular vote, which was sufficient to secure the office. The coming to power of this extreme but minority government led to a deep polarization of the Chilean society that has persisted. The government, as expected, nationalized the copper mines, and although Allende initially respected the constitutional processes, difficulties in achieving objectives and the intransigence of the extremists of his own party resulted in arbitrary actions by Allende and finally to the violence and chaos that ended in his downfall. The policies of this period were dominantly statist; the bureaucracy swelled and initiative was discouraged. However, the approach never had a fair trial because of chronic mismanagement.

After the Pinochet coup, the economic system veered 180 degrees to a complete market economy, with the policies pretty well determined by the followers of the Chicago school of Milton Friedman—at first with considerable success, but then came a crash at the beginning of this decade. While responsibility for the situation can be ascribed to some extent to rigidity of free market absolutism, it does raise the question of whether free enterprise can function effectively in an otherwise unfree society; in Chile, a society of repression and violence, which, among other things, silenced even constructive criticism of the economic measures. In Chile, therefore, we have a textbook case of the operation of three completely different economic and social approaches within a few years. None of them was finally successful, but the failures carry many political and economic lessons for other countries and underline the need for a subtle pragmatism.

Throughout the discussions and illustrated amply by the cases, the issue of the desirable extent of government intervention in the economy kept cropping up. The examples of development we analyzed here seemed to many of the participants—the majority of whom obviously accepted the free market system—as cautionary tales. Nevertheless, there was no great enthusiasm for pure Friedmanism. We took the path of moderation and applauded the concept of strong and uncorrupt governments that listen to the advice of their economists, institute wise policy guidelines, and create environments responsive to the working of the market and propitious to entrepreneurship, and at the same time are sensitive to the problems of income distribution and mindful of welfare needs. None of our cases quite met this simple ideal.

Another recurring theme was the distinction between growth and development. As one participant put it, "Growth can be achieved by governments; development is a matter for the people." Throughout the cases it was clear, nevertheless, that the economic policies did reflect national characteristics. And, after all heads of governments are themselves people. Strong personalities such as Marcos of the Philippines or the prime minister of Singapore stamp their personalities on economic arrangements as well as the nature of their societies.

Two major topics were hardly touched upon in the discussions: the impact of technology and the population explosion. We have mentioned the technology dilemma of the Third World briefly in connection with the NICs, but the question is still more important for countries at an earlier stage of development. As we have noted, the most highly industrialized countries are now experiencing a new wave of the technological revolution. It is likely to lead to the widespread automation of manufacturing and to have a heavy impact on the agricultural and service sectors, producing changes in employment, income distribution, and the nature of society. As with earlier technological innovations, countries already advanced and with strong capacities for research and development will profit first and to a great degree. Most of the developing countries have not yet been able to assimilate and exploit the fruits of the original industrial revolution and lack the infrastructures, educational levels, and skills to profit fully from the new wave. Technological developments tend to favor the most advanced and to increase disparities.

The immediate threat to the developing countries is, as we have seen, the erosion of their advantage of low wages. The emerging technologies diminish the cost of labor relative to the other factors of production and thus the advantage of low-wage countries is diminished also. In the case of fully automated installations it becomes nil, and the entire advantage is gone. This fact indicates a paramount need for developing countries to reassess their industrialization strategies; continuation of the existing approaches to industrialization through the import of traditional plant and processes can lead only to obsolescence.

J. J. Servan Schreiber, in *Le Defi Mondial*, suggests that the new technology presents a unique opportunity to countries of the

Third World to "leap-frog" from their present conditions of underdevelopment over the situation of the traditional technology of the nations of the North to become advanced technology-based economies. This would entail the flooding of the developing world with microprocessors and minicomputers. The approach has received some support from President Mitterand of France, but many consider it diversionary. The developing countries have in many instances very high rates of unemployment and underemployment, and are experiencing an explosion of population. To encourage the widespread introduction of labor-unintensive activities would simply worsen the situation. For most developing countries the greatest needs are for capital and jobs. An economy based on microelectronics would demand capital and would not create jobs. Moreover, these countries in general lack sophisticated research and development facilities and advanced skills. To introduce packaged microelectronics equipment in these circumstances would still further increase their dependence on the industrial giants of the North and the Far East, and would be seen as technological colonialism. Even if the "leap-frogging" notion is rejected, it is certain that the advanced technologies can assist in the development of the Third World, but their wise use may prove to be a slow, subtle, and costly process.

Increasing population is the most serious world problem after that of nuclear control. Its immediate and direct effect will be felt mainly in the countries of the South. The prospects are well known from the statistics of the United Nations. While there has recently been some diminution of fertility rates in some of the most hard-pressed countries, the absolute size of the world population will rise substantially during the rest of this century to around 6.2 billion by the year 2000. This means that a million new inhabitants will appear on our planet every four to five days, or, to use a topical comparison, there will be an increase amounting to the size of the population of Grenada twice a day until the end of the century. In terms of sheer numbers, population will be growing faster in 2000 than it is today, with 100 million people added each year as compared with 75 million in 1975.

Although total population will have increased by around 40 percent by the end of the century, the effect will be very different in different regions. It is expected that the increase will be 75 percent in Africa, 65 percent in Latin America, 55 percent in South Asia, 24 percent in East Asia, about 17 percent to 18 percent in the United States and the USSR, and only 7 percent in Europe. The immediate problem will be to ensure that the world will be able to produce sufficient food and other basic essentials to sustain the multitudes. The food prospects are good when considered on technical grounds, although even here there are many obstacles to be overcome, for example, with regard to the cost and availability of energy for many countries. The increasing difficulty of obtaining fuelwood for cooking is indeed one of the most serious aspects of the world energy crisis. The main difficulties in providing food will be economic and political. After all, even in the food-surplus world of today there are more than half a billion people chronically undernourished and malnourished. The hungry are the poor, and their plight in the midst of plenty is a reflection of the imbalance in the distribution of wealth both within and between countries. Thus, the problem of providing food for the coming population increments is inextricably part of the continuing, overarching difficulty of trying to secure equitable distribution of wealth and resources.

It is evident, then, that the population issue is intimately connected with all the other features of development, such as the availability and sustainability of land for agriculture, water, energy, forests, the upgrading of human resources, levels of technology and industrialization, the management of mineral and other resources, maintenance of the environment, and the attainment of social and cultural as well as economic objectives. These are among the tangle of issues that we loosely term development and that demand the attention of many disciplines in addition to those of economics and political science. It is exceedingly important that methodologies be worked out for a realistic inclusion of the demographic element in the planning of development.

The vexations of population will strike the countries of our two regions in different ways. The problems may be less acute for Latin America, which still has considerable room for expansion and for increased food production. The main difficulties may continue to be of a sociopolitical nature, particularly in relation to land-tenure systems which are probably even now the main obstacles to development in contrast to growth. For East Asia the population problem is already well understood. The draconian measures taken by China may or may not succeed, but they must be watched with concern and interest by the other countries of the region. It is extremely important that intensification of agriculture be pursued by all the countries of the region because, by the end of the century, the productive capacities of the food-surplus countries are likely to be strained. Further, climatic conditions and natural disasters must be taken into account, for both can intervene to the detriment of food supply. An approach to food self-sufficiency is therefore of prime importance.

Toward the end of our meeting, Frederick Turner raised the question as to whether development studies are at a dead end. I think that the answer is emphatically no, as Turner himself suggests in the concluding chapter. There will be an ever-increasing need for understanding the tangled web of interacting elements of the process that we call development. National case studies, such as the present ones, should remain important and will need to be deepened and refined, but there will also be a need for new approaches of a multidisciplinary nature that attempt to link and understand the interactions between the various elements of development. It is in this connection that the creation of global development models as well as the national equivalents, as suggested by Professor Guetzkow, could contribute greatly.

A still more important question is whether policies and attitudes toward development are at a dead end. It is my opinion that this is indeed the case. The failure of the recent decades of development based mainly on the transfer of capital and technology indicates that the transfers have been insufficient; the time span too short; the process inefficiently executed; or the underlying assumptions wrong. There is a growing appreciation of the interdependence of nations. The recent petroleum crises have persuaded even the economically strongest of their vulnerability with regard to access to energy and raw materials on which their industries depend, and to political events in distant places over which they have no control. In addition, the developed countries have felt many of the unwanted consequences of rapid quantitative growth of their economies in terms of environmental deterioration and a multitude of social difficulties.

In light of the impasse in North-South relations, it is time for a new start in attacking the problem of development. We should look not merely at the disparities between the industrialized countries and the developing countries but at worldwide development—the weak and the strong working interdependently. Within such a concept, the most useful way to assist the weakest may be to encourage and aid their self-reliance, in other words, their capacity to manage interdependence. Within the concept one would expect a strong development of regionalism, another subject that we have avoided in our discussions, despite the favorable beginning of cooperation through ASEAN. All this provides a rich menu for a further encounter.

9.

The Future of Development Studies

Frederick C. Turner

Despite the current discouragement of some of the scholars who have contributed greatly to the study of political and economic development in the past, the future of development studies remains crucially important. At first, it is disconcerting to see that eminent scholars have become so disillusioned with the field as to see development economics in serious decline[1] and to call for abandonment or a complete reorientation of developmental paradigms. [2] Yet, when we do not expect the developmental literature to have become conclusive or exhaustive, we can at least see that the literature of the past provides a necessary background for the monographs of the future. Since the 1950s, the literature has tested a wide range of generalizations, expanded the traditional studies from Europe and North America to include other nations and regions, and provided case studies on issues and national experiences that establish the guidelines for later research. Moreover, the issues of development are so vital to improving the quality of human life around the world that they *will* be studied, come what may. What we need to do is to study them in the most expeditious and relevant ways possible, building not rarified generalizations or isolated case studies but rather an informed and comprehensive literature, one that will prove useful to policy planners as well as to scholars.

Looking to the future, and keeping in mind the issues raised in the other chapters of this volume, fourteen areas of investigation stand out as especially significant. They do not exhaust the considerations to be kept in mind for research in the late 1980s and in the 1990s, but they do point to some of the directions for these studies to take.

Cultural Relativism

First, in an overall sense, it is necessary to recognize that contributions to policy alternatives as well as to intellectual understanding may come from nations on all continents. Just as we appreciate—all too painfully—that the early studies were mistaken in seeing development as an inevitable and a self-reinforcing process, so it was also misleading to expect the experience of Europe and North America in the nineteenth century to encapsulate that of Third World countries in the twentieth. In fact, some of the most promising work in the decades ahead could point to ways in which some nations in the former areas can learn from some nations in the latter. The English, or the Soviets, or the North Americans may have a great deal to learn from the experience of Japan, or Taiwan, or South Korea, not only in terms of strategies for economic growth or cooperation in the workplace but in terms of a broader cultural cohesiveness as well.

Development studies are at a stage, therefore, where the comparisons and the national models can become truly international in scope. It is to be hoped that the ethnocentrism of the past will be overcome, by way of the areas and topics selected for analysis, and the backgrounds of the scholars involved. If de Tocqueville perceived the United States far more accurately than did indigenous scholars in the early nineteenth century, this same role may be played at the turn of the twenty-first century by foreign social scientists for a number of the "more developed" and the "less developed" nations. The comparisons will become more helpful when they are systematic and empirical, when they can be quantified at least to a degree, and when they can be related to extant hypotheses or theories. In this sense, a framework of analysis can be useful.

Economic Growth

To begin such a framework, one needs to measure performance first, and the most fundamental benchmark here is the level of economic growth. How rapidly are given nations growing in terms of the level of aggregate national income, and how consistent are the patterns of this growth over years and decades? The contrasts are very great in terms of these measures. Mexico, the Ivory Coast, and Japan have grown rapidly and consistently for decades, while Ghana has lowered its standard of living just as consistently over the same decades. Brazil has experienced both periods of rapid advance and years of moving backward in national income levels, while the experience of growth in Argentina has been so erratic as seriously to undercut citizens' expectations for the future.

Concerning the recent development experience of the nations listed in table 9.1, the most fundamental question is why some nations grew so much more rapidly than others. The contrasts are truly striking between, on the one hand, rapid economic growth in Japan and Korea and, on the other hand, much more sluggish growth in Chile and Argentina. Of course, given a total per capita income that is so much larger, Germany increases its per capita income in real terms much more than does South Korea, even if Germany's rate of growth is less than half the Korean, but the variation in rates is dramatic indeed. Considering growth over a period as long as twenty years sometimes masks exceptionally varied rates of increase within the period; in these cases, it obscures the negative growth of the Chilean economy in the early 1970s and its rapid growth later in the decade, the major falloff in South Korean growth in 1980 and 1981, and the fact that United States GNP rose by 4.2 percent between 1960 and 1973 but only by 1.8 percent between 1973 and 1982. These comparisons over an extended period downplay the impact of particular leaders and policies in any given year, focusing attention instead on some of the underlying structural contrasts among the nations.

The data in table 9.1 also question generalizations that are frequently made about economic growth. In the 1970s, South Korea and Taiwan were headed by military figures and spent heavily on national defense, yet their economies prospered; Paraguay, headed by a general who has survived in office for three decades, had a much more mediocre record, despite rapid growth at the end of the decade. Just as military leadership does not prevent or assure swift economic expansion, so neither does the level of population

Table 9.1

Economic Indicators, Selected Countries: Income, Growth, Inflation, Literacy

	GNP per capita, 1980 (dollars)	Average Annual Growth in GNP per Capita (%)	Average Annual Rate of Inflation 1970-1980 (%)	Adult Literacy, 1977 %
Argentina	2,390	2.2	130.8	93
Brazil	2,050	5.1	36.7	76
Chile	2,150	1.6	185.6	—
China, P.R	290	—	—	66
France	11,730	3.9	9.7	99
Germany, F.R.	13,590	3.3	5.1	99
Indonesia	430	4.0	20.5	62
Israel	4,500	3.8	39.7	—
Japan	9,890	7.1	7.5	99
Korea, R.	1,520	7.0	19.8	93
Paraguay	1,300	3.2	12.4	84
Philippines	690	2.8	13.2	75
Switzerland	16,440	1.9	5.0	99
U.K.	7,920	2.2	14.4	99
U.S.A.	11,360	2.3	7.1	99
U.S.S.R.	4,550	4.0	—	100

Source: *World Development Report, 1982* (New York: Oxford University Press, 1982)

increase. Economically, Brazil grew more than twice as fast as Argentina even in per capita terms during the 1960 to 1980 period, while the Brazilian population was also growing more than twice as fast as the Argentine population. In other respects, militarism significantly curtails personal freedom, and unrestrained population increase makes it far more difficult to raise living standards for most citizens, but, in evaluation processes of development, we need to go far beyond the stereotypes that condemn the generals or the population explosion as the culprits behind underdevelopment. The specific data on comparative levels of economic growth confirm this beyond question, and they also point to specific case studies and institutional contrasts that we need to investigate in detail.

Distribution of Income

Fernando Henrique Cardoso was quite right recently when he wrote, "It is now time to reorient efforts to measure success in development by indicators centered on the *quality of life* and on *equality* in the distribution of goods and services."[3] In terms of human welfare, the distribution of income is fully as important as the level of per capita income and the rate at which it is rising or falling, and moreover, the growth of per capita income levels in most developing countries in recent decades means that—hypothetically, if not politically—more egalitarian distribution can occur without disrupting the lives of the most affluent. As a moral issue, the distribution of income faces leaders in all nations, and steep inequalities are least defensible in countries with the highest levels of aggregate wealth. Thus, as pointed out in the pastoral letter "Catholic Social Teaching and the U.S. Economy" issued by North American bishops in November 1984, it does indeed seem especially disgraceful to have thirty-five million people living at or near the poverty level amidst the vast affluence of the United States.[4]

As table 9.2 demonstrates, no countries approach the ideal of fully egalitarian distribution, but some countries are much more egalitarian than others. Among the various nations in table 9.2, South Korea and Israel reveal the most equal distribution. Such data establish the parameters within which we need to consider issues related to distribution, but the experience of various nations indicates far more about its impact in development.

What are the underlying determinants of income distribution? Weede and Tiefenbach conclude that South Korea and Taiwan have far more egalitarian distribution than do the Latin American countries because of the need to mobilize mass support against threats from North Korea and mainland China.[5] The interpretation also fits the situation of Israel, which, surrounded by hostile neighbors, has one of the lowest Gini coefficients of inequality in table 9.2.[6] To the extent that this view is correct, it has interesting implications for Latin America, suggesting that the perceptions of dangers from the United States and other states are significantly less than the threats that neighbors seem to pose for the South Koreans, the Taiwanese, and the Israelis.

Another result that appears from the comparative study of income distribution is that, if the people and the leaders of a

Table 9.2

Income Distribution, Selected Countries

	Income Received by Top 5 (%)	Income Received by Top 10 (%)	Income Received by Bottom 10 (%)	Gini Coefficient
Argentina (1961)[a]	32.0	40.7	1.8	.4895
Brazil (1960)[a]	39.9	49.1	1.2	.5896
Chile (1968)[b]	31.0	41.3	1.9	.5065
France (1962)[b]	24.7	37.2	0.5	.5176
Germany, F.R. (1960)[a]	35.4	43.0	1.9	.5053
Hong Kong (1971)[b]	23.3	33.7	2.1	.4301
Indonesia (1971)[a]	33.7	40.7	2.7	.4625
Israel (1957)[c]	13.1	22.7	2.5	.3143
Japan (1962)[b]	18.8	28.8	1.7	.3868
Korea, R. (1966)[b]	12.1	21.0	3.9	.2650
Philippines (1961)[b]	28.8	40.3	1.6	.5128
Taiwan (1964)[b]	16.7	26.1	3.0	.3290
U.K. (1960)[b]	15.6	25.8	2.3	.3546
U.S.A. (1960)[b]	16.3	26.7	0.8	.3865

Source: Shail Jain, Size Distribution of Income: A Compilation of Data (Washington, D.C.: World Bank, 1975). The dates after each country are those for which the distributions of income are given.
(a) By income recipients.
(b) By households.
(c) By wage earners.

nation opt to distribute and consume the wealth of the nation to the exclusion of concern for producing new wealth, they and their children will have a far lower standard of living than they might have had. Thus Uruguay, the "Switzerland of Latin America" in the 1930s with its advanced social legislation and its pride in widely enjoyed wealth, by the 1970s underwent a military coup and found economic growth just matching the population increase year by year; productivity in the export agricultural sector stood still, and the country could not afford the cost of welfare and old-age pensions, no matter how much people enjoyed them. Similarly, Argentina, which had ranked about sixth in the world in per capita income in 1928, by 1982 fell to about thirty-sixth,[7] after decades of income redistribution under Peronist governments and reversals of those policies under the military governments that ousted the Peronists. In a third case in point, during the 1970s the Costa Ricans enjoyed lavish government spending, but with a foreign debt of over $3 billion and a falloff in world prices for coffee, sugar, and bananas, the government of Luis Alberto Monge in 1982 and 1983 had to emphasize hard work once again, cutting public expenditures drastically, escalating taxes, and encouraging new export industries while curbing imports and sharply lowering the standard of living from what citizens had come to expect.[8]

A final question from a distributionist perspective is: Has a given government helped the poor to help themselves? This is a useful issue for citizens to consider for administrations like that of Ronald Reagan's in the United States, though voters paid little attention to it in reelecting President Reagan to a second term in 1984. It is proportionally even more important in the Third World, where those virtually without savings make up a far greater part of the population. The writing of John F. C. Turner and others has suggested that in Latin America, for example, the poor—such as the migrant poor in the shantytowns—must take charge of their own lives to work their way out of poverty; government cannot do it for them. In relation to the high proportion of citizens in Asian nations who live in rural areas, John Friedmann has recently articulated the same sentiment.[9] In evaluating both rural and urban poverty, therefore, we should ask how much has the central government facilitated citizens' efforts to aid themselves, how successful have the efforts been, and have they led to a sense that the poor can participate in broader political decisions as well.

Technology

Technological change is a vital ingredient in this process of innovation. We are only now coming to see the range of impact on development that technology has, to appreciate that all countries require technological capability to meet the national priorities that they establish. The kinds of technological adaptation that national leaders encourage involve some of the most important decisions that they have to make.

For any given nation, for example, shifts in the technology used may improve military capability or the price of exports, each of which has little to do with the quality of life enjoyed by most citizens. On the other hand, technological change may greatly affect this quality of life, if it improves food production or health, reduces unemployment or underemployment, or cuts balance of payments problems by substituting for costly foreign imports. Especially important here is the level and the direction of indigenous technology, the application of scientific research to the particular patterns of resources and production found in each nation-state.[10] Studying the transfer of technologies among nations, and the rise of effective indigenous technologies in some nations can point the way to both specific innovations and effective strategies of innovation in the future.

Demographic Analyses

One of the most broadly significant technologies is that involving health and conception. The unprecedentedly rapid increase in population through the world has depended upon it, and so may the efforts to stabilize national populations in the decades ahead. As in other areas where technology is applied, it is never an autonomous variable. It always interacts with the social structure and the cultural preconceptions of citizens in a given place and time. This will be as true for the "morning-after" pill and the new male contraceptives in the proximate future as it has been for the loop, the IUD, and the vasectomy in the recent past.

In addition to analyzing the acceptance and the effects of new technologies that people may use to space or to limit the number of their children, demographic studies need to focus upon a variety of other changes in population and the government policies that shape them. Employment and education become critical problems when population growth has been great in the past. In Mexico, for example, although the nation adopted a comprehensive program of government support for "responsible parenthood" in 1972, in 1984 the labor force was still growing at 3.5 percent a year, with job opportunities increasing by only about 1 percent a year.[11] Internal migration and rapid urbanization put major strain upon the delivery of government services in the cities, even though it is in considerable part the pattern of better services in urban areas that attracts rural people to them in the first place.[12] If governments are to maximize personal freedom, if they are not to limit migration as strictly as do the Soviet Union and the People's Republic of China, then they must find other ways to deal with precipitate urbanization and with the other results of the dramatic increases in national populations that have already occurred.

Public Indebtedness

An issue that has taken on far more salience since the early writing on development is public indebtedness, especially the level of foreign debt. With recession characterizing so many nations in the early 1980s, their low demand for imports has curtailed the ability of many Third World nations to pay back large external debts through export sales. The dangers of this situation, where tens of billions of dollars of potentially productive investment funds instead go from Third World nations to the international banks year after year merely for debt service, have only recently come to be recognized for what they are. The situation has caught distinguished economists as well as bankers off guard; for example, as late as 1980 Albert Fishlow praised what he called "debt-led, rather than export-led growth" in Brazil, saying that he wished "to stress the special character and importance of Brazilian integration into world capital markets as a condition of success of the model."[13] By 1984, with the Brazilian debt close to $100 billion and yearly debt service at over $18 billion, with a level of per capita income that had gone dramatically backward and a level of privation that caused acute discomfort, "debt-led" growth seemed far less attractive just four years later.

It is, therefore, useful to compare nations in terms of their borrowing to finance development, especially to ask: (a) How large is the external debt, in absolute, per capita, and value-of-exports terms? (b) How effectively has the borrowed money been used to finance projects that can help in time to repay it? and (c) What policies in the future should be adopted by borrower and creditor nations, by the International Monetary Fund, and by financial institutions in the private sector?

Foreign Ties and Dependency

Until quite recently most economists have assumed that the ties between the wealthier and the poorer nations could benefit the latter substantially. Yet, is this still true in the 1980s after serious recession in the West, the growth of protectionist initiatives there, and the dangers that recession and protectionism pose for Third World nations that have based their development strategies upon increasing exports? Do the reversals of recent years in the international economic system demonstrate that Third World nations have become overly dependent upon capital or markets abroad, perhaps even affirming the strictures of the "dependency theory" that grew up in the 1970s?

The answers to these questions may well be yes to the first and no to the last. It may be time for many nations in the Third World to concentrate upon more internally oriented models of growth, distributing income more widely, expanding internal markets, and reorienting some production and employment to fill domestic needs better rather than concentrating as strongly upon the export sector. Yet a pragmatic reorientation of some resources to the domestic market does not validate the "dependency" literature for a number of reasons: because careful historical analysis shows the perspective to be wrong in many cases;[14] because dependency theorists actually vary greatly in their analysis;[15] and because in *some* cases, such as the Ivory Coast, nations that remain highly dependent have achieved most in raising living standards for their people.

Counterbalancing the earlier literature are recent emphases on interdependence. Dependency is a two-way process, because, as Heraldo Munoz argues convincingly, the wealthier countries of the center are tied significantly to the developing countries of the periphery through their need for strategic raw materials, labor that is cheap even in terms of productivity, and markets in the Third World.[16] Direct foreign investment is by no means limited to that from the United States, Europe, and Japan, for recent case studies have demonstrated that public and private overseas investment also rose dramatically in the 1970s from such nations as Korea, Taiwan, Hong Kong, Brazil, and Argentina.[17] Keohane and Nye have articulated this growing interdependence of nations, particularly in economic terms.[18] Many central events of the past fifteen years buttress the interdependence perspective, such as the fourfold increase in oil prices that OPEC countries imposed on the center and the periphery alike in the early 1970s, or the heavy indebtedness of Brazil or Mexico in the early 1980s that simultaneously has threatened institutions and prosperity in both lending and borrowing nations.

Another recent approach deserving further consideration is the "world-systems analysis" suggested by Immanuel Wallerstein and his associates.[19] Drawing upon classic elements of Marxist theory, it focuses attention not on development within individual nation-states but rather among nations worldwide. In this context, it becomes especially important to ask how, for any developing nation, its level of income and choice of products (industrial, agricultural, extractive) relate to its patterns of trade, what proportion of the profits generated within the nation are reinvested there, and how economic structures affect the relations among social classes. Potentially useful in directing attention to the transnational dimensions of development, the approach nevertheless concentrates, as did early dependency theory, upon the notions of "core" and "periphery" that came from the Economic Commission for Latin America in the late 1940s. Like the original theorizing of Parsons, Easton, and Almond, it still remains at a highly abstract level. Later, when the developing countries have been more systematically studied in terms of transnational ties to multinational corporations, foreign governments, trade union movements, religious institutions, and the emerging cooperation among socialist and conservative parties, the countries may turn out to vary widely in the degrees of their international connections.

Underlying the approaches of dependency theory or world-systems analysis is the assumption that the wealth of the more affluent countries has come from their exploitation of the developing countries. This is a fundamental reason that Marxian analysis has been so popular in the Third World, and, if accepted, it justifies far greater assistance from the affluent to the developing nations in terms of higher prices paid for Third World exports, foreign assistance, and the restructuring of international institutions. Thus the Brandt Commission typically called for "a large-scale transfer of resources to developing countries" between 1980 and 1985,[20] yet no such transfer has taken place, essentially because the arguments and the current distribution of political and economic power among nations have not been sufficient to convince the affluent to share a greater proportion of their wealth.

Appeals to goodwill or to past exploitation are not sufficient to change behavior. It is only when the leaders and the voters in the richer nations become convinced that their future prosperity *does* depend on prosperity in other nations that their behavior will change.

Cultural Adaptation

Another international dimension of development is cultural assimilation and adaptation. Foreign merchants have stimulated commerce and entrepreneurship in many contexts, as have the Chinese in Southeast Asia or the Levantines in Latin America.[21] How they have done so and how indigenous groups have reacted to their doing so form chapters in the developmental experience of many nations. All too often, there are jealous and chauvinistic reactions against them and their success, encouraging political leaders to restrict or expel them, as Idi Amin Dada drove out the Asian merchants from Uganda, whose economy Amin virtually destroyed. Even where the case is not as extreme as in Uganda, studying the role of entrepreneurs from minority groups can be useful, suggesting both ways that their civil rights may better be protected and ways that their economic contributions may be encouraged.

Another link between foreigners and the indigenous population encompasses cultural adaptability, the degree to which citizens in various countries can adapt to foreign techniques of production and the attitudes that partially go along with the new techniques. Nations vary strikingly in this regard. In 1983, for example, the People's Republic of China was producing automobiles patterned after those of the Soviet Union thirty years before and signed an agreement with American Motors to begin building Jeeps in Beijing, whereas, with a legendary ability to accept foreign technology and improve on it, the Japanese automobile industry had so outdistanced its North American competitors as to capture a quarter of the U.S. market. The adaptation to foreign processes of production varies according to fundamental characteristics of the culture in the recipient country as well as according to how welcoming the host government is to foreign firms. Understanding the elements in each culture that affect adaptation would facilitate the roles of both entrepreneurs and government officials.

Political Stability

Political stability, change in governments, and alterations in types of governments remain a central concern of developmental studies, one that can be investigated somewhat better than it could be a quarter century ago. The most seminal work in this area remains Samuel Huntington's 1968 study, *Political Order in Changing Societies*, a work that was widely read and accepted in Third World nations as well as in the United States and Europe.[22] Perhaps because its coverage is so broad and its conclusions so forcefully argued, or because Huntington and his students soon turned their attention to other issues, the major propositions of the volume have yet to be reconsidered in other contexts. To understand political stability in greater depth, we require a series of case studies that investigate in detail the interests and the perspectives of the groups most responsible for undermining a regime or for keeping it in power. Such investigation stability is not only essential in countries like South Korea or Chile, where dramatic changes in regime have taken place, but just as necessary in countries like Taiwan or Paraguay, where the hallmark has been regime continuity over a long period.

Another avenue for political stability studies involves the wider utilization of survey data. As Juan Linz suggested, regime change finally comes down to "a conflict about legitimacy formulas,"[23] and legitimacy can be studied best through survey research. Data banks and the archives of survey research firms are replete with studies of the political attitudes of national populations and subgroups before, during, and after shifts in government, shifts that occurred with elections, with military coups, or with the death or resignation of chief executives. Furthermore, detailed evaluation of survey data in authoritarian countries has recently suggested that the data are surprisingly accurate when compared with other measures of public attitudes,[24] so that, with care, these data may also be used to illuminate the perspectives and the issues surrounding stability.

The Level of Demands

Demands from the populace can curtail or enhance the capacity of leaders to further their developmental policies. We should thus ask, in terms of both economic rewards and participation in mak-

233

ing poltical decisions, how much do the occupational and interest groups of a given society demand? Given the need to husband and reinvest economic resources, and the need as perceived by many national leaders to centralize allocative decisions rather than letting others have veto power over them, a high level of demands may seriously limit the ability of the central government to implement its objectives.

A major issue for the 1980s is how can wage demands be kept at competitive levels, that is, how can management salaries and blue-collar wages not exceed the levels needed for finished products to compete in the domestic and the international markets. Such salary and wage restraint has been a significant dimension of growth and prosperity in Sweden, with the close working relationship between organized labor and the Social Democratic party. From even more striking success in this regard, Japan has become a fascinating case study, with North Americans increasingly interested in studying the patterns of production and worker-management relations that seem so successful there. In one of the most thoughtful commentaries on this theme, Harry Oshima concludes that "the main lesson to be learned from Japan's postwar experience is not so much that other countries should import the various institutions which were successful (although some of them may be imported in modified form) but that managers and workers can be motivated (and owners can be induced) to play for lower stakes and that all this is crucial to the growth of GNP and its distribution."[25] If there are indeed systematic ways to lessen demands in the short run, to "play for lower stakes," then the inducements need to be studied in detail.

Political Participation

In the study of political participation among nations, survey data can establish fundamental comparisons of attitude, and then these data can, as in the classic seven-nation study by Verba, Nie, and Kim, be compared with levels and varieties of participation and with socioeconomic and institutional data from each nation.[26] How much do citizens really *want* to participate in political decisions? Who wants to participate, on what sort of issue, at the local, regional, national, and international levels? How effective is the participation of various groups, given the institutional structures and the political issues of specific nations? How do increasing technological complexity and reliance upon experts limit the opportunities for participation?[27]

Recent work points to self-imposed limitations on participation, to different utilization of institutions among countries, and to the values obtained during study abroad. Notwithstanding United States concern with "democracy" and Soviet concern with "building socialism" in the Third World, many citizens in the Third World are far more concerned with improving their material standard of living than with gaining new opportunities for political participation.[28] Other analysis shows that Koreans tend to use political organizations far more than do Kenyans or Turks to bring their views to the attention of the national government.[29] It remains intriguing to investigate the participation and impact of scientists and technocrats who were trained overseas, to assess how their training affected their view of what they should be doing in their societies as well as their technical capacity to do it.[30]

Another dimension of participation involves patterns of perception among political elites and the degree to which the elites of a given society fear or actively encourage wider degrees of participation by the rank and file. Following the work by G. Lowell Field and his students on elites and particularly elite consensus in the process of development,[31] future studies can approach these issues with new data, especially survey data. Such work in Brazil demonstrates that elites there, while deeply divided among themselves, nevertheless "dread mass politics," as Peter McDonough puts it,[32] suggesting that the much-discussed return to democracy there may be more arduous than many expect.

Attitudes and Values

The traditional literature on political culture alerts us to look for the values and attitudes citizens possess: What is their sense of national community, trust in one another, and support for the current government and for the rules of the political game? How do these perceptions affect their effectiveness in working together, shaping political stability and economic growth? Instead of trying largely to estimate the levels of "trust" or "legitimacy" for national populations as a whole, upcoming development studies may, in addition, more comprehensively compare values in different nations, while other studies investigate attitudes within specific segments of national populations, tracing how attitudes change over time and in relation to what specific events the change is most likely to occur.

Thus, Gallup International is engaged in a survey project costing several million dollars, comparing human and religious values in the populations of more than sixteen nations in Europe, North America, and Latin America. A summary book on all the nations is planned, and then separate books for each country will more deeply probe the patterns of values in each national context. The early studies in development focused upon nations in the Third World and borrowed conceptual schemes from Europe and North America to apply or test there, and it remains worthwhile to test such constructs in other parts of the world. But, with a different approach, Gallup seeks to ask the same questions in all parts of the world, even including Eastern Europe and parts of the Soviet Union.[33]

Leadership

Leadership remains a central variable in politics and in economic development. As Anderson, von der Mehden, and Young emphasized long ago, leaders in developing nations are not "instruments" in a process of modernization but, rather, people involved in highly complex problem solving.[34] Some are better at it than others, because of their own capabilities, the resources at their command, or the tractability of the problems. Each of these dimensions deserves detailed scrutiny in various national contexts, especially because from a clearer understanding of effective leadership may come more thoughtful and effective leaders in the future.

Looking more directly at political leadership—which was a central concern of the classical philosophers—can thus help to provide better guidance for policymakers. In terms of encouraging leaders to appreciate broad strategies through which they can lastingly affect their societies, it would be useful to have more case studies like Wayne Cornelius's classic analysis of institutional reforms under Lázaro Cárdenas,[35] who fundamentally reshaped the Mexican political system. In terms of governmental responses to crisis, students of leadership should look at such cases as South Korea, which minimized the cost of the oil price rises of the 1970s by sending construction crews to Saudi Arabia to earn vast amounts of foreign exchange,[36] a wise move that made the impact of the high energy costs far less damaging in Korea than in other Third World nations. Both overall strategies and specific policy innovations come into clearer focus when we look from the vantage point of the leaders involved.

The Military

Finally, given the predominance of the military in so many nations, patterns of military rule should be investigated and compared. Why are some military governments far more successful at economic growth, or redistribution, or political tolerance than others, and how can success in such areas be encouraged? How do courses at the national military academies and the superior war schools affect officers' conceptions of their societies, the institutional structures of those societies, and the relationship of military officers to them? Does the new literature on the military in one part of the world help us to understand it on other continents? That is, for example, does the emerging literature on "redemocratization" in Latin America[37] need to be seen in terms of events on the Iberian peninsula, and does the literature raise questions that should be investigated in Asia and Africa as well?

Useful—and counterintuitive—information comes from careful comparisons of various national patterns of government spending on the military. As table 9.3 makes clear, it is not whether a nation is run by military leaders but rather the security threats that it faces that primarily determine what part of the national wealth goes to the military. Israel, a vibrant democracy, spends nearly a third of its GNP on defense, whereas Brazil, a military-led state for many years spends under 1 percent. States threatened by the Soviet Union, such as the United States, the United Kingdom, and the People's Republic of China, all support heavy defense expenditures, and in passing it is interesting that the per capita weight of defense spending has been exactly the same for Argentina and Chile, two nations recently in military confrontation over the Beagle Channel. Another important conclusion to come out of expenditure comparisons is the rarity of the Mexican case, where the leaders of a nation feel secure enough to spend more than six times as much on education as on defense, and where

Table 9.3

Military Expenditures, Selected Countries

	Defense Expenditure as percentage of GNP, 1979	Central Government Expenditure, Per Capita, 1979 (in 1975 dollars)	
		Defense	Education
Argentina	2.5	37	22
Brazil	0.8	11	15
Chile	4.2[a]	37	40
China, P.R	5.7	12	7
Germany, F.R.	2.8	222	21
Israel	29.8	1,083	246
Korea, R.	5.5	44	24
Mexico	0.5	8	50
Paraguay	1.2	9	10
Philippines	2.2	15	16
Singapore	5.1	164	100
Switzerland	2.1	187	65
U.K.	5.4	249	45
U.S.A.	4.6	376	51

Source: *World Development Report, 1982* (New York: Oxford University Press, 1982)
(a) Data are for 1978.

civilian leaders also have enough political power to impose this decision on the military establishment. In terms of training for economic development, it is advantageous to spend at least something more on education than defense, as table 9.3 reveals to be the case for Brazil, Chile, Paraguay, and the Philippines. Of course, the initial data require further elaboration; in Paraguay, for example, the major benefit to military officers and the major costs to the system come not through government salaries but through control of contraband. But the data of table 9.3 do evidence the central role of security concerns in military spending, and therefore the need to reduce threats of warfare and violence, not only to protect human life but also to allow vastly more funds for the development process.

An emerging focus for joint research that *cannot* be studied through quantitative comparisons turns to the ways that military leaders deal with their civilian assistants and advisers. Guillermo O'Donnel has recently demonstrated in detail how military governments in Argentina, Chile, and Brazil in the late 1960s and the 1970s depended upon the developmental strategies of civilian "technicians" far more than has been recognized in the past.[38] In the South Korean case, it appears that a significant element in the impressive economic growth over the past two decades has come from a modern application of the Confucian ethic of leadership, from the fact that national leaders have given major responsibility for implementing development goals to administrators chosen for their talent and training, a meritocratic elite that has undertaken its tasks with great competence. It would be helpful to see just how unique this approach really is.

Conclusions

Approaches to development in the 1980s look quite different than they did a quarter-century ago. Some of the old issues, like economic growth and political participation, remain central to the field, but other issues, such as the roles of technology and external debt, have gained prominence as well. We now have far more data on some topics, such as income distribution, and far more material for comparative case studies, such as those of modernizing military regimes. Our ability to collect and analyze some sorts of information, such as survey research data, has increased dramatically, and a rich store of survey data awaits secondary analysis by a new generation of social scientists. Perhaps the greatest change from the 1950s, the area where the old orientations now appear most dated and quaint, is our appreciation that useful paradigms of development can appear in nations throughout the world, that they are not some exclusive prerogative of the West to be shared like foreign aid with other countries.

A special concern of development in the 1980s is that of self-reliance, moving away as far as is possible from dependence upon other nations and eliminating as far as is feasible vulnerability to worldwide economic conditions such as recession and volatile demand. In one sort of situation, the dramatically increased prosperity of the Ivory Coast over the past two decades demonstrates that great progress may occur with considerable foreign ties, like those of the Ivory Coast to France. Yet dependence upon foreign markets and loans as in the case of Brazil, or markets and military defense in South Korea, significantly limits the options open to national decision makers. The resulting push for greater self-reliance among Third World nations does not, as Johan Galtung argues,[39] require heightened struggle and conflict with the wealthier nations. When China or Tanzania pursued more autarkic strategies, neither the West nor the Soviets prevented it, although the losses in education and technology that China experienced in the Cultural Revolution stand as a stark warning against *one* form of inward-looking development. Instead of rejecting technological innovation, developing nations need to adapt technologies to their won indigenous needs, working to produce more efficiently the food, clothing, and shelter that their people require. A strategy of filling domestic needs from domestic production, rather than relying too heavily upon export earnings, can also help to reduce the inequalities in living standards within Third World nations as well.

When seen in terms of self-reliance and of the fourteen issues outlined above, the study of development in the 1980s becomes more a framework of questions than a set of answers. At first, this may seem superficial, a betrayal at the very least of the aspirations of developmental theorists twenty-five years ago. Yet it is also far more realistic. Development studies is not and should not be a separate discipline; it is fruitful precisely because it brings together economists, political scientists, sociologists, and others, because it works to integrate insights from different disciplines as well as different parts of the world. As Harold Lasswell wrote in 1941, "Although they are neither scientific laws nor dogmatic forecasts, developmental constructs aid in the time of scientific work, stimulating both planned observation of the future and renewed interest in whatever past events are of greatest pertinence to the emerging future."[40]

The conclusions of developmental studies are and will long remain short-range or middle-range at best, yet here they can bring far more balanced insights to researchers and policy choices to public officials. These investigations do not tantalize researchers with Nobel prizes or the chance to uncover the double helix, but they do offer opportunities to understand both specific nations and social processes far better through explicit theorizing and a vast extant literature. To the extent that the findings of this literature are appreciated by those who govern, the studies can inform more appropriate public policies as well. Surely this is compensation enough in a world so much in need of better theory and better policy.

Notes

1. Albert O. Hirschman, "Ascensâo e declinio da economia do desenvolvimento," *Dados* 25, 1 (1982). The indictment is particularly telling because Hirschman has been one of the most thoughtful and articulate contributors to the literature.

2. Harry Eckstein, "The Idea of Political Development: From Dignity to Efficiency," *World Politics* 34 (July 1982).

3. Fernando Henrique Cardoso, "Towards Another Development," in *From Dependency to Development: Strategies to Overcome Underdevelopment and Inequality,* ed. Heraldo Muñoz (Boulder, Colo.: Westview Press, 1982), p. 310.

4. In fact, the bishops' statement in neither an attack on the Reagan administration nor on the capitalist system, as some of its initial critics have stridently claimed. The bishops were careful to issue their statement after the 1984 elections in order to reduce its partisan impact; as their spokesmen pointed out, the concerns of the church are of far more than four years' duration. The pastoral does not attack the fundamental principles of capitalism; rather, it seeks to soften the impact of capitalist acquisitiveness on those who live in material poverty. It is with a sense of moral concern for the disadvantaged and the traditional North American appreciation of social equity that the bishops seek to reduce unemployment through public programs to rebuild roads and bridges, to reduce the tax burden especially for the "working poor," and to relate United States foreign aid increasingly to reducing endemic poverty overseas rather than simply to military and strategic alliances.

5. Erich Weede and Horst Tiefenbach, "Correlates of the Size Distribution of Income in Cross-National Analyses," *Journal of Politics* 43 (November 1981): 1041.

6. Without income distribution in mind, Christopher Lucas makes the general comparison, calling Taiwan "a sort of Far Eastern Israel" and going on to describe it as "a small beleaguered nation threatened by hostile powers, a country whose industrious people are prepared to defend themselves against subjugation from without and who have worked hard to achieve the material prosperity that is the goal of so many developing countries," a state whose people reject "the drab socialism of a proletarian" neighbor and where "ability and talent are rewarded and capitalist incentives flourish." Christopher J. Lucas, "The Politics of National Development and Education in Taiwan," *Comparative Politics* 14 (January 1982): 223.

7. Frederick C. Turner, "The Aftermath of Defeat in Argentina," *Current History* 82 (February 1983): 58. On the policies of the Peronist years, see also Frederick C. Turner and Jose Enrique Miguens, eds., *Juan Peron and the Reshaping of Argentina* (Pittsburgh: University of Pittsburgh Press, 1983).

8. A useful summary of problems facing the Costa Ricans is "Costa Ricans Work to Rebuild Economy and Maintain Stability," *Wall Street Journal,* 3 May 1983.

9. Friedmann writes, "It is not a matter of reaching 50,000 or 100,000 peasant farmers with an impressively financed program of irrigation, where the construction work is supervised by Dutch, Taiwanese, or Israeli engineers. This approach never leads to anything other than a showpiece. If the rural masses are to see a substantial improvement in their lives, it is they themselves who will have to do the work, who will have to organize themselves, and, rising from below, transform the social and physical conditions of their existence. In such a development. . . central government must act to inspire, to empower, to guide, to facilitate, to promote, to assist, and to support. It must not plan, command, administer, or implement projects of its own unless in support of the entire effort and therefore beyond local capacity." John Friedmann, "The Active Community: Toward a Political-Territorial Framework for Rural Development in Asia," *Economic Development and Cultural Change* 29 (January 1981): 261.

10. Alexander King, "Interdependence and Self-Reliance: Science and Technology in an Alternative Approach to World Order" (paper presented in Tunis, April 1983). See also Alexander King and Aklilu Lemma, "Scientific Research and Technological Development," in *Reshaping the International Order: A Report to the Club of Rome*, coordinated by Jan Tinbergen (New York: E.P. Dutton, 1976); Richard S. Eckaus, *Appropriate Technologies for Developing Countries* (Washington, D.C.: National Academy of Science, 1977.)

11. Christopher Swan, "Mexico Seen through the Eyes and Lives of Its People, Rich and Poor," *Christian Science Monitor*, 7 March 1984, pp. 1, 32. For analysis of the Mexican initiatives to curb its population increase of nearly 3.5 percent, see Frederick C. Turner, *Responsible Parenthood: The Politics of Mexico's New Population Policies* (Washington: American Enterprise Institute, 1974). In Brazil, one of the largest and most powerful nations in which to study development strategies, Thomas Sanders and his associates on the American Universities Field Staff have defined employment as *the* most critical national problem, and they have come up with a multidisciplinary approach to study it in the late 1980s.

12. On the problems of urbanization in Latin America and the responses of different governments to them, see Frederick C. Turner, "The Rush to the Cities in Latin America: Government Actions Have More Effect Than Is Generally Recognized," *Science*, 4 June 1976. On migration more generally, see *Third World Migration and Urbanization: A Symposium*, a special issue of *Economic Development and Cultural Change* 30 (April 1982).

13. Albert Fishlow, "Brazilian Development in Long-Term Perspective," *American Economic Review* 70 (May 1980): 95.

14. Among the most interesting and best-documented case studies of the inapplicability of dependency theory are Paul B. Goodwin, Jr., "The Politics of Rate-making: The British-owned Railways and the Union Civica Radical, 1921-1928," *Journal of Latin American Studies* 16, pt. 2 (November 1974); Paul B. Goodwin, Jr., "Anglo-Argentine Commercial Relations: A Private Sector View, 1922-43," *Hispanic American Historical*

Review 61 (February 1981). For a more general critique of the dependency perspectives, see Tony Smith, "The Case of Dependency Theory," in *The Third World: Premises for U.S. Policy,* ed. W. Scott Thompson, (San Francisco: ICS Press, 1983).

15. One of the most reasonable and widely accepted views of dependency is Fernando Henrique Cardoso, "Associated-Dependent Development: Theoretical and Practical Implications," in *Authoritarian Brazil: Origins, Policies, and Future,* ed. Alfred Stepan, (New Haven: Yale University Press, 1973). Cardoso says that, in Brazil, dependent development has allowed rapid economic growth and social mobility, but that at the same time, in Brazil and elsewhere, "part of the industrial system of the hegemonic countries is now being transferred, under the control of international corporations, to countries that have already been able to reach a relatively advanced level of industrial development" (pp. 156-57). More radical and more controversial views of dependency may be found in Peter Evans, *Dependent Development: The Alliance of Multinational, State, and Local Capital in Brazil* (Princeton: Princeton University Press, 1979), and in the various articles in *Latin American Perspectives.*

16. Heraldo Muñoz, "The Strategic Dependency of the Centers and the Economic Importance of the Latin American Periphery," in *From Dependency to Development: Strategies to Overcome Underdevelopment and Inequality,* ed. Heraldo Muñoz, (Boulder, Colo: Westview Press, 1982).

17. See eds., Krishna Kumar and Maxwell G. McLeod, *Multi-nationals from Developing Countries* (Lexington, Mass.: D.C. Heath, 1981).

18. Robert O. Keohane and Joseph S. Nye, *Power and Interdependence: World Politics in Transition* (Boston: Little, Brown & Co., 1977), esp. pp. ix, 8-19.

19. The best summary of the approach is Terence K. Hopkins and Immanuel Wallerstein, *World-Systems Analysis: Theory and Methodology* (Beverly Hills, Calif.: Sage Publications, 1982).

20. *North-South: A Program for Survival. The Report of the Independent Commission on International Development Issues under the Chairmanship of Willy Brandt* (Cambridge, Mass.: MIT Press, 1980), p. 276.

21. For comparative comments on the roles of these two groups, see Yuan-Li Wu, "Chinese Entrepreneurs in Southeast Asia," and William Glade, "The Levantines in Latin America," *American Economic Review* 73 (May 1983).

22. Samuel P. Huntington, *Political Order in Changing Societies* (New Haven: Yale University Press, 1968).

23. Juan J. Linz, "Crisis, Breakdown, and Reequilibrium," in *The Breakdown of Democratic Regimes,* eds. Juan J. Linz and Alfred Stepan, (Baltimore: Johns Hopkins University Press, 1978), p. 92.

24. Brian H. Smith and Frederick C. Turner, "The Meaning of Survey Reseach in Authoritarian Regimes: Brazil and the Southern Cone of Latin America Since 1970," in *Statistical Abstract of Latin America,* vol. 23, eds. James W. Wilkie and Adam Perkal, (Los Angeles: UCLA Latin American Center Publications, 1984).

25. Harry T. Oshima, "Reinterpreting Japan's Postwar Growth," *Economic Development and Cultural Change* 31 (October 1982): 42. On a more narrow theme, Oshima writes that "the historical significance of Japan's postwar economic growth is the demonstration that the labor force under capitalism can be motivated to produce efficiently without relying entirely on material rewards, but through making the workplace a 'joyful place to work.'" With cool detachment and a note of prophecy, he concludes that "Japan will certainly surpass the United States if there is complacency concerning the superiority of present American ways of working, producing, selling and innovating" (ibid., pp. 41, 43). On the historical background of Japanese growth, see Cyril E. Black and othes, *The Modernization of Japan and Russia: A Comparative Study* (New York: Free Press, 1975).

26. Sidney Verba, Norman H. Nie, and Jae-on Kim, *Participation and Political Equality: A Seven-Nation Comparision* (New York: Cambridge University Press, 1978. See also Sidney Verba, Norman H. Nre. and Jae-on Kim, *The Modes of Democratic Participation: A Cross-National Comparison* (Beverly Hills, Calif.: Sage Publications, 1971); Sidney Verba and Norman H. Nie, Participation in America: Political Democracy and Social Equality (New York: Harper & Row, 1972).

27. For some useful commments on ways to maintain broad participation while relying for information of those with technical information, see Stephen Wexler, "Expert and Lay Participation in Decision Making," in *Participation in Politics*, eds. J. Roland Pennock and John W. Chapman, (New York: Lieber-Atherton, 1975).

28. Commenting on the failures to institutionalize wider participation in Yugoslavia, which once seemed a promising model to many Third World leaders, Thomas Oleszczuk proposes that most Yugoslavs have tried to gain "prosperity in return for obedience." Oleszczuk, "The Liberalization of Dictatorship: The Titoist Lesson in the Third World," *Journal of Politics* 43 (August 1981): 822. Considerable confirmation of this conclusion comes from survey work done in Yugoslavia. See Jan F. Triska and Ana Barbic, "Evaluating Citizen Performance on the Community Level: Does Party Affliation in Yugoslavia Make a Difference?" in *Political Participation in Communist Systems*, eds. Donald E. Schulz and Jan S. Adams, (New York: Pergamon Press, 1981).

29. Ersin Kalaycioglu and Ilter Turan, "Measuring Political Participation: A Cross-Cultural Application," *Comparative Political Studies* 14 (April 1981): 132.

30. One of the most suggestive of these analyses remains A. H. Halsey, "The Education of Leaders and Political Development in New Nations," in *Comparing Nations: The Use of Quantitative Data in Cross-National Research*, eds. Richard L. Merritt and Stein Rokkan, (New Haven: Yale University Press, 1966). More recently, important studies are being done by the Study Group on International Communication of the International Political Science Association.

31. G. Lowell Field, *Comparative Political Development: The Precedent of the West* (Ithaca, N.Y.: Cornell University Press, 1967); G. Lowell Field

and John Higley, *Elites in Developed Societies: Theoretical Reflections on an Initial Stage in Norway* (Beverly Hills, Calif.: Sage Publications, 1972); G. Lowell Field and John Higley, *Elitism* (London: Routledge & Kegan Paul, 1980); and John Higley and Gwen Moore, "Elite Integration in the United States and Australia," American Political Science Review 75 (September 1981).

32. Peter McDonough, "Repression and Representation in Brazil," *Comparative Politics* 15 (October 1982): 90.

33. For more details on the human values project, write to its director, Gordon I. Heald, Social Surveys Limited, 202 Finchley Road, London NW3 6BL, England.

34. Charles W. Anderson, Fred R. von der Mehden, and Crawford Young, *Issues of Political Development* (Englewood Cliffs, N.J.: Prentice-Hall, 1967), p. 8.

35. Wayne Cornelius, "Nation Building, Participation, and Distribution: The Politics of Social Reform under Cárdenas," in *Crisis, Choice, and Change: Historical Studies in Political Development,* eds. Gabriel A. Almond, Scott C. Flanagan, and Robert J. Mundt (Boston: Little, Brown & Co., 1973). For a contrasting appreciation of the Cárdenas presidency from a Marxist perspective, see Nora Hamilton, *The Limits of State Autonomy: Post-Revolutionary Mexico (Princeton: Princeton University Press, 1982).*

36. This point is especially well made by Anthony Sampson in *The Money Lenders: The People and Politics of the World Banking Crisis* (New York: Penguin Books, 1983), pp. 221-25).

37. See especially eds. Howard Handelman and Thomas G. Sanders, *Military Government and the Movement Toward Democracy in South America* (Bloomington: Indiana University Press, 1981); eds. Cynthia McClintock and Abraham F. Lowenthal, *The Peruvian Experiment Reconsidered* (Princeton: Princeton University Press, 1983).

38. Guillermo O'Donnell, "As forças armadas e o estado autoritário no Cone Sul de América Latina," *Dados* 24, 3 (1981).

39. Relying upon the old notion of world centers that exploit the periphery, Galtung writes, "The politics of self-reliance has been and will continue to be resisted both from within and from without. It will be a politics of struggle because of the vested interest in the present world order for those at the top . . . . We are not heading for a nice linear, or even exponential, growth in the phenomenon of self-reliance around the world; the resistance will also gain increasing momentum." Galtung, "The Politics of Self-Reliance," in *From Dependency to Development: Strategies to Overcome Underdevelopment and Inequality,* ed. Heraldo Muñoz (Boulder, Colo.: Westview Press, 1982), pp. 175-76.

40. Dwaine Marvick, ed., *Harold Lasswell on Political Sociology* (Chicago: University of Chicago Press, 1977), p. 176.

CONTRIBUTORS

Toshio Aoki (Ph. D., Kyoto University, Japan) is executive director of The Overseas Economic Cooperation Fund (OECF), in charge of the Association of S. E. Asian Nations (ASEAN). He has also served as the secretary of a diet member (Liberal Democratic Party); established joint ventures of forest development in Sulawesi Island, Celebes, etc. for Kokusaku Pulp & Paper Co., Ltd.; and managed several OECF loan departments throughout southeast Asia.

John C. H. Fei (Ph. D., Massachusetts Institute of Technology) is professor of economics at the Economic Growth Center, Yale University. He has taught at Antioch College, Cornell University, and Yale University. His primary research interest lies in the areas of economic development, theory, and policy. His books include The Development of a Labor Surplus Economy, The Transition in Open Dualistic Economies, and *Growth with Equity.*

Takao Fukuchi (Ph. D., University of Tokyo) is professor of economics at Tsukuba University in Japan and a member of the UN Latin American Economic Council. He was chief researcher of the Economic Planning Agency of the Japanese Government and also director of its Economic Research Institute. Fukuchi has contributed many articles to professional journals in Japan.

Ilpyong J. Kim (Ph. D., Columbia University), the editor of this volume, is professor of political science at the University of Connecticut and specializes in comparative and international politics, with a focus on China and East Asian governments and international relations. He is chairman of Columbia University's Faculty Seminar on Modern Korea, and was visiting research scholar at Harvard University's Fairbank Center for East Asian Research. Kim was also senior Fulbright professor at the University of Tokyo and International Christian University in Japan. He has published six books, including *The Politics of Chinese Communism, Communist Politics in North Korea, The Great Power Politics and the Korean Peninsula,* and contributed twenty-seven articles and chapters to professional journals and edited volumes.

Ung Soo Kim (Ph. D., University of Washington) is professor of economics at the Catholic University of America and a retired lieutenant general in the Republic of Korea Army. He teaches courses in econometrics and economic development in Asia, and has contributed articles to academic and professional journals.

Alexander King (Ph. D., Royal College of Science) is chairman of the International Federation of Institutes for Advanced Study, receiving a Doctorate of Science in Chemistry. He is a member of the Club of Rome, which produced *The Limits to Growth.* Articles of his dealing with science, technology, and development have appeared in numerous professional journals.

Sidney Klein (Ph. D., Columbia University) is professor of economics at California State University, Fullerton, and is author or co-author of five books and well over a hundred articles, papers, and book reviews. He has taught at Hong Kong University and the University of British Columbia, as well as Columbia University, Rutgers University, UCLA, University of Hawaii, Portland State University, and other U.S. institutions. In 1976 he received the Distinguished Teaching Award of the Western Economics Association.

Paul A. Kuznets (Ph. D., Yale University) is associate professor of economics at Indiana University in Bloomington, where he teaches courses in economic development and modern Asian economic history. Before joining the Indiana University faculty in 1964, Kuznets worked in the research department of the Federal Reserve Board in Washington, D.C. He is the author of *Economic Growth and Structure in the Republic of Korea* and many articles on Korean economy.

Charles W. Lindsey (Ph. D., University of Texas at Austin) is associate professor of economics at Trinity College, Hartford, Connecticut. He has held visiting professorships at Atenio de Manila University (the Philippines) and the University of the Philippines. He was also a research fellow at the Institute of Southeast Asian Studies in Singapore. Lindsey has published widely on industrialization and foreign investment in the Philippines.

Paul E. Sigmund (Ph. D., Harvard University) is professor of politics and director of the Latin American Studies Program at Princeton University. He is the author of ten books on political theory and Latin American politics, including *The Ideologies of Developing Nations*, *The Democratic Experience* (with Reinhold Niebuhr), *The Overthrow of Allende and the Politics of Chile*, *Multinationals in Latin America: The Politics of Nationalization*, and *The Politics of Income Distribution in Mexico*. He is currently at work on a book about Chile, focusing on the post-Allende period.

Edward C. Steward (Ph. D., University of Texas at Austin) is Professor of Cross-Cultural Communication at International Christian University in Tokyo, Japan. He has authored many books and contributed numerous articles to professional journals, including *American Cultural Patterns: A Cross-Cultural Perspective* and "Outline of Intercultural Communications."

Frederick C. Turner (Ph. D., Fletcher School of Law and Diplomacy, Tufts University) is professor of political science at the University of Connecticut and a member of the Executive Committee of Board of Directors and the Roper Center. He has written especially on Latin American politics, with books on Mexican nationalism, Catholicism, and political development. He has received grants from the National Science Foundation and the National Endowment for the Humanities to conduct survey research in Latin America. More than forty of his articles have been published in professional journals. His most recent book, *Juan Peron and the Reshaping of Argentina*, edited with Jose Enrique Miguens, appeared in 1983.

Sources

The primary source of this volume was derived from papers presented in Committee IV ("Developmental Experiences in East Asia and Latin America") at ICUS XII ("Absolute Values and the New Cultural Revolution"). The symposium, one of six sponsored by ICUS, of the International Cultural Foundation, Inc., was held at the Chicago Marriott Hotel, November 24-27, 1983, and had as its organizing chairman, Ilpyong J. Kim. The honorary chairman was Alexander King.

Supplemental papers include "Economic Crisis in the Philippines" by Charles W. Lindsey (originally published in the "Asian Review") and "The Japanese Model of Modernization: Present and Future" by Edward C. Stewart (originally published in the Proceedings of the Tenth ICUS.)

INDEX

The numbers in parenthesis behind the page numbers refer to footnote(s) on that page. The numbers in **bold face** type refer to sections written by the person, but not necessarily sections referring to the person.